Children's Unspoken Language

of related interest

Giggle Time – Establishing the Social Connection
A Program to Develop the Communication Skills of Children with Autism
Susan Aud Sonders
ISBN 1 84310 716 3

Profiles of Play
Assessing and Observing Structure and Process in Play Therapy
Saralea E. Chazan
ISBN 1 84310 703 1

Small Steps Forward
Using Games and Activities to Help Your Pre-School Child with Special Needs
Sarah Newman
ISBN 1 85302 643 3

How We Feel
An Insight into the Emotional World of Teenagers
Edited by Jacki Gordon and Gillian Grant
ISBN 1 85302 439 2

First Steps in Parenting the Child Who Hurts
Tiddlers and Toddlers
Second Edition
Caroline Archer, Adoption UK
ISBN 1 85302 801 0

Next Steps in Parenting the Child Who Hurts
Tykes and Teens
Caroline Archer, Adoption UK
ISBN 1 85302 802 9

Children's Unspoken Language

Gwyneth Doherty-Sneddon

Jessica Kingsley Publishers
London and Philadelphia

The right of Gwyneth Doherty-Sneddon to be identified as author of this work has been asserted by her in accordance with the Copyright, Designs and Patents Act 1988.

First published in the United Kingdom in 2003
by Jessica Kingsley Publishers
116 Pentonville Road
London N1 9JB, UK
and
400 Market Street, Suite 400
Philadelphia, PA 19106, USA
www.jkp.com

Copyright ©2003 Gwyneth Doherty-Sneddon
Second impression 2003
Third impression 2004

Library of Congress Cataloging in Publication Data
Doherty-Sneddon, Gwyneth, 1968-
   Children's unspoken language / Gwyneth Doherty-Sneddon.
      p. cm.
   Includes bibliographical references and index.
   ISBN 1-84310-120-3 (pbk.: alk. Paper)
      1. Nonverbal communication in children. I. Title.
BF723.C57 D64 2003
155.4'1369--dc21

British Library Cataloguing in Publication Data
A CIP catalogue record for this book is available from the British Library

ISBN-13 978 2 843 120 8
ISBN-10 1 84310 120 3

Printed and Bound in Great Britain by
Athenaeum Press, Gateshead, Tyne and Wear

To Charlotte and Dylan

Acknowledgements

I would like to thank everyone who has helped me complete this book. There are too many to mention individually by name but include all of the children, parents and teachers who have been involved in the research throughout my academic career.

Thanks also to colleagues James Anderson and Lesley Bonner for your comments on the manuscript.

I give a special acknowledgement to my family for their encouragement, support and inspiration, especially Jim for the motivation to write the book and my own children for teaching me so much.

Contents

Chapter 1

Introduction

An important part of learning to be a competent, social human being is learning how to send non-verbal information. Equally important is learning how to understand it. Children acquire these skills throughout childhood. The aim of this book is to document this important part of child development. Children express their knowledge and understanding of situations, concepts and people in non-verbal ways before they can articulate the same information in words. So non-verbal communication provides an invaluable window through which to see children's social, emotional and cognitive development. Understanding these important channels of communication can help parents and professionals working with children to facilitate children's learning and development.

In many cultures an important issue in child development, for parents and professionals alike, is the unfolding of language. A major event for most parents in a child's early years is when she speaks her first word (typically this happens around 12 to 18 months of age). In contrast, we seldom hear parents report when their children first began pointing to ask for something, or when they first used an action like flapping their hands to represent a bird. Why should this be? My understanding is that people just aren't looking for these signals because they don't expect them to be important. However, many early non-verbal signals occur before children begin to speak, and are important indicators of their growing understanding about the world in which they are living.

Because children, particularly the very young, lack the language skills to express their knowledge and understanding, we often seriously underestimate their abilities. This is a great folly on our part and I hope the current text goes some way to rectify this. What you will find as you read on is that there is a wealth of information in non-verbal signals. Sometimes we respond to these cues without conscious awareness. Sometimes we remain entirely ignorant of them. Even worse, because of inaccurate 'folk psychology', we often misinterpret non-verbal cues and draw the wrong conclusions. This book aims to document some of the ways in which children communicate, over and above what they say.

There are many good books that describe how children acquire language. In contrast to these, this book examines the development of a range of non-verbal communication skills over a wide age range: from birth to late primary school. It documents milestones for parents and professionals to look for, but more importantly provides a way for these adults to read non-verbal acts and see behind them into the child's developing mind. While other popular books exist which document the social psychology of non-verbal behaviours, these primarily address what we know about adult behaviour. The current text is unique in that it specifically looks at non-verbal behaviour in child development. Furthermore, the issues addressed are broader than social effects and include impacts on cognitive development.

Non-verbal communication

Non-verbal communication is diverse in the forms that it takes. As you will discover, there are a number of 'channels' of non-verbal communication (Argyle 1996):

- hand gestures
- eye gaze
- facial expressions
- touch
- posture
- spatial behaviour

- physical appearance
- non-verbal vocalisations
- smell.

At first glance these channels all look very different; for example, we move our faces in different ways compared with the movements we make with our hands and whole bodies. However, when we really think carefully about these different channels of communication, we see that they share many similarities. Essentially they all carry information about what's going on inside us, including how we feel and what we're thinking. Sometimes we deliberately send information through these channels of communication, sometimes we do this automatically. There is a certain unity about these diverse behaviours, especially when we explain them through theories of social interaction. One of these, equilibrium theory, describes how the different channels of non-verbal communication work together to maintain a balance of intimacy and dominance within all social relationships (Argyle and Dean 1965).

Essentially equilibrium theory proposes that every social relationship has an unspoken intimacy distance. The better we know someone, the 'closer' the relationship. This intimacy distance is kept in 'equilibrium' by balancing a number of factors. Every channel of non-verbal behaviour has a part to play in establishing and maintaining this intimacy distance; for example, we are far more comfortable making eye contact with, touching and standing closer to people we know than those we have just met. Furthermore, there are many unwritten rules about these behaviours, which change depending on the specific relationship.

Thinking about how social relationships function in this way is very important when we consider children's social and communication development. In certain respects children can be blissfully unaware of some of the rules about these behaviours; for example, children don't learn to avoid eye contact until they are around four or five years old. Indeed, the rules about interaction style between adults and children typically vary greatly compared with adult–adult communication. This has a huge impact on how children behave and respond in social situations and how we respond to them. Chapter 2 describes equilibrium theory more fully. Furthermore, in that chapter it is used to explain certain features of adult–child interactions. A specific example is made of the effects that live video links have on child witnesses.

Social interaction

Non-verbal communication is important in children's development in many ways, as you will see. One way is fundamental: non-verbal communication gives children an important way of interacting with other people. Being able to communicate effectively is central to every aspect of our lives. The word communication derives from the Latin *communico*, meaning 'to share'. So whenever we share our thoughts or feelings with someone else we communicate. Sharing meaning is one of the most important parts of caring for children. By communicating with them we help them to develop and grow.

Human beings are social animals. Our sociability is something that is ingrained within us and integrally linked with our abilities to communicate with one another. We see this clearly when we look at the sorts of behaviours that babies are born able to do. We know that from birth infants are responsive to faces, voices and touch. They also have a number of inborn qualities designed to keep adults attentive to their needs; for example, babies are cute and attractive. Particular features that contribute to this attractiveness include a relatively large forehead and eyes and bulging cheeks (Lorenz 1942). Seeing people with these features naturally induces nurturing behaviours in most adults. In other words, babies and their parents are automatically predisposed to interact with one another. The quality of these interactions has important consequences for the development of children. Many researchers have shown clear evidence of the beneficial effects of good quality interaction on social, emotional and mental development.[1] No baby or child is an island. Development is driven through interaction with both the physical (Piaget 1972) and social (Vygotsky [1934] 1962) environments.

What are the critical features of good quality interaction? Two important characteristics are sensitivity and responsiveness. By sensitivity I mean the ability of the parent to understand the child's needs and wants.

Responsiveness is the likelihood that this understanding will be acted upon appropriately; for example, to illustrate sensitivity, consider a baby crying. How good is the parent at determining what is wrong? Is the baby tired, hungry, thirsty, too hot or too cold, or just plain bored? There are lots of indicators that tell us the root of the problem. These include the specific qualities of the cry and also other non-verbal behaviours such as mouthing or ear rubbing. This doesn't just apply to infancy. The non-verbal behaviours of older children remain extremely informative. Adults differ in terms of how well they read these cues. A lot of the time it's just down to experience and getting to know the child. We all have natural skills for interacting with children and I'm a great believer in using gut instincts. However, much of human communication is so automated that we lose sight of important signals. Explicitly describing these and explaining them in relation to psychological frameworks can help us understand them better.

In addition to sensitivity, the other quality of adult–child interaction is how responsive the adult is to the child's signals and cues. In other words, how likely and how quickly will the adult respond? This is often determined by parenting 'rules' set down within cultures. These can give parents mixed messages; for example, 'babies should never be left to cry'; 'babies shouldn't be spoilt and picked up too quickly'. It is my view that on the whole children should be responded to quickly. The degree of sensitivity and responsiveness that parents show to their children affects the children's confidence that their parents will be there for them. As will be discussed in Chapter 6, this in turn influences the security of attachment of the child to parent which has knock-on effects on social, emotional and cognitive development.

One example of trying to harness infant communication, in order to promote parental sensitivity and responsiveness, is the use of 'baby sign languages'. I will describe one of these systems in Chapter 3. These are designed to give infants another way of communicating with people in order to make them more effective at doing so before they can speak. This book shows that the idea of using non-verbal behaviours to facilitate and improve interactions with children extends well beyond infancy and still has important applications even when language is well established.

So interacting effectively with our children requires that we understand them. Sometimes this is easy, sometimes extremely difficult. Knowing how to 'read' their non-verbal communication can help us to do this accurately. From birth the only clues we have as to what a baby wants or feels are the things that he does. Later in development non-verbal signals are normally combined with speech, but remain a crucial part of the child's communicative repertoire.

Principles of communication with children

Here I will describe a few principles that I think capture the essence of communicating with children. This is not meant to be an exhaustive list. These give a general framework within which to think about and understand the phenomena you see every time you interact with a child. The principles apply to both language and non-verbal cues. There are four that refer to both children's and adults' contributions. The other three principles describe additional characteristics of effective adult communication towards children. Use these principles to ask questions of communicative situations. For example, if a child is trying to explain something to you but you can't understand what they're getting at, or a baby is crying and you can't fathom why, you might ask yourself some of the following questions:

1. Are you attending to all the communicative cues available to you?

2. What visual messages is the child sending you?

3. Is s/he gesturing?

4. Is s/he looking at you or avoiding eye contact?

5. Is s/he intentionally directing your attention?

6. Is s/he doing something s/he has learned to do in other similar situations?

By asking these sorts of questions when children are struggling to communicate, or when we are struggling to understand them, can help us see 'hidden' meanings. The seven principles are shown in Table 1.1.

Table 1.1 Principles of child communication	
Child and adult communication	*Adult style*
1. Intentionality	5. Adults should be attentive
2. Visual cues	6. Responsiveness ·
3. Communication is innate	7. Scaffolding
4. Communication is learned	

Principle 1: Intentionality

Non-verbal behaviour is a term that can be used to refer to all types of non-language behaviours; for example, a child playing with a toy could be classed as non-verbal behaviour if it does not involve the child speaking. However, most of what I write about in this book is a special class of non-verbal behaviour. A lot of the time I'll be talking about non-verbal communication where the behaviour is used to communicate or share information with another person. The distinction between non-verbal *behaviour* and *communication* is determined by whether or not the action is used intentionally. So if I yawn because I'm tired or bored you will get information about how I'm feeling and will make various inferences about this. If I yawn deliberately to show you that I'm bored this is subtly different. You get essentially the same signal and may respond to it in a similar way. However, if you detect the intentional nature of what I've done this adds a whole new dimension to the action and you will start to think things such as, 'Why is she trying to tell me she's bored, what does she want me to do?'

When we look at infancy, particularly the early months, most of the information we get from the baby's behaviour is not given intentionally. The behaviours are nevertheless very informative. For example, babies are born with a set of reflexive behaviours, such as crying, sucking, grasping, the babinski (a reflexive movement of the foot observed in newborns when the sole of the foot is stroked), the startle, and several others. These reflexes are important external indicators of the baby's internal brain development. Deviations from the norm would alert paediatricians to an underlying problem. While they are very informative, the baby does not do them intentionally to signal information. Over the first year of life these reflexes change, some disappear, others change from reflexive to voluntary actions. For example, the grasp reflex, where infants will grasp tightly any object placed in the palms of their hands, is replaced by voluntary grasping where babies deliberately hold on to objects.

Babies also learn to use some of their behaviours intentionally to influence other people. For example, crying is initially entirely reflexive in response to negative internal states such as hunger or cold. By the time most babies are nine months old they are getting the idea that they can use crying to get other people to do certain things. For example, infants begin using crying deliberately in order to get picked up when they want a cuddle. This instrumental crying has certain characteristics that you can recognise. It typically has a different sound to it, being less 'sincere' but escalating if not responded to. You might notice that your baby cries and then stops to listen to see whether you are coming or not. If not, s/he resumes crying with more commitment than before. The same behaviour can sometimes be intentional (and therefore truly communicative) and sometimes not. It is important to understand both sorts of cues, but the main focus of this book will be the behaviours that develop into later communication signals.

Whenever we look at children's behaviour we should consider whether they are intentionally trying to tell us something. While all behaviours are informative, responding to early attempts to communicate as intentional fosters communicative development. I discuss this more fully in Chapter 3. No matter what the behaviour is, think about whether the baby is using it intentionally. Treating infants in this way promotes their development and will help you recognise when true communication begins. However, we do have to be careful about the signals we encourage as communication cues. It is not pleasant for baby or carer if children learn to use crying and whining as their primary communication signals. Encouraging intentionality is good for development. However, being aware of when undesirable cues are being used intentionally is also important in order to avoid reinforcing them.

Principle 2: Visual cues

The most striking characteristic of children's communication is their reliance on visual communication cues. A shared visual context in which to interact and the non-verbal signals that this affords (such as eye gaze, facial expression and hand gestures) are central to children's abilities to communicate their own thoughts and feelings as well as to understand other people. Furthermore the rich repertoire of visual cues that children employ provides us with a window into their emotional, physiological and cognitive states. They provide us with many different types of information ranging from the emotions to indices of thinking. Without these visual cues (for example, when we speak on the telephone) children's communication is greatly impoverished. I won't go into this in any depth here since it is the main focus of the book.

Principle 3: Communication is innate

A pervasive question across the wide field of psychology is whether we are born with our various human qualities and skills or whether we learn them from others. This debate centres on the nature–nurture argument. The study of communication development also considers this question. A number of factors are often taken as evidence that a particular skill or characteristic is inborn (or innate). First, if there is evidence of the skill (for example, emotional facial expressions) in lower animals, particularly those that are not thought to possess human-like thinking abilities, this suggests that the skill has its origin in our evolutionary past. Second, if the skill is found in all cultures or is 'universal', the argument is made that it must derive from the human genetic make-up since variable learning experiences across cultures have not influenced its occurrence. Third, if human babies develop the skill very early in life, before it is likely that they have learned it, this is also evidence that they have been born with the skill or at least significant precursors to it.

These three ways of tapping the nature–nurture question will be used throughout this book. As you will see, there is often evidence for inborn foundations of non-verbal communication, but what children experience and learn interacts with this and matters a great deal.

Principle 4: Communication is learned

Although every child is born with a considerable genetic endowment that should unfold to produce a good communicator, what they experience during their childhood years greatly influences the fulfilment of this. Children have a lot to learn about how best to use their non-verbal skills and how to read other people's cues. Children use cues such as eye gaze and facial expressions before they fully understand their meanings and the rules underlying them. Understanding this 'unspoken language' develops well into primary school and for some aspects of face processing right up until adolescence. Experiencing good quality interactions allows children to practise and develop their communication skills.

Principle 5: Adults should be attentive

This is perhaps the most obvious thing I'm going to say in this book. We don't gain any information from children's communicative signals if we don't attend to them. Watching for their non-verbal cues, as well as listening to what they say, is more than half the battle in understanding children's communication. What I say in this book will help you interpret and explain what's in front of your eyes. Being attentive is of course central to being sensitive to children's needs.

Principle 6: Responsiveness

I have already mentioned responsiveness as the necessary companion to sensitivity in providing quality interaction for children. There is seldom only one correct answer to a parenting problem (for example, night-time waking). Whatever the approach taken, responding within a reasonable timescale and in a consistent way to children's requests or needs allows them to develop a sense of self-efficacy, to learn what the boundaries are and to feel confident about the carer's availability. All of these are important in children's development. Responding to children's communication attempts fosters their growing understanding of communication.

Principle 7: Scaffolding

Good communication provides the essential bridge between the adult's mind and knowledge and that of the child. It is how information is transmitted from one to the other, providing an essential source of learning. While a lot of child development can be argued to result from individual discovery and exploration, a significant part of development results from social interaction and what children learn from this. This is central to Lev Vygotsky's theory of child development ([1934] 1962) described more fully in Chapter 3. Scaffolding refers to the support given by the adult to the child in assisting their understanding. This concept can be applied to teaching children anything from stacking cups in infancy to algebra in high school. In order to scaffold effectively, the adult has to be able to judge accurately the child's abilities and level of knowledge in order to give new information and help at appropriate times. Making these judgements involves understanding what children are communicating about their knowledge in their speech and non-verbal signals.

In this book I devote a chapter to each of four channels of non-verbal behaviours that highlight interesting aspects of child development – hand gestures, eye gaze, facial expression, touch. A brief summary of each of these chapters follows.

Hand gestures

For me some of the most intriguing aspects of non-verbal communication are hand gestures. In these visual signals there is a wealth of unspoken information that is seldom consciously acknowledged, but nevertheless plays a crucial role in human communication. In Chapter 3 I describe contemporary work on gesture showing that while the eyes may be the windows to the soul, hand gestures can provide a window into the knowledge and understanding held by an individual. As you will see, this is especially true with children who often struggle to express themselves in verbal speech simply because they do not yet have the necessary language skills to do so.

There are many different types of gestures, all with different developmental time courses. Some types of gesture precede verbal expression and allow us to see evidence of understanding or knowledge before a child can tell us this in speech. Gesture can be a precursor to verbal expressions in both infancy and later childhood. Furthermore, parental awareness and

helps dev. understanding.
aid what child is
trying to see

use of gesture can have important effects on the development of their child. It may be possible to use children's gestures to make adults better teachers, sensitising them to children's ever-changing levels of understanding.

Eye gaze

In Chapter 4 I describe the evolutionary and developmental significance of eye gaze, including the most recent research showing what infants do and do not know about other people's eyes. Babies begin to look at their caregiver's eyes at around two and a half weeks of age. This mutual eye contact is an important source of social communication for both baby and adult. It has been linked to a number of aspects of social and emotional development and also has a significant emotional effect on caregivers. Eye contact and other aspects of gazing behaviour play an important role in children's mental development. For example, if a baby of around six months (possibly earlier) sees you turn your head, s/he will often follow the direction of your gaze. It appears that this is important in a number of ways, one of which facilitates language acquisition. If you are saying 'what a lovely doggie' to a baby, it helps to ensure that the child attends to the thing you're talking about rather than something else that might catch his attention. Whether such 'glance tracking', as it has been called, involves the baby reflecting in any way about your focus of attention is a source of some controversy at present.

Certain types of gazing behaviours have important consequences. For example, looking away from the person you are speaking to while you are working out an answer to a question increases your chances of successfully thinking through the problem. Averting your gaze seems to reduce the level of distracting information (from the other person), allowing you to concentrate better. Until recently we did not know whether children did this. Some of my recent work suggests they do, but perhaps not consistently until the primary school years. Chapter 4 finishes by describing how gaze aversion can be used as a cue to children's thinking and in particular their readiness to learn.

Facial expressions

Children develop abilities both to produce and understand faces throughout childhood. Human beings are incredibly influenced by faces. We use our faces to express different types of information, ranging from different emotional expressions (for example, happiness, sadness and disgust) to facial gestures (such as raised eyebrows to signal disbelief). Other important types of information we get from faces, discussed in Chapter 5, include visual speech (or lip-reading) and individual identity.

There are a number of inborn mechanisms underlying our abilities to understand and use faces; for example, newborn babies make disgust expressions in response to bitter tastes. Just moments after birth, babies prefer looking at pictures of faces compared with pictures of other objects. However, the fine-tuning of facial expressions and our understanding of them develop with age. Children's abilities to control their facial expressions improve well into primary school. Being able to understand and produce appropriate facial expressions is essential to children's social development and acceptability. Problems with understanding faces have been linked to certain developmental disorders such as autism. However, even for normally developing children there are considerable individual differences in ability. This can be one factor in whether children are popular within their peer groups or rejected by them. Other aspects of face processing also develop over a long period of time. The ability to identify faces develops well into the teenage years. Fundamental differences in the ways that younger and older children process faces are described.

Touch

Touch is a very important part of human social relationships and has important influences on development. Touch is perhaps the most primitive channel of non-verbal communication in evolutionary terms. It is like 'social glue' for many non-human primate groups, helping to maintain social bonds through grooming and touch. There is plenty of scientific evidence that monkey and human infants who are deprived of social and touch contact suffer significant negative consequences. For example, infant monkeys raised in isolation are entirely inept in their social relationships with other monkeys once introduced to a group.

Appropriate and positive levels of touch can bring about a number of social, emotional, mental and even physical benefits. For example, touch has been used as an effective therapy with premature infants. Research has shown that premature babies who receive 'touch therapy' recover faster from a number of medical conditions often associated with premature birth. Furthermore, their long-term cognitive development is also more favourable. Touch is perhaps the most rule-laden channel of non-verbal communication. Some of the rules in relation to adults and children will be discussed alongside some of the anxieties that exist in many cultures relating to interpersonal touch.

Applying knowledge

This book will enable professionals working with children and parents to understand children better by increasing their awareness of non-verbal behaviours. It is not enough just to read the book; it is essential that you practise observation of the things you've read about. Whenever I lecture on these topics I always use video clips showing examples of behaviours which help to consolidate what I'm saying. Every behaviour I've described in these pages is entirely natural and an integral part of everyday interactions. This is partly why we sometimes don't notice what's going on right in front of us. To help remedy this, at the end of each chapter I have given a list of things you can look for and try out. These lists are there to get you started. What you notice and your subsequent understanding will increase as you become a practised watcher of non-verbal behaviours.

I finish this introductory chapter with a story that clearly illustrates the important role which non-verbal signals play in children's communication. A few years ago when my daughter Charlotte was two years old, we had friends visiting from Denmark. Both parents spoke excellent English, but their daughter, also aged two, spoke only Danish. Since Charlotte knows no Danish this gave the two children an interesting situation to overcome. They couldn't use any words to communicate with one another and yet had a day ahead of them during which they had a captive playmate.

All the parents had different expectations as to how the children would get along; in fact they became best of friends. They played together happily for many hours, laughing excitedly and obviously enjoying one another's company. They managed to negotiate games and the use of toys without speaking. For them, not being able to speak a word to one another did not interfere with their plans and they were able to accomplish together what they wanted without any common language. Of course it could be argued that the tasks they set themselves were limited and that others would have proved more difficult. This is true. However, what the story serves to show us is that while language is important it is not always the bottom line in communication. We have many other non-verbal ways with which to express ourselves. In everyday, face-to-face conversation non-verbal communication gives us a huge amount of information. It is the development of non-verbal skills that is the topic of this book.

Note

1. Good interaction with the primary caregiver is particularly important. But it is also important in all the child's close relationships. In this book I often refer to parents and especially mothers. Most of what is discussed can be extrapolated to other carers and usually when I say mother I mean primary caregiver.

Chapter 2

The Balancing Act
of Social Relationships

In this chapter I am going to describe a social psychology theory (equilibrium theory) that is a useful framework for understanding important aspects of social relationships. I will first discuss two factors that characterise all social relationships – how much we like/dislike other people and whether we are dominant or submissive to them. These characteristics of relationships go some way to explain the numerous rules of engagement that exist within and across cultures. We will then look at the evidence that, contrary to popular beliefs, even quite young children have an appreciation of these rules similar to those of adults. Some advice is given relating to establishing a positive interaction style when greeting and communicating with children. Finally I will describe a study of the use of live video links for interviewing child witnesses. The results of this study are interpreted using equilibrium theory.

Social relationships refer to any relationship between two or more people. These are of course extremely varied in nature, ranging from: relationships between babies and their mothers; close friendships; acquaintances; sexual relationships. Despite the variety, all can be described in broad but similar terms.

Interpersonal attitudes and social relationships

One common denominator in social relationships is that they all involve 'interpersonal attitudes'. Interpersonal attitudes are very similar to emotions, but differ in one important way. If we feel angry, happy or sad we are experiencing emotions. If these experiences are directed towards someone else (for example, you are angry with someone), this is an interpersonal attitude (Argyle 1996). The expressions of emotions and interpersonal attitudes are very similar and typically involve certain characteristic non-verbal cues.

People's behaviours within social relationships can be described in terms of two general interpersonal attitudes:

- whether they are friendly versus hostile
- whether they are dominant or submissive. (Foa 1961)

These vary independently on different continuums. In other words, changes in friendliness can occur while the level of dominance remains the same, and vice versa. Figure 2.1 illustrates this. Think carefully about the various relationships you have. You can, with a little thought, characterise all your relationships somewhere on these dimensions. For example, how submissive are you to your boss? How much do you like her? It is quite possible to really like someone who is dominant over you. At the same time we sometimes dislike people who are 'submissive' to us. Try plotting where on a copy of Figure 2.1 these relationships would go. In particular, plot where you would put your children in relation to you. How you see your relationships with your children in terms of these dimensions will influence the parenting style you take. Permissive parents are typically warm and loving towards their children but are often very submissive, allowing their children excessive amounts of control. Authoritative-reciprocal parents are very warm and typically are neither submissive nor domineering with their children. They take a middle line, exerting authority over their children but at the same time allowing them to make decisions where appropriate. Authoritarian parents generally lack warmth and can be hostile while at the same time asserting a very dominant position (Baumrind 1967). I've highlighted possible areas in Figure 2.1 that indicate where we might expect to find different types of parents.

Remember the plots refer to parental attitudes *towards their children*, not the other way around. The parenting style adopted has important effects on children. This is not the place to go into this. In short, children of authoritative-reciprocal parents tend to fare better in their social and emotional development than either of the other two groups.

Liking/friendliness and dominance are signalled by the non-verbal cues listed in Table 2.1. All of these signals tend to add together to give an overall impression of liking or dominance. So the more people smile, gaze and touch, the greater the liking between them. In fact it's quite easy to judge how close a relationship is (or how close the participants would like it to be!) just by observing these sorts of behaviours. As relationships change and fluctuate, so too do the non-verbal signals sent between individuals. Couples in love gaze at one another far more than those not reporting to be in love (Rubin 1970). In contrast married couples experiencing difficulties in their relationship look less at one another (Beier and Sterberg 1977).

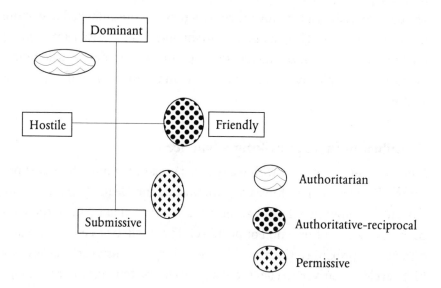

Figure 2.1 Interpersonal attitudes
Source: adapted from Argyle (1996)

The same range of cues is used in signalling dominance. For example, asserting dominance is associated with 'staring down', touching the other person and a non-smiling face. Note that the particular pattern of cues of dominance differ depending on whether or not the hierarchy is established or in flux. In an established hierarchy the more dominant person often gazes less and adopts a more relaxed posture: essentially saying, 'I'm top dog and I don't need to try and impress.'

Non-verbal cues are typically combined with other information; for example, we tend to disclose more personal information to people we like and feel close to than to those we do not. Non-verbal signals of liking and dominance seem to have a more powerful effect than anything we actually say. In one study it was found that non-verbal cues had about five times the effect of verbal messages in terms of whether the speaker was judged to be friendly or hostile (Argyle, Alkema and Gilmour 1972). So what we say matters less than *how* we say it.

Our personalities also influence our use of these cues. People who are extroverts typically use non-verbal signals of liking and affiliation more frequently. They tend to gaze and smile more, stand closer and even gesture more. All in all, extroverts come across as more animated than more introverted people. This can be important and make it easier for them to establish new friendships and relationships. In contrast, people who report being lonely typically don't gaze, smile and gesture as much (Trower 1980).

Equilibrium theory: striking a balance

It has been suggested that within any given social encounter there are both approach and avoidance forces at work (Argyle and Dean 1965). So we are attracted to other people, but at the same time repelled by them (perhaps because of a fear of rejection or hostility). There will be a certain intimacy distance or proximity (increased by close physical distance, but also by high levels of non-verbal cues such as eye gaze and touch), where the motivation an individual has to approach another person exactly balances their motivation to avoid them. At this point the intimacy distance is said to be in equilibrium and the parties involved feel comfortable with the proximity.

The level of proximity is signalled by the sorts of affiliation cues listed in Table 2.1. The greater occurrence of affiliative behaviours, the more intimate or emotionally close the relationship. If the level of intimacy changes (for example, one person gets too close or gazes too much), this can be very uncomfortable. If an imbalance in equilibrium occurs, this is compensated for (Argyle and Dean 1965). For example, if someone makes more eye contact with us than we find comfortable, we typically increase physical distance by backing away or reduce our own level of gaze.

Table 2.1 Non-verbal signals of liking and dominance		
Non-verbal channel	*Liking/friendliness (proximity)*	*Dominance*
Proximity	Closer, forward lean.	Raised position; takes up more space.
Orientation	More direct.	Direct.
Gaze	More gaze and mutual gaze.	In established hierarchy less gaze (relatively more while talking); when establishing dominance more gaze.
Facial expression	More smiling.	Non-smiling, frowning.
Gesture	More lively, similarities.	Pointing at the other or their property.
Posture	More open, similarities.	Full height, hands on hips; relaxed in established hierarchy posture.
Touch	More touching (appropriate).	More touching of other.
Tone of voice	Higher pitch, upward pitch contour.	Loud, lower pitch, greater pitch range.

Source: adapted from Argyle (1996, pp.88, 97)

This also explains why people often reduce eye contact when someone asks them a personal question (Patterson 1973). The question increases intimacy to an uncomfortable level and one way of compensating for this is to reduce eye gaze.

Compensation to redress the imbalance in equilibrium doesn't always happen. Sometimes when someone moves closer, looks too much or touches us, we reciprocate. This might happen if the increase in intimacy is interpreted as pleasant (we think the person is being friendly). If we interpret the proximity in a negative way (embarrassment) then compensation occurs (Patterson 1976).

Cultural differences

Different cultures have very different rules about appropriate intimacy distances. Cultures are generally described as being either 'contact' or 'non-contact' (Watson 1970). Contact cultures (such as Arab, southern European and Latin American) are typically more tolerant of closer physical distances, gaze more, gesture more and touch more. In contrast, non-contact cultures (such as northern European and Japanese) generally maintain their equilibrium at greater distances. So contact and non-contact cultures differ in terms of their proximity behaviours. Contact cultures prefer 'social closeness' while non-contact cultures prefer relative 'social distance'. This is important when people from different cultures communicate. Different non-verbal norms can be a source of considerable tension. For example, people from Mediterranean areas might find British people 'cold'. In return people from Britain may find them overbearing.

Training in cross-cultural contact can be extremely beneficial to ensure that one's style of interaction doesn't cause offence. It has been suggested that these cultural differences are acquired at an early age (Hall 1966). In the next section I will describe some evidence for this, but also highlight ways that children's understanding of intimacy distance differs from that of adults.

Children's proximity behaviours

We know relatively little about children's proximity behaviours. Indeed this is one area where our folk psychology generally lets us down. People often violate adult expectancies when interacting with children, expecting the rules not to apply to children in the same way. However, even babies are sensitive to behaviours relevant to proximity norms. How many of us have suffered well-meaning house guests who on arrival immediately pick up small children and smother them in kisses before the child is comfortable with that level of closeness? Essentially the adult has violated the child's 'personal space bubble'. Children react negatively to this by pushing the adult away and even crying. The lesson to be learned is that we have to respect the personal space of children and reserve overly warm greetings to those we are familiar with. If we don't do this we risk sending the message, 'I am dominant over you and don't have to respect your space.'

Adults have different expectations about children's spatial behaviour depending on the age of the child. Five-year-olds who invade adults' personal space in a public place (e.g. bumping into them in a queue) are responded to in a positive way by the adults. In contrast, eight-year-olds are typically ignored and ten-year-olds are responded to negatively (Fry and Willis 1971). So as adults we tolerate the breaking of intimacy distance rules if the perpetrator is a young child, but not if they are ten years of age or older. There are lots of possible reasons for this. Perhaps we simply don't expect young children to be aware of the rules or to obey them. Furthermore, young children are far less threatening than older children and therefore any violation of personal space is unlikely to be interpreted as a threat or signal of dominance. This idea is supported from observations of behaviour within social groups of non-human primates where physical contact from infants and juveniles is tolerated to a greater degree than from adolescents and adults.

Greeting children

Considering non-verbal signals of affiliation and dominance can help make greeting and welcoming young children more pleasant. Showing children that you are pleased to see them is obviously important, but at the same time we must respect their space. There are a number of factors that give adults 'power' over children. One very basic one is that we are bigger than children and this automatically signals dominance to them. Also adults are normally the responsible ones taking care of the children. So there is an inherent *asymmetry* in adult–child interactions. Typically both parties see the adult as having the upper hand. We can use non-verbal signals sensitively in order to redress the balance. Greetings should obviously show warmth and sometimes affection. Just be vigilant for compensation behaviours that indicate you're coming on too strong. Here are some suggestions for successful greetings:

1. If possible we should try getting down to a child's physical level, thus avoiding the height advantage.

2. Leaning forward with arms straight and backwards is a postural sign of hostility exhibited by toddlers and pre-school children. Figure 2.2 shows a four-year-old child in conflict with her mother. She demonstrates the classic forward posture with her chin raised. Her arms are not straight since she has learned that hands on hips is a sign that people often use when arguing. She is using this deliberately to emphasise her point. Children often present this behaviour towards one another when they are in conflict. Adults often greet small children when standing by leaning their bodies forward while keeping their legs straight, in order to approach the child's face more closely. However, this stance is rather like the small child's hostility posture and may be read as such by them. Much better to get down to their level by bending the knees in order to approach their height.

3. Keep a straight-on orientation. It shows that you are attending to the child. Take time to maintain this until the child breaks the greeting and moves off. A side-on orientation can seem distant and disinterested.

4. Make mutual eye contact but don't stare. Smile.

5. If greeting children emotionally close to you, you may want to give them a kiss or a hug. Be careful that this is OK with them.

Outward signs of affection like this can be embarrassing in front of their friends. This might be reserved for certain occasions.

6. Get the balance right. The closer your relationship, the closer the greeting. Always look for signs that the child is compensating for an uncomfortable imbalance in equilibrium; for example, by averting her gaze or trying to distance herself.

Children's understanding of intimacy distance

Figure 2.2 A conflict posture by a four-year-old girl. The forward lean is a classic characteristic of this. The hands-on-hips feature is an enculturated feature that she has

Pre-school children do not fully understand the social rules surrounding eye gaze, but nevertheless have some sense of what is appropriate and what is not. In one study, pre-school children typically responded to an adult staring at them in a shopping mall by staring back. In contrast, older children generally looked away (Scheman and Lockard 1979). However, in this study the authors report a child who violated adult gaze norms and stared back, but who obviously appreciated that the constantly gazing adult was not behaving normally. On his way past the small boy punched the experimental confederate.

In her dissertation a student of mine investigated proximity and intimacy behaviour in pre-school children (Gooch 1999). There was little evidence that three-year-old children adjusted their gaze behaviours to close proximity with an adult. However, there were some important differences in other behaviours depending on whether or not the children sat close to (48cm) or at a distance (95cm) from an adult while doing a card-sorting task. First, the children were more likely to initiate conversation when they were further away. Second, they engaged in fewer self-touching gestures when far away (self-touching gestures can be a sign of anxiety and emotion) (Souza-Poza and Rohrberg 1972). Both of the findings therefore suggest that the children were more at ease when the adult was at a greater distance. The results show that children as young as three years of age are sensitive to changing social distances.

Other work has shown that approach and avoidance forces are present in children as young as four years. In one study, when approached by an experimenter individual children typically withdrew and when the adult withdrew the children approached. Withdrawal generally happened at a distance of one foot and approach at three feet (Peery and Crane 1980). Furthermore pre-schoolers' approach distance to an unfamiliar adult is further away when an adult looks at them as they approach. So looking at a child closes the intimacy distance, making it less likely that unfamiliar children will approach. Girls generally acquire this knowledge sooner than boys (Eberts and Lepper 1975). This reflects the fact that girls generally acquire the rules of socialisation faster than boys. I find that when beginning work with a new group of young children it is best to sit quietly busy with a task and only look at and engage them once they have approached me. Once a child has engaged then lots of smiling and gazing are the order of the day. The approach can't be forced and should be done at the child's pace.

So children are sensitive to the effects and norms of proximity. Certain situations that violate these norms are stressful for them. Another such situation is crowding. Forced and undesired close proximity can be stressful for adults (Baum, Aiello and Calesnick 1978). Similar effects have been shown in children. In one study ten-year-old children spent time in groups of four under either high or medium levels of spatial density. Crowding had a number of negative effects on the children ranging from stress-related physiological arousal to social/emotional effects like feeling tense and annoyed (Aiello, Nicosia and Thompson 1979).

There are optimal distances for working with children, as there are optimal distances for talking with adults. The distance will depend on how well the child and adult know one another and what task they are doing together. This has implications for one-on-one teaching in the classroom and for the interviewing or assessment of children. A relatively close physical distance can be desirable to maintain task engagement. However, allowing the child to position themselves within reason may help avoid anxiety, particularly if the child is not familiar with the adult. This is less of an issue when the child and adult know one another well.

I am not suggesting that close working and contact should be avoided, quite the contrary. In the chapters that follow I describe the numerous benefits of gesture, gaze and touch for children's learning, communication and development. What I am saying here is to be aware of maintaining a comfortable distance for the child. The importance of this for effective communication is shown very clearly in the next section. I describe one particular situation where distancing children from adults can be of real benefit – the interviewing of child witnesses by unfamiliar adults.

Certain cultural differences in interactional style are found from an early age. It has been noted that lower income black American adults use a closer interaction distance than middle income white Americans (Hall 1966). The same cultural differences have been observed in six- to eight-year-old white and black American children (Aiello and Jones 1971). So at least from the early primary school years children are already adopting intimacy distances that they consider appropriate. These cultural differences have been learned from observing norms within cultural groups.

All in all, even very young children appear to be sensitive to the rules surrounding intimacy distance, which suggests that equilibrium norms exist for them. In addition to this, parents actively teach their children about appropriate interactional distance, moving them closer or further away and showing them how to stand (Hall 1966). Some developmental disorders are associated with particular problems in understanding the rules of social contact. In contrast to typically developing children, those with Asperger's syndrome (a developmental disorder on the same continuum of deficits as autism – see Chapter 4) seem less aware of personal space and the rules about intimacy distance. Furthermore they are less sensitive to encroachments of personal space. They often stand too close to others, unaware of the discomfort this entails (Attwood 1998).

Live video links with child witnesses

It is clear that while there are certain differences in very young children's proximity behaviours compared with adults, the balancing of relationships is no less critical for them. Furthermore, how successfully this is accomplished influences many aspects of children's lives including the interactions they have with their family, peers and teachers. It is never more important to consider these issues than when an adult is trying to obtain information from a child, particularly emotion-laden information. This is of course relevant when children are required to be witnesses in the legal system.

This is often a very traumatic experience for children, especially those who have been victims of crimes. One way that the legal system has tried to accommodate child witnesses and to alleviate the trauma for them is via the introduction of video links into courts where the children have to testify. I have done some research in this area which I will describe briefly since it illustrates the importance of social factors in children's communication as well as the role of visual signals.

Video mediated communication (VMC) refers to a class of remote communication systems which includes visual access for speakers, video phones, live close circuit television (CCTV) links and desktop video conferencing. One specific application of such technology is live video links (live links) that are installed in many UK courts to facilitate the giving of evidence by child witnesses involved in crimes of violence or sexual assault (Davies and Noon 1991; Flin, Kearney and Murray 1996; Murray 1995). The live link allows the child to give evidence from a room remote from the main courtroom, thus avoiding the need to confront the accused or enter the sometimes intimidating atmosphere of the court.

Essentially a typical link consists of a camera that relays the child's image from their remote room to the courtroom where it is displayed on TV monitors visible to the jury, judge, lawyers and defendant. Cameras in the courtroom in turn send an image of either the examining lawyer or the judge back to a monitor in front of the child. So a two-way, live cross-examination can take place without the child setting foot in open court. There are many issues surrounding the use of the live link, not least the importance of giving children the informed choice as to whether they use it or not. However, these issues are not the topic of discussion here. What is important for us is the communicative impact of such links. In other words does using live links affect the quality of evidence given?

Video links may have negative or positive effects on evidence quality for different reasons. Negative effects may result from the attenuation of visual communication cues (such as eye gaze, gesture or facial expression). As you will see from this book, these cues can be central to children's abilities to communicate. Furthermore live links do not deliver these in the same way as face-to-face access. In contrast, a positive influence may result due to a decrease in social and emotional pressure when the social distance between the child and questioner is increased. I propose that the influence of the live link is dual-edged in these ways.

Visual communication

First, if attenuation of visual cues is to be considered to have a negative effect, it must be shown that visual communication signals are important in normal interaction. Much of this book is devoted to convincing you of this and I'm not going to repeat the arguments here. A question that remains is whether video-mediated visual signals can substitute for those found in face-to-face interaction. A number of studies illustrate that in many ways they do not. For example, I have found that with adults video-mediated conversations do not carry the same efficiency benefits as had previously been found for face-to-face interactions (Doherty-Sneddon *et al.* 1997). The superiority of face-to-face communication over audio-only interaction is described in Chapter 3. So if live links decrease access to important information, we might expect a reduction in evidence quality.

Social and emotional effects on testimony

In contrast, the social and emotional benefits provided by the live link could *facilitate* the giving of evidence. There is evidence that providing social support and decreasing intimidation increases the accuracy of children's reports (Goodman *et al.* 1991). One important factor in children's testimony is their ability to deal with leading and misleading questions. Furthermore, children's suggestibility is a situational factor that can be exacerbated by stress (Baxter 1990). In addition children interviewed by a warm, supportive interviewer are more resistant to misleading questions about an event than children interviewed in an intimidating manner (Carter, Bottoms and Levine 1996). An experimental study compared the evidence of eight- to ten-year-olds given either in a mock courtroom or at school. Children questioned in court gave a less accurate recall of events and rated the experience as more stressful than those interviewed at school (Saywitz and Nathanson 1993). So reducing stress should have positive effects on the quality of children's evidence.

Stress and intimidation are reduced in live-link testimony in a number of ways. The main fear children have prior to testifying is of seeing the accused in court (Flin *et al.* 1990). Furthermore, those children who are most worried about seeing the accused have the most difficulty answering questions. Using the link means that the child does not have to confront the accused. Another way to reduce stress is by distancing the child from the questioner (often a stranger who is acting as a 'hostile' lawyer). There is considerable evidence that video-mediated communication involves a 'lack of social copresence' (Sellen 1995). In other words, people report feeling distanced from the person at the other side of a video link. An intimidating stranger should therefore be less frightening on a screen than face to face.

A number of studies have evaluated the use of the live link. On the whole, significant emotional benefits are found. The live link reduces stress in child witnesses and improves the quality of their evidence. Live-link children are rated as more fluent and audible; they are happier and are more likely to be judged as competent to swear the oath (Davies and Noon 1991). However, the authors also report that live-link testimony took significantly longer than the open court (50 minutes versus 24 minutes); the judicial assessment of competence took longer on the live link (three minutes versus two minutes); and importantly, judges were found to be less empathic to the live-link witnesses. So while there are very important benefits to be gained both emotionally and in terms of children's abilities to express themselves, there are also some drawbacks relating to the efficiency of the process and to how those viewing the child's testimony feel towards the child.

Both prosecution and defence lawyers agree that the use of live link enables some children to give evidence who would otherwise be unable to testify (Flin *et al.* 1996). However, there are communicative problems associated with the use of video links. For example, children fail to understand questions more often across the link and they provide less detail. The aim of the child witness work I've done at Stirling was to investigate the communicative impact of the live link in an experimental setting (see Doherty-Sneddon and McAuley 2000).

My study involved a comparison of interviews between adults and children, carried out either via high quality video links or face-to-face interaction. We were interested in the following:

- how accurately children recalled a sequence of events
- how readily they gave this information
- what communication strategies they employed to express this information (e.g. relying on entirely non-verbal versus verbal expression)
- the suggestibility of children to misleading questions.

Our focus was on the way in which the different modes of giving testimony (face to face versus live link) affected communication strategies and how this influenced the quality of information given.

We predicted that there would a 'communicative cost' associated with the use of the video condition in that visual and social cues would be attenuated. However, this attenuation may be advantageous to this type of communication (an unfamiliar adult questioning a child). The increase in social distance through the use of video mediation might decrease the intimidation felt by the child, resulting in more accurate and efficient 'testimony' and a decrease in susceptibility to misleading questions.

The study

Groups of six-year-olds and ten-year-olds took part in the study. The children came to the University of Stirling for the experimental sessions in pairs and were collected by a researcher in a departmental car. A sequence of events was staged upon their arrival. The researcher 'found' a ball and a box in the car and told the children that she did not know to whom they belonged: 'someone else using the car must have left them there'. The children then accompanied the experimenter to 'Fred's' room. They were told that Fred took care of lost property. He was not there and so the experimenter left a note for him. Each pair of children experienced the same sequence of events. Later they were interviewed individually and asked about the events and various details surrounding them; for example, the colour of the notepaper, the picture on the wall in Fred's room, the name of the corridor where Fred's room was, whether the experimenter dropped the ball, and so on.

Three interviewers took part in the study. Each pair of children was interviewed by the same person, one child in the face-to-face condition across a table, the other child across the video link. Each interviewer therefore carried out equal numbers of face-to-face and video-mediated interviews. A phase approach was adopted based on the *Memorandum of Good Practice* (Home Office/Department of Health 1992) for practitioners who interview children. This involves moving from very open questions that allow the children to put their evidence in their own words to increasingly specific questions which can be necessary to get at the required information. Interviewers had an interview protocol that they used to keep track of the information the child gave them. They were given a list of 28 pieces of information that they were asked to elicit from the child in any order. Following the main part of the interview, the children were asked a series of leading questions, three of which were true (positive response correct) and three of which were false.

Positive effects of live link

In several ways the video condition interviews were the same as those carried out face to face, resulting in the same total amount of correct information and generally the same questioning style. The video condition therefore is comparable to face-to-face interviewing in these respects. It does not result in a decreased efficiency of the interview process.

The differences that did emerge between the visibility conditions reflected a positive impact on evidence quality. Amongst the findings were that less incorrect information was produced in the video condition interviews and younger children were more resistant to misleading information. We suggest that these effects are due to a common underlying cause – an increase in the child's perceived social distance from the adult that results in decreased intimidation and increased confidence.

Incorrect information primarily occurred in response to specific and closed questions. So the interviewers had to 'pursue' this information with some effort and increasingly specific questioning. These points of information therefore seemed to be the hardest for the children to recall and were more likely to result in incorrect responding – perhaps because the children were more likely to guess. Age of the children had a significant effect on the number of incorrect responses, with older children giving fewer incorrect pieces of information. In addition, more incorrect information was produced in the face-to-face interviews. Video-mediated interviews were therefore more accurate in that they elicited less incorrect information. It appears therefore that both groups of children were less likely to guess when unsure of an answer in the video link interviews.

Age had a significant effect on how resistant children were to *misleading questions*, with older children more resistant than younger children. More interesting for the current study was that this age difference was evident only in the face-to-face interviews where the six-year-olds disagreed with the adult 47 per cent of the time, and the ten-year-olds disagreed 81 per cent of the time. The level of resistance to such questions in the younger children increased in the video condition to approximately the same level as that of the older group of children (76% and 83% respectively). A distinct benefit therefore exists for the younger children in relation to their ability to disagree with misleading questions in the live link interviews.

These findings support the suggestion that 'distancing the child from the questioner may serve to ease communication' (Westcott, Davies and Clifford 1991). Furthermore, face-to-face interaction with a stranger asking questions is likely to be intimidating for children. So there are informational benefits when social distance is increased through video-mediated interactions. Using the live link helped strike the correct social equilibrium between adult and child and was of benefit to the children.

Practical issues regarding using live link

Negative effects found using the link appear minor compared with the positive benefits, but nevertheless deserve consideration and are indeed informative. One potentially negative impact of the video condition was that interviewers had to expend more effort managing the younger children who were more likely to move off camera and were on the whole more restless in the video condition. One reason for this is inherent in the system: the camera angles only have a limited field of view and both parties have to stay within that. Furthermore, this underlines the importance of careful consideration of camera angles when setting up such a system – a wide-angle shot will give greater leeway. Using a wide-angle shot brings other costs such as an increase in peripheral visual information which may be distracting; and a decrease in size of the image of the speaker, again causing an attenuation of visual cues.

Another negative effect of the video condition was the loss of gestural information. Although gesture frequency was not very frequent in the interviews, 18 out of the 32 children used some gesturing which delivered information that they never articulated in speech.[1] Furthermore, 5 out of the 16 video-mediated interviews contained a gesture of this nature that was not visible across the link. While a relatively small amount of information was transmitted in gesture, it had a one in three chance of going unseen in the video condition. Given this, it is conceivable that certain information (perhaps key to the testimony) could be lost over the link. Again this should be addressed by those involved in the trial procedure. At the very least, camera angles should be set appropriately and judges, jury and lawyers should be made aware of the potential for gesture-only information – particularly from younger witnesses or those describing difficult information.

Summary

In many ways, therefore, video condition interviews do not differ from face-to-face interviews. Our results suggest that where differences do occur, primarily they have a positive impact on evidential quality. It is suggested that such effects are mediated by an increase in children's confidence under the live link condition. Negative effects include the attenuation of visual cues, although such informational loss is more than outweighed by the benefits afforded by increasing children's confidence.

Video links are therefore an important contribution to the legal system. Furthermore, by applying what we know about the social psychology of human relationships and the role of non-verbal signals in human communication, we can understand the particular benefits and problems associated with their use. It is clear that the benefits obtained by interviewing children across live links rather than face to face are at least partly mediated by social factors. In other words, live links are one way of increasing the intimacy distance and thereby redressing the equilibrium within adult–child interactions. This can afford children new confidence with which they can deal more effectively with the adult's questions.

The benefits found with live links exemplify the sorts of benefits afforded more generally by applying equilibrium theory to adult–child interactions. Careful consideration of intimacy distance, especially when the parties are unfamiliar, can help put children at ease. This is reassuring and can increase the children's confidence. This in turn is likely to facilitate how forthcoming they are in any context – be it the classroom, courtroom or simply at home.

Note

1. It is likely that this partly reflected the material the children were being asked to recall. A more demanding topic may have resulted in more gesture.

Suggested reading

1. Baumrind, D. (1967) 'Child-Care Practices Anteceding Three Patterns of Preschool Behaviour.' *Genetic Psychology Monographs 75*, 43–88.

2. Argyle, M. and Dean, J. (1965) 'Eye-Contact, Distance and Affiliation.' *Sociometry 28*, 289–304.

3. Peery, J.C. and Crane, P.M. (1980) 'Personal Space Regulation: Approach-Withdrawal-Approach Proxemic Behaviour during Adult–Preschooler Interaction at Close Range.' *Journal of Psychology 106*, 63–75.

4. Doherty-Sneddon, G. and McAuley, S. (2000) 'Influence of Video Mediation on Adult–Child Interviews: Implications for the Use of the Live Link with Child Witnesses.' *Applied Cognitive Psychology 14*, 379–392.

Key points

1. Non-verbal communications signal interpersonal attitudes: affiliation and dominance.

2. Degrees of affiliation and dominance explain different parenting styles.

3. Every social relationship has a comfortable intimacy distance which has to be kept in equilibrium through the adjustment of proximity cues.

4. There are important cultural differences in proximity behaviours.

5. Children are sensitive to many of the same proximity issues as adults.

6. Different rules surround adult–child versus adult–adult interactions.

7. Live video links result in valuable emotional and informational benefits for child witnesses.

Things to try

The following are some suggestions for things to try with children, which will, it is hoped, help to illustrate some of the points made:

1. Ask the child to place dolls together 'as though they're playing together or talking', and when they are friends or strangers. If the child understands the relationship between physical distance and intimacy distance, she should place the dolls closer when pretending they are friends than when they are strangers.

2. Understand that if you are asking the child about something he doesn't want to talk about, he will avert his gaze or reduce direct orientation to distance himself.

3. Avoid getting angry or irritated with a child when you are trying to extract information as this is extremely counterproductive. In doing so you will reduce your affiliative signals and increase your dominance cues. For example, you are likely to frown and stare the child down. This will be intimidating for the child, greatly reducing his ability to express himself effectively.

4. Observe the child's interactions with other people. There is generally a 'settling in' period when children meet someone they are unfamiliar with. With time they will increase their degree of approach, particularly if they feel relaxed.

5. Try making sure you give positive signals when greeting children. Show that you're pleased to see them and ready to engage with them. Adapt the level of closeness (touch, orientation, gaze) depending on how well you know the child and on the situation.

6. Think of parenting style in terms of the interpersonal attitudes affiliation and dominance. Parents often don't realise how hostile or domineering their style is. We get out of children what we put in. Negative styles of parenting typically result in increased hostility in the recipient children.

Chapter 3

Hand Gestures

Hand gestures are movements of the hands made while communicating. In these visual signals there is a wealth of unspoken information that is seldom consciously taken on board, but nevertheless plays a crucial role in human communication. Contemporary work on gesture is showing us that while the eyes may be the windows to the soul, hand gestures can provide a window into the knowledge and understanding held by an individual. As you will see this is especially true with children. Unfortunately most of the time we are 'blind' to these cues in that we are not consciously aware of them. Even worse, at times we misinterpret children's non-verbal gestures. Children communicate with us in many ways and only one of these is what they say.

In this chapter we look at the development of hand gestures from infancy through to primary school. The important impact that gestures have on a baby's developing sense of communication is described, as are the potential social and mental benefits that this brings. I will describe ways that gestures can be used to gauge mental development and the acquisition of understanding. We will see that hand gestures often deliver a significant amount of information that is never expressed in speech which has important implications for adults teaching children.

While some gestures have a definite form that map to commonly understood messages, many do not. Most gestures we make happen while we speak, and their meaning is integrally linked with the context in which they are made and what we are saying. It is therefore difficult to come up with a 'dictionary of gestures'. There are two types of exceptions to this:

some of the emotional gestures used in infancy and toddlerhood; and emblematic gestures used by adults. I will discuss these briefly, but most of this chapter relates to gestures that are harder to define by their form alone. The important thing to remember is to look for the gestures and make sensible interpretations based on their context and accompanying speech (if any).

Evolutionary history of gesture and speech

Traditionally gesture and speech have been seen to develop as independent systems of expression and communication. Some researchers have recognised a close relationship between gesture and speech and suggested that, in evolutionary terms, language originated in gestural communication which then transferred to vocalised speech. So, before language as we know it had evolved, our distant ancestors may have used gesture to communicate. Modern gestures, it is argued, are a residue of earlier gestural languages. In this vein, gesture is a primitive mode of representing our thoughts that speakers may fall back on when they find it difficult to express something in words (Werner and Kaplan 1963). The attitude that gestures are somehow less demanding than speech is advocated by some of the most recent advances in this field and is one to which I am not opposed. Where I disagree is in the notion that speech has superseded gesture. Instead, I hold the view that gesture is fundamentally integrated in modern-day language and an integral part of our ability to communicate.

So is our use of hand gestures a skill we are born with and are gestures specifically a feature of human communication? Addressing these questions is important when considering how children develop hand gestures as part of their communication repertoires. If gestures are a primitive and basic form of communication, we might expect the use of gestures by animals lower in the evolutionary scale than ourselves. Furthermore, we would expect to see them occurring early in human life and to be culturally universal. When we examine hand gestures in this way we find rather a mixed story. First, a few gestures occur naturally with non-human primates; for example, chimps will use an upturned, extended hand to beg for food. However, in general the existence of gestures in the animal kingdom is very rare indeed. Second, while we see hand gestures in all cultures of the world, there is considerable cross-cultural variability in the form that they take (or how they look). This suggests that the functions which gestures play in human communication may be partly inborn, but the specific use of gesture within any given culture is learned.

There is a handful of culturally universal emblematic gestures, for example, the shrug. Some researchers have proposed that these may be inborn. Also, human infants begin making gesture-like movements in the first few months of life, suggesting that they occur naturally and without learning. These quickly develop into intentional signals that they use to communicate. Furthermore, many such gestures actually precede and may indeed facilitate language development. It seems that there must be a considerable amount of inborn knowledge about gesture that quickly unfolds. Using hand gestures to communicate seems to be uniquely human and at the same time open to the forces of cultural learning.

Types of hand gestures

Very broadly speaking, there are three main types of gestures:

- emblems
- illustrator gestures
- emotional gestures.

The main focus of this chapter will be the development of emblems and illustrators. We will return briefly later in the chapter to look at emotional gestures.

Gestures that can stand alone

Emblematic gestures are those that can be directly and easily translated into verbal words. They have a definite meaning that is understood without having to say anything. Examples are the 'thumbs up' hitchhike sign; the 'thumb and index finger' OK sign; and the 'V' for victory sign. Within our own culture and in a number of others these are similarly understood. There are however many important cultural differences in the forms and meanings of emblematic gestures. Without an awareness of cultural differences such gestures are a sure way of getting yourself into difficulties in other countries. For example, the thumbs up sign in Iran is an obscene gesture and signs like our OK have sexual connotations in countries such as Ethiopia and Mexico. The cultural diversity of these gestures illustrates that their specific use in different countries is culturally learned. Children therefore learn these gestures and their meanings in the way that they learn their own native languages. Cultural differences are described in more detail towards the end of the chapter.

It is not well documented when children actually start to use these gestures and to understand them. In many ways this will depend on their exposure to them, just as children's vocabularies and speech develop faster if they are spoken to frequently. This explains the efforts of parents every-where to avoid exposure of their little ones to some of the less desirable emblematic gestures. Furthermore, gestures are typically not taught to children in a deliberate way, it is something they pick up over several years of being immersed in their culture. One exception to this is the very explicit way that hand waving is taught to children. During the first half year of life parents will wave their children's little arms saying 'bye bye' and other similar expressions. Babies start being able to do this themselves around nine months of age.

It is also around nine months that babies start to play peek-a-boo, to raise their arms as a request to be lifted and to imitate actions like eating out of context. All of this represents their increasing ability to represent things mentally in their minds. Hand gestures allow them a way of expressing these thoughts. Another form of gestures that babies adopt easily are baby sign languages. These are essentially contrived systems of emblems designed to facilitate pre-verbal infant communication and are described later.

Gestures that are tied to speech

The development of *illustrator gestures* is well documented. Illustrator gestures are the hand movements that we do while speaking and so the study of illustrators applies primarily to children who have begun to talk. Pre-verbal babies do move their hands while they babble and chatter, some very expressively. Indeed these movements are in close synchrony with the timing of the stream of vocalisations. This temporal relationship between speech and movements may reflect an underlying link between gesture and language in the brain. We'll discuss this later in the chapter. As infants mature, the hand movements become finer and begin to resemble proper gestures.

We all gesture to some extent as we speak, some of us more than others. I am a high frequency gesturer and find it difficult to explain things without considerable movement of my hands – a great source of amusement to my students when I lecture on this topic. Some people gesture less, but almost everyone gestures to some extent. The amount we gesture depends on what we're talking about, with gesture generally increasing when we are describing difficult material, or if we become emotionally excited about the topic.

Illustrators are typically difficult, if not impossible, to interpret without some knowledge of what is being spoken and/or the context of what is going on. We are generally unaware of our own use of such gestures, and it is my experience that we seldom take any *conscious* heed of other people's gestures. This is especially true when we speak with young children. We often recount proud tales of what our youngsters say in words, but rarely what they say in gestures. I hope to show in the rest of the chapter that this is a major oversight if we are fully to appreciate what young children are expressing.

There are many different sub-types of illustrator gesture. These perform a number of different functions. For example, they can repeat, clarify or even add to information expressed in speech. Table 3.1 shows some of the ways in which different types of illustrator gestures have been described (McNeill 1992). It is important to categorise gestures in this way, since the likelihood of seeing a child perform each of the different categories changes with the child's age. 'Pictures in the air gestures' and pointing are produced frequently by younger children while metaphoric and beat gestures are all but absent in the early years. The changes we see in children's use of gesture reflects their ever increasing mental abilities.

The different categories of gesture listed in Table 3.1 will be useful to refer to as I describe the development of hand gestures in children.

Table 3.1 Types of illustrator gestures	
Illustrator type	*Example*
Iconic	Visual 'picture in the air' of an object or action described in speech: e.g. drawing a circle in the air when saying or trying to say 'circle'.
Deictic	Pointing to indicate spatial location of things being discussed.
Metaphoric	'Picture in the air' of an abstract concept: e.g. using two hands like weighing scales to represent balancing ideas or options.
Beat	'Beat' out the rhythm of the speech: e.g. short up and down movements used along with words emphasised in speech.

Development of speech and gesture

McNeill (1985) considers a number of lines of argument which support the notion that language and gesture are integrally linked. I will describe a couple of these. First, gesture and speech seem to develop together in children. As children's abilities to express themselves with symbolic language increase, the nature of their gestures also changes. With development, children's gestures move from being very concrete representations of what they depict to being more symbolic. For example, a three-year-old might describe someone running by actually running on the spot – a concrete representation of running. In contrast, an eight-year-old is likely to use a more symbolic representation; for example, two fingers 'running'.

Another source of evidence for the close link between gesture and speech are the particular patterns of gesture loss that accompany speech loss with different types of aphasia in adults. Aphasia refers to a number of syndromes caused by brain damage (perhaps due to stroke or head injury) that involve complete or partial loss of speech. Very broadly speaking there are two main types of aphasia: Broca's type and Wernicke's type. These result from damage to Broca's area and Wernicke's area of the cerebral cortex respectively. The cerebral cortex is the outermost part of the brain and is associated with what we generally consider our ability to think.

Broca's aphasia is characterised by a significant, if not complete, loss of vocal speech. Any speech is slow and laboured. What remains for these people is an understanding of what they are trying to communicate and other people's communication directed to them. Furthermore, they produce many and often elaborate iconic gestures. I have seen adult Broca's aphasics who have almost no speech completing a complicated communication task (the map task, described later in this chapter) to the same level of accuracy as normal 14-year-olds (Merrison, Anderson and Doherty-Sneddon 1994). The reason they managed to communicate so well was through the use of iconic gestures; for example, drawing pictures in the air of the things they were trying to describe.

In contrast, people with Wernicke's aphasia speak fluently, rapidly and grammatically. However, they show little understanding of their own speech or that of other people and therefore communicate very poorly. Furthermore they make little use of iconic gestures, but often accompany their speech with beat gestures.

The contrast between Broca's and Wernicke's aphasics clearly shows that communication is not all about language. A case report of a three-year-old boy with communication difficulties illustrates the same point (Blank, Gessner and Esposito 1978). The child's sentence structure and vocabulary development were age appropriate. Furthermore, the way in which he said his utterances (his tone of voice and pitch patterns) was also appropriate. However, he failed to use the language that he had to communicate. Like Wernicke's aphasics, he showed no understanding of what it means to communicate. Interestingly, he also failed to understand or produce non-verbal communication. The root of his problem therefore seemed to be an underlying deficit in understanding about communication.

If you look at the vast literature on children's verbal language development, you will find that by and large most studies have considered this development to occur independently from non-verbal factors. Non-verbal behaviour has been assigned implicitly a rather peripheral role in communication. As I hope you will see, this has been a gross oversight and one rectified by a number of contemporary lines of research. Gestures become increasingly refined and develop alongside speech rather than being phased out.

The need to attend to gestures over and above what someone expresses in words is especially important when the person in question has little or no language. This includes very young children, children with specific or non-specific language delay and learning difficulties. Furthermore the gestures we should look for include not only the common forms such as pointing and reaching, but also more idiosyncratic gestures that may be specific to a given child. For example, carers of autistic children often report 'knowing what a child wants' on the basis of particular non-verbal behaviours that are difficult to interpret by people unfamiliar with the child.

Symbolic gesturing and language development

Words as symbols

In order to look more closely at some of the issues surrounding the relationship between hand gestures and speech, let us now turn to what happens *before* children can speak. Language is a wonderful system that human beings have evolved in order to communicate with one another. Any language in the world is essentially a set of symbols that we can use to represent the world and things in it. I should emphasise here the word *symbol*. A symbol is exactly what its name suggests – a symbolic representation of something. This contrasts with concrete representations that more directly (concretely) illustrate what they refer to. Let me use an example to show this distinction. The word 'dog' written on a page (or spoken) is a symbol meaning 'dog' in English. Someone who does not speak or read English will have no way of knowing this. The word itself gives no indication as to its meaning unless you know the particular language. There are many other just as arbitrary symbols or words that stand for the same thing in other languages; for example, 'chien' in French. In contrast a more concrete representation for 'dog' would be a picture of a dog or perhaps acting out 'dog-like' behaviours, such as pretending to bark. These concrete representations of 'dog' are likely to be understood regardless of any language barrier – although onlookers may think you're rather strange.

Gestures as symbols

Traditionally, researchers studying children's development, and parents too, have treated children's first spoken words as indicating that the infant has begun to be able to think about things symbolically and to use symbols to express themselves to other people. What we know now about children's use of gesture teaches us that there is more to this aspect of development than verbal expressions. More recently we have begun to look at the precursors of language and here we see that children gradually acquire the arbitrary symbols which they use to communicate about the world and their thoughts. Children often progress from expressions that are concrete representations of what they refer to, like saying 'baa baa', to more symbolic representations like the word 'sheep'. As the expression becomes more symbolic (or is more 'distant' from the thing it refers to) it places greater demands on the child's mental abilities since the child has to maintain that representation in his mind without support from the environment (Goodwyn, Acredolo and Brown 2000). So encouraging young children to use concrete representations for new events or objects they come across can help scaffold or support their expressive abilities.

This concept of 'distance between the symbol and what it refers to' has been useful when considering the use of hand gestures in early communication. Early gestures typically are concrete expressions of thought. Later in development the child has the ability to use truly symbolic communication in both gesture and speech. The onset of intentional communication is signalled by infants beginning to use gestures to express their wishes and interests. These early gestures are sometimes called *performative gestures*. There are other names but this will be fine for our purposes. Babies begin using true performatives when they are about ten months old. For example, they can tell us what they want by purposefully reaching towards something or pointing at it. The development of these purposeful gestures, where the baby is deliberately trying to express a thought, desire or wish, is based upon earlier reaching behaviours. A little later infants also direct other people's attention towards objects by holding them up or giving the object to the other person (Bates *et al.* 1979). This shows that on some level they appreciate that other people have thoughts and interests too. So gestures give us another way of judging a child's ability to think symbolically. These gestures may play an important role in paving the way for related aspects of mental development and in particular the child's acquisition of language. Let's look now at some evidence for this.

Does gesture develop into language?

There are two opposing perspectives on how infants learn to communicate. The first assumes continuity between verbal and non-verbal behaviour; that development of language is related to achievements in other domains such as mental and social competence; and that verbal and non-verbal communication share common underlying processors. In other words, development of gesture and experience of using gesture (and other forms of communication) influence language learning. For example, a baby who frequently experiences people responding to her pre-verbal attempts to communicate her wishes acquires a good sense of what communication is all about. She is therefore in a good position to decipher language to which she is exposed.

From as young as three months, babies reach toward objects that they want. By six months this reaching becomes very purposeful. Mothers vary in their responses to this. Imagine a scene where mother Sarah is pushing Megan (ten months) in her buggy around a shop. Megan reaches towards some biscuits. Is she just trying to grab them or is she trying to *tell* mother that she wants them? How Sarah responds will depend on a number of things, one being Megan's age and another whether Megan accompanies her reach with gazing at Sarah. If she thinks that Megan has tried to communicate with her, Sarah ought to respond to her. This needn't be by giving her the biscuits but perhaps at least by saying 'no we're not buying these today' and offering something else. To Megan this is far more meaningful than if her mother just ignores her gesture and turns the buggy away from the shelf. Interpreting reaching as intentional helps develop proper pointing gestures (emerging around ten to twelve months).

Another gesture that looks very like true pointing but isn't is using the index finger when exploring objects. From around nine months babies will investigate objects by poking at them with their index fingers. This helps them to develop a pincer grasp (involving their index finger and thumb) with which to get hold of small objects. At about this age babies get good at using this grasp when eating finger foods like peas and raisins. Babies will therefore 'point' to objects in this way, showing an intention or desire to explore them. However, this is not accompanied by looking at their carer and is not communicative. In other words they would like to touch and poke the object but are not asking for it. Having said this, responding to these gestures as being communicative will facilitate the infant's growing understanding of gesture as communication.

Once children understand real pointing and use it communicatively it becomes an extremely important part of a toddler's communication repertoire. Around 18 to 28 months children often combine one- and two-word utterances with pointing in order to produce a more complex 'sentence'. For example, the word 'give' plus a point towards an apple allows the child to express 'give me the apple' (Goldin-Meadow 1999). So there is considerable evidence that pre-verbal experiences feed into the development of language.

The second opposing view is that there is discontinuity between verbal and non-verbal behaviour, with language acquisition depending upon specific processes that are different from those controlling gestural behaviour. For example, a common assumption among psychoanalysts is that non-verbal behaviour reflects and is controlled by the unconscious, whereas language is controlled by conscious processes (Freud 1915). The discontinuity approach proposes that language acquisition is not contingent upon development of pre-linguistic, non-verbal abilities.

My loyalties definitely lie within the continuity camp. Theoretical arguments for and against these approaches will not particularly add to this book or your enjoyment of it, so I'll spare you the details. I will however describe some more of the scientific evidence that has swayed my own opinion. I believe that communicative experiences have an important effect on infant and child development. Babies and small children have a considerable repertoire of pre-verbal communication tools that allow them to be actively involved in their communicative environments.

Consider an example of two mothers with differing approaches to how best to deal with infant crying. Fiona believes that if she responds too readily when her baby cries she will 'spoil' him and he will cry more often in order to get attention. In contrast, Jacki never leaves her infant to cry if at all possible. Which baby will cry more? Which will learn more quickly about using signals intentionally to communicate with another person? In all likelihood Jacki's infant will fair better. Quickly responding to babies' needs allows them to exert control over you and their environment, making them sure of your availability. It also gives them a chance to experience being a communicator. A lack of response is likely to foster feelings of passivity, helplessness and insecurity. Indeed babies whose parents respond to crying quickly and sensitively end up crying *less* than those whose parents do not.[1]

Bates *et al.* (1979) examined children's verbal and non-verbal abilities between nine and thirteen months of age. She found that 'communicative' gestures – for example, pointing and looking at an object in a social context – were related to children's abilities to say words and understand them. The tendency for gesture ability to relate to language ability became stronger as the children got older, suggesting that, rather than becoming more divergent, these modes of communication become increasingly related with development. This means that verbal and non-verbal systems of communication are interrelated, as a continuity approach would assume.

Through social interactions with others, infants develop an ability to form intentions to communicate. If children practise 'talking' with others about objects and events by gesturing to them, it makes it easier for them to refer later to these things with language. The step from pre-language gesture to speech can be seen as a shift in infants' strategies to communicate. So babies develop an increasing awareness of what communication is and at the same time widen their repertoire of signals to use. Gestures and other signs allow infants to practise communicating and this has an important impact on their development.

Linda Acredolo and Susan Goodwyn from the University of California, are two psychologists who clearly believe that non-verbal communication abilities and experiences influence language development in a definite way. For a number of years they have studied babies' use of gestures – those that the infants make of their own accord and those that are deliberately taught by their caregivers. In one of their studies they looked at the impact of teaching parents a 'gesture language' that they in turn could teach their pre-verbal infants to use for communication (Goodwyn *et al.* 2000). In other words they taught the parents a system of baby signs to use when interacting with their infants. The gestures were typically fairly concrete representations of what they referred to: for example, 'flapping arms' to stand for 'bird'; 'palms up and out' to stand for 'where is it?'.

The parents and babies took part in the study from when the babies were 11 months old to three years old. Other parents also took part but were not told to use signed gesturing with their babies. Instead they focused on consciously labelling verbally as many objects as they could while interacting with their infants. A third group of parents and babies was given no instruction at all. The study showed that the babies whose parents had taught them sign gestures did better on a number of measures of verbal language development than those who had not received this special treatment. They were better both at expressing themselves verbally and understanding other people's speech. Furthermore, little advantage was found for the verbal training group, showing that the advantages in the signing group were not due to the families' involvement in research looking at language per se. It seems as though experiencing *using gestures* to express yourself *before* you can do so verbally gives you an advantage in terms of acquiring language. In many ways this makes good sense. Concrete representations, like the signs used, are easier for babies to understand than the more abstract words that language provides. Practising with these easier 'building blocks' helps smooth the way for the harder task of tallying verbal words with objects.

I should point out that this was far from a foregone conclusion. Many parents and professionals working with deaf children have voiced the concern that exposure to gestural sign language might impede vocal language acquisition. In fact this has been shown not to be the case for deaf or hearing children (Goodwyn *et al.* 2000; Schlesinger and Meadow 1972). In addition, exposure to such sign systems in infancy can have a positive impact on both the baby's self-esteem and the bond between child and caregiver. This is likely to be mediated by reducing the frustration experienced by both parties because the sign system gives the infant a clearer way of expressing himself prior to having verbal words at his disposal.

Earlier work by these researchers showed that babies between 11 and 24 months of age use gestures of their own accord to refer to objects (in other words to name things). Interestingly, the girls in their group of infants were more likely to gesture than the boys. The use of gestures also predicted verbal vocabulary development, with children who produced a higher number of gestures increasing their verbal vocabularies faster. There have been some claims in the research literature that this early naming by gesture is easier than naming by speech. In fact, Goodwyn and Acredolo (1993) conclude that although babies begin using such gestures slightly earlier than verbal words, the difference in age of onset is much smaller than previously thought. A baby has to have developed the necessary thought processes in order to 'know about naming' before doing either. Once these are in place, gesture may be slightly easier than words.

An important point to re-emphasise is the intentional nature of human communication. By the end of the first year of a child's life, she has a variety of non-verbal communication signals available to use *intentionally* in order to influence other people around her. The practise and experience of doing so provides the basic knowledge about what it means to communicate with others that motivates the child to learn language (Sugarman 1983). Furthermore, the behaviours that link into this developing sense of intentionality are often not obvious and may include gestures which are idiosyncratic to certain children. For example, mothers of breast-fed infants may report that their infants push back towards the breast when hungry. Whether a mother responds to this behaviour as intentional or not may well have an effect on the child's later behaviour.

Encouraging pre-verbal children to communicate by using hand gestures is beneficial for their development. You can make up your own gestures to teach children. Early on choose movements that make concrete 'pictures' of what they represent. For example, a gesture for 'do you want some milk?' for a breast-fed infant might be to tap a breast. Children will also devise their own gestures; all you have to do is look for them and respond appropriately.

Experiences that babies have before they can speak not only influence vocabulary development, but also other aspects of conversational skills. Work with very young infants shows that as early as eight to twelve weeks of age certain hand and arm movements are synchronised with mouth movements (Trevarthen 1977). This suggests that there may be an inborn (innate) co-ordination of hand and mouth movement. Such innate abilities may, together with a responsive caregiver, provide a framework within which the infant learns the fundamentals of communication. Early infant–carer interactions have been called 'pseudo-conversations' because of the apparent 'taking of turns' by infant and caregiver to 'say' something. Imagine a carer and baby engaged in face-to-face 'play'. The baby coos and babbles. When she stops the carer interjects something in response, such as: 'What a lovely story, tell me another.' The carer stops her speech in readiness for the baby's next contribution. A number of scientists believe that these exchanges are caused by an innate temporal organisation of the infant's behaviour that produces spurts of activity and vocalisation. Care-givers respond to this by fitting their behaviour into this sequence. Some psychologists propose that these 'pseudo-conversations' help babies learn about verbal co-ordination and conversational turn taking (Bruner 1975).

Parents should be encouraged to play these conversational games with infants from an early age. Obviously daily care of an infant involves many interactions. It is beneficial to make a little time each day to have a face-to-face conversation where adult and baby are engaged, for the sake of it, with one another. By doing this, both parties have a valuable opportunity to learn about each other. Here are some suggestions to help get a successful face-to-face conversation going:

1. The baby and adult should be facing one another directly, the baby lying in a comfortable, secure seat that allows freedom of movement. The full-front, face-to-face orientation is very stimulating for infants.

2. Ideally the baby should be as upright as possible. There are a number of types of baby seats and bouncers that suit the purpose.

3. Very small babies (particularly less than eight weeks) might protest at being in such a seat. In which case the baby can be placed on the carer's lap, still in the face-to-face orientation, with her back and head supported by the carer's arms and hands. This obviously disallows gestures. Nevertheless very young babies will get lots of stimulation from the carer's face.

4. The baby's face should be level with the adult's. We seldom have conversations with people where one of us is elevated and hanging over the other. The same should go for adult–baby interactions.

5. The baby should have a clear view of the adult's face, arms and hands (unless position (3) is being used).

6. The conversation should be relaxed and not forced. The baby should be allowed to lead. She will make movements and vocalisations in spurts. The adult should go with the natural flow and interject in between these periods. Remember that most of us are very good at talking to babies; it's something that comes naturally.

7. As you get to know the baby and she gets older, you will become better at recognising the cues she sends. She will also become more adept at influencing your behaviour by her own.

You must get the point

Not only do we often miss non-verbal messages altogether, but also we see the signal and misinterpret it. One example of a gesture that adults sometimes misunderstand, when it is used by a toddler, is the declarative point. Imagine a scene where a mum, Sally, has taken her 18-month-old son, Jack, for a picnic near a river. Jack has been exploring his surroundings while Sally watches carefully. He walks over to a large oak tree and starts to pick some daisies. He then heads towards the river but Sally shouts out, 'No Jack, you mustn't go near the water, come back and see Mummy.' Jack dutifully returns to Sally for a few minutes. He then heads off for some more daisies. He stands up and points at the river and looks at his mum for some time. Sally responds with a note of annoyance in her voice, 'No Jack, Mummy told you not to go near the river.' Sally has interpreted Jack's point to mean 'I want to/intend to go over there', and now he's in trouble. In all probability Jack will be rather bemused by his mother's irritation, since all he was doing was *commenting* on the river, drawing his mother's attention to it. The point is his way of saying 'there's the river/it's making a nice noise/it's very pretty'. He isn't *requesting* a trip over to it. The point is his way of sharing his thoughts with her, and an important indicator of his mental development.

The mismatch between Jack's intention and Sally's interpretation reflects the division of early pointing into two main types: *protoimperatives* that are requests and *protodeclaratives* that are comments (Bates, Camaioni and Volterra 1975). We can't blame Sally for her misinterpretation since she has been responding to Jack's pointing gestures as *requests* for several months. For example, he often points to objects he wants, like his favourite book, meaning 'give me the book'. However, he also *comments* on objects by pointing at them, and giving and showing them to people. On the picnic he is using his point (in conjunction with a *prolonged* gaze at his mother) to comment on the river without necessarily intending to go there. When the pointing and glance is brief, toddlers are more likely to be signalling their intention to approach the object of their attention. Using gesture to comment on things is communicatively more advanced than using it to request things and indicates that the child has developed an important social understanding – that other people have mental states.

We see evidence for this assertion in the study of communication by autistic children. Autism is a pervasive developmental disorder, characteristics of which are more fully described in Chapter 4. Particularly relevant here is the fact that autistic children often use gestures to request things but they rarely use pointing just to share interest with another person (Baron-Cohen 1989). The lack of protodeclarative behaviours, such as showing objects and directing other people's attention, along with a lack of pretend play, can be indicative of developmental delay. If combined with a lack of monitoring eye gaze, these features can predict the development of autism (Baron-Cohen, Allen and Gillberg 1992). Similarly children with Asperger's syndrome do not use protodeclarative pointing or show objects to others in ways that typically developing children do. These gestures are outward signs that the toddler is beginning to think about and understand that other people have thoughts and their attention can be manipulated. A lack of understanding about other people's minds is a crucial feature of both Asperger's syndrome and autism.

Another common mistake made by adults is to misinterpret a toddler's showing of an object (in order to comment on it or to elicit an opinion from an adult) as meaning that he is giving the object. For example, a 17-month-old boy has experienced that when out for walks some objects but not others evoke negative reactions from his parents. So picking up flowers is allowed while poking at bees on flowers is not. Handing mum a piece of litter gets a negative reaction but collecting stones does not. How should we interpret the following action from this toddler? He has been looking at the autumn leaves on the ground while walking with his mum in the park. He picks up a large red leaf and runs to her holding it out. She thinks he is offering her a gift and says, 'That's a beautiful leaf. Is that for me? Thank you.' However, before he reaches her he throws the leaf away and runs off again. Has he meant to tease his mum? Probably not. What he has wanted to find out is whether he is allowed to pick up leaves. By holding the leaf out towards his mother he is not offering it but asking her opinion. Once he has the information he wants (leaves are good), the leaf has served its purpose.

Older children: beyond infancy

Much of what I have described so far may leave you thinking that non-verbal communication becomes replaced by language. For the sorts of naming functions we've been considering this is in large part true. However, for many roles that non-verbal communication plays, this is not so. The development of communication skills involves learning to use signals in different channels, learning to integrate these signals in appropriate ways and learning how to apply and combine the signals in different communication situations. Rather than look for qualitative changes between young children and adults in their communication styles (with children being very non-verbal and adults very verbal) it may be more fruitful to look at changing patterns of both verbal and non-verbal behaviours. The fact that children are less articulate than adults with verbal communication is not the only reason for their generally different communication abilities. Their holistic communication acts, including verbal and non-verbal components, are different from those of adults. In other words, children's skills with and use of gesture change with age. This is clearly illustrated by the changing patterns of gesture use as children get older.

Gesture change in pre-school

In general very young children (pre-schoolers and in early primary school) use a lot of concrete gestures that closely resemble what they refer to. Pantomimic gestures, as the name suggests, involve acting out the 'to be expressed' information. This often means that these gestures are very large, concrete representations of objects or events. For example, a toddler describing another child's tantrum at play group might act out the tantrum. Children often need this form of expression to get their message across and it is important to give them the time (and sometimes the space) to do so. In contrast older children and adults are likely to use gestures that are more symbolic. Many adults use a lot of gesture while communicating and indeed some of the best communicators are animated gesturers. However, adults seldom use the child-like pantomimics we see in youngsters. An example already given is that, when describing running, children often run on the spot whereas adults might instead gesture 'run' with two fingers.

An important milestone in the development of pantomimic gestures occurs between the ages of three and five years. During this time the form of these gestures changes (O'Reilly 1995), reflecting an increase in the symbolic nature of the gestures. For example, when describing actions involving tools, three-year-olds will typically use a body part to represent the tool. In other words, they use a body part as a concrete substitute for the tool. If you ask a child of this age to describe (without speaking) how they brush their teeth they will often show you by pretending their index finger is a toothbrush. In contrast, if you ask a five-year-old child to do the same thing, they will hold their hand as though they are holding an invisible toothbrush and pretend to brush. So the specific form of gestures used can give us an insight into the underlying symbolic abilities of the child: the more advanced, the less concrete the gesture. In other words, gesture indicates aspects of how children are thinking because it helps them to represent their thoughts to the external world. In addition, it can also help us gauge the degree to which these thoughts have developed. Seeing a child use increasingly symbolic gestures lets us know that he is developing abilities to think using symbolic mental representations.

Choosing a strategy

Children's understanding of the appropriateness of certain gestures also changes with age. For example, when asked to direct someone's attention to a set of objects at a distance, four-year-olds often point. However, this is ambiguous because it is hard to tell where someone is pointing when the objects are far away. In contrast, nine-year-olds and adults prefer to verbally name objects when they're far away, although they are just as likely to use pointing when referring to things close at hand (Pechman and Deutsch 1982). This suggests that not just isolated language or non-verbal skills are lacking in young children, but a lack of knowledge about how to use such communicative tools efficiently. Increased language skills offer more communicative options, but what must also develop is an increased awareness of how effectively to employ the skills that are available. It can be very frustrating for children when they are unable to get their message across. Young children fail to see the inappropriateness of certain signals and may not understand why they're not understood. A confounding problem is that young children tend to blame their listeners for communi-cation failures and become quite irate that their 'perfectly adequate' messages are misunderstood. It can be helpful in such circumstances to suggest a change in strategy with an explanation as to why. For example, if a child is pointing at a distance and you can't tell what they're referring to, try and explain to them why you cannot understand. Follow this up with a helpful line of questioning to get the necessary information.

Deaf children born to hearing parents

One thing that emerges from the literature on children's communication is that there is a powerful, inborn drive or need to communicate. Even in adverse circumstances communication typically finds a way. This is clearly demonstrated by deaf children born into hearing families who do not know sign language. In this situation the child is in a difficult predicament. He cannot hear the language being spoken around him in order to learn it and his parents do not yet know an appropriate visual sign language. Susan Goldin-Meadow has done some fascinating work in this area. She found that in these circumstances the children develop their own lexicon of signs to communicate with those around them. In other words they develop their own informal set of sign-language signs. Furthermore, this gesture system remains stable over several years. The individual signs are combined into strings of gestures rather like sentences. Stringing gesture like this is not found in the spontaneous gestures of hearing people (either adults or children). The gesture systems produced by the deaf children are more like language than the non-verbal gestures that hearing children and adults use to accompany language. This 'gesture into language' transformation takes place when the gesture system has to carry the full burden of communication; that is, when it becomes the primary mode of communication (Goldin-Meadow 1999). This is a little like the sort of behaviour you might find yourself engaging in when trying to communicate a reasonably complex message across a noisy room at a distance. What is interesting about deaf children of hearing parents is that they fall back on a system of gestures when they have no access to spoken language. In the next section we will see that hearing children also rely heavily on gesture when their limited language skills prove insufficient.

Illustrative gestures add to speech

Gestured information adds to the information given in speech for normal hearing adults and children. Furthermore, some studies have shown that gestures which accompany speech are taken on board automatically by naive listeners who watched video recordings of people narrating stories (McNeill, Cassell and McCullough 1994). Researchers asked children and adults to watch Sylvester and Tweetie-Pie cartoons and then tell the stories back to another person while being video taped. This work showed a number of interesting features in the development of gestural communication. First, adults and children often gave information in their gesture that they never in fact said in speech. What is more, the people who watched the recordings of the storytelling unconsciously incorporated this information into what they 'thought' the storytellers had actually said. For example, in one cartoon scene, Tweetie-Pie's Granny punches Sylvester the cat out of a window. One participant described this by saying, 'Then Granny threw Sylvester out of the window.' This was accompanied with a *punching* hand gesture. People who watched the video recording of this account sometimes said in their own telling of the story, 'Granny *punched* Sylvester out of the window' (McNeill *et al.* 1994).

So even though they had not actually *heard* that Granny had punched Sylvester they had *seen* this gestured. This had the same effect as if the first storyteller had said that Granny had punched Sylvester out of the window (McNeill 1985; McNeill *et al.* 1994). Evidence from research such as this clearly shows that we often articulate information in gesture which we never say. In addition, listeners are perfectly capable of capitalising on this extra source of information.

Figure 3.1(a) shows a sequence of stills of a six-year-old child taking part in my own work. She is describing a Tom and Jerry cartoon she has just watched. The first series of stills shows what she was doing while she said, 'Then Tom poked his ear.' What she says doesn't make much sense unless you see what she is doing non-verbally. In conjunction with her visual behaviour it is clear that she means that 'Tom pricked his ear and oriented it all around the room' – a sentence you're unlikely to get verbally from a six-year-old.

Figure 3.1(b) shows the same child saying, 'Then he took the doctor's ears.' Again this sentence makes little sense and could easily be misinterpreted if attention is not given to what the child is 'saying' non-verbally. Her visual behaviour helps illustrate that she is referring to a stethoscope.

If we are truly to appreciate all that children are 'saying' to us we must attend not only to what they say but also to what they gesture. It is clear in the examples I've given what information is added in hand gestures. You may well be asking how much this actually adds to the informational content of children's communication in general. In other words, are these examples fairly isolated incidents that would have little impact in the grand scheme of a child's overall communicative abilities? I would argue that gestures significantly increase children's abilities to communicate. Essentially, when children and indeed adults begin to struggle to say what they want in words (i.e. the topic becomes challenging), they tend to fall back increasingly on non-verbal strategies. So adults gesture more often when describing difficult versus easy material. The thing with young children is that they are more likely to find a wider range of material challenging.

Figure 3.1(a) A six-year-old describing Tom the cat 'poking his ear'

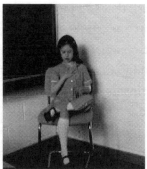

Figure 3.1(b) A six-year-old describing 'a doctor's ears' (stethoscope)

Remembering as pictures or words

Another reason why young children may retain certain parts of information in a form that they gesture but do not express in speech is that they may remember it visually. When we store something in our memories we can do this verbally and remember it as a series of words and sentences that describe the memory (this is a gross simplification). Alternatively we might remember the event as a visual image, rather like a picture in our mind. It could be that certain types of gestures represent pieces of knowledge or information that we have stored in our brains in visual form. This would explain the frequent use of pantomimics when children narrate back visual events they have seen, like cartoon stories. Sometimes children do not verbally encode information because they have limited vocabularies. They may not have a verbal label for the item and therefore when representing the event in their minds that item is left visually encoded. Certainly young children (of around five years of age) have a bias to remember drawings that they see in a visual code. In contrast, by the time children are ten years old they are more likely to remember the same drawings verbally; that is, to remember them as verbal descriptions rather than pictorial images (Hitch *et al.* 1988).

Measuring gestured information

The communicative impact of hand gestures for young children is illustrated in some of my other research. I'll describe part of this in detail because it gives a useful task that you too can use to elicit children's communication strategies. In one study I asked pairs of six-year-olds, ten-year-olds and adults to complete a communication task called the map task (Doherty-Sneddon and Kent 1996). The main point of the study was to see how well the participants could communicate when they couldn't see one another, compared with when they could. The reasoning behind this was that if non-verbal signals really matter and actually influence how much information is communicated, then performance ought to be worse when these cues are not available.

The map task involves two people assigned to the role of instruction giver or instruction follower. Each is given a schematic map of the same location. Figure 3.2 shows an example of a pair of maps I've used with children (you can photocopy these and enlarge them to A3 size if you want to try this yourself). At the beginning of the task the instruction-giver's map has a route through the location while the instruction-follower's map does not. The aim of the task is for the instruction giver to tell the instruction follower about the route so that he can reproduce it on his map as accurately as possible. The pair of maps shown include a completed instruction-follower's map (done by a pair of six-year-olds). The children are told that there may be differences between the maps (some discrepancies between the maps were incorporated into their design in order to produce points of difficulty). In face-to-face interactions, the pair of children sit opposite one another with their maps positioned so that they can see one another, but not one another's maps. Figure 3.3 shows two six-year-olds playing the map task. At other times a screen is placed between the pair to produce the unseen context where they cannot see one another at all, but can talk normally.

A useful feature of the map task is that it provides an objective, quantifiable measure of communicative success. By calculating the area (in sq cm) between the original 'correct' instruction-giver route and the route drawn by the instruction follower, a map deviation score is produced for each conversation. In other words, as well as having a sense of how well a conversation has gone, we can actually measure how much information was successfully passed between the pair.

You can try the map task with pairs of children and observe what happens. Alternatively an adult can do the task with a child either as the instruction giver or instruction follower. Each role will elicit a different set of communication skills. The instruction-giver role shows strengths and weaknesses in ability to articulate information in a way that another person can effectively understand. Watch for when the instruction giver chooses to use gesture and when they do not. Look also for how they monitor whether or not their partner has understood their instructions. For example, do they explicitly ask them using phrases like: 'Do you understand what I mean?'; 'Have you done that?' Do they monitor their partner's facial expressions to try and gauge comprehension? The instruction-follower role is good for determining children's listener skills. Do they realise when they don't have sufficient information? Do they signal this verbally or non-verbally with gaze and facial expressions? Try the task face to face and also when you can't see one another (either use a screen between you, sit back to back or better still try doing the task over the telephone). You'll soon see just how important non-verbal communication is – you don't miss the water until the well runs dry!

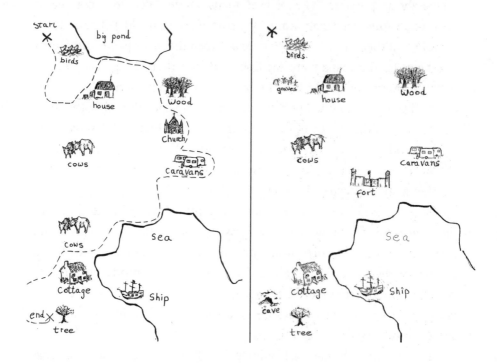

Figure 3.2 One of the pairs of maps used by the children in our research: on the left the instruction-giver's map; on the right the instruction-follower's

For the study the children's maps were identical to maps used with adults in terms of how complex they were. The only difference was that they had features labelled with words which young children would find easier to read. For example, a feature labelled on the children's maps as 'hut' was called 'thatched mud hut' on the adult maps. The adult study showed that adults adapt well to unseen communication (Boyle, Anderson and Newlands 1994), as we would expect given our adept use of telephones. Interestingly, their communication was less efficient when they couldn't see one another. They had to say more in order to complete the task. Such effects illustrate that, even for effective adult communicators with good language skills, visual signals add information that has to be replaced by speech if they cannot see one another.

When we looked at the children we found a rather different scenario. The younger children, on the whole, performed less well than the older children. This is hardly surprising since we'd expect older children to do better. The six-year-old children's routes were around 37 per cent less accurate than the 11-year-olds'. However, the striking thing was that this was only the case when the children *could not see one another* while doing the task. In face-to-face communication, the six-year-olds did just as well as the 11-year-olds. The younger children's performances were much better when they could see one another compared with when they could not. Their performance dropped considerably when they could not see one another's non-verbal cues.

In contrast, the older children adapted well to not seeing one another and communicated to a reasonable standard regardless (Doherty-Sneddon and Kent 1996). So six-year-olds communicated as effectively about the map task as 11-year-olds when interacting face to face, but they did not adjust to being unable to see one another in the way that 11-year-olds did, and their task performance suffered.

This study was the first of its kind to show, in a tangible way, the specific difficulty that very young children have in communicating without a shared visual context. We have found the same face-to-face benefit with other groups of young children doing a number of different types of tasks and are confident that this is a robust effect. We do not however need special communication tasks to see the difference that being able to see made to communication for young children. Anyone who has ever had a telephone conversation with a three-year-old will be able to testify to that.

One reason why the younger children did not adapt to unseen communication was that they used more communicative gesturing than both older children and adults and did not abandon this non-verbal strategy when they couldn't see one another. In the map task study we crudely defined gestures as intentional and communicative if the children raised their hands deliberately above the level of their map supports to ensure their partner could see the gesture (the little girl in Figure 3.3 is doing this). It was therefore obvious that these gestures were used intentionally to communicate a piece of information. The younger children were quite dependent on this type of signal and often fell back on the strategy when words failed them. In addition, when they could not see one another they *still* tried to use these gestures to communicate. I had quite a time keeping the youngsters on their seats and not jumping up to peek around the screen between them. In other words, even when gesturing was not appropriate (i.e. they couldn't see one another) the younger children still did it because they simply couldn't articulate the necessary information in words.

Very young children (pre-school and younger) often do things like nodding in agreement or pointing at objects (without the necessary verbal additional accompaniments) when talking on the telephone, even though their listener cannot see them. Although adults also gesture and nod on the phone, they accompany these actions with speech that expresses the same information; for example, 'mhm' with nodding.

Figure 3.3 A pair of six-year-olds perform the map task face to face.

The following is an extract of a face-to-face map task dialogue between two six-year-olds. The underlined words represent speech that was accompanied by communicative gesture. The speech marked by * represents non-verbal vocalisations which were used to add effect to the gestures they accompanied.

G = instruction giver 4; H = instruction follower 4

Turn 1   (G): Ehm, now do three straight lines.

Turn 2   (H): Straight?

Turn 3   (G): Uh huh.

Turn 4   (H): <u>Like this?</u>

Turn 5   (G): <u>No.</u>

Turn 6   (H): <u>Like this, like this?</u>

Turn 7   (G): <u>No</u> * 'dunk' 'dunk' * <u>straight down the way.</u>

Turn 8   (H): <u>Down?</u> Then * <u>do do do</u> *.

Turn 9   (G): <u>No just three lines straight down the way</u> just three.

This example illustrates how poor the verbal attempts could be with young children doing this task. The instruction giver wants the instruction follower to draw three straight lines vertically down. He does not at first specify that the direction is down. In Turn 4 the instruction follower shows that he has misinterpreted the instruction to mean horizontal straight lines when he accompanies his utterance with a gesture showing a horizontal line straight across. In Turn 5 the instruction giver says 'No' and gestures straight lines vertically down the way, but has not yet verbalised the downwards information. The instruction follower then asks 'Like this, like this?' while gesturing curving lines first vertically down and then horizontally across. The instruction giver repeats his instruction in Turn 7, this time verbalising that the lines are to be drawn down the way, and again accompanies the utterance with gestures designating straight lines vertically down the way. The instruction follower is still confused and accompanies his utterance 'Down?' with a downwards gesture, but accompanies 'do, do, do' with horizontal curvy gestures. The exasperated instruction giver then repeats his instruction accompanying his verbal utterance with vertical downward gestures, and for the first time verbalises all the relevant information. Communication between six-year-olds is not always so desperately painful. This example illustrates what happens when their communication skills are pushed to the limit.

It is therefore crucial to look at children's gestures as we listen to their speech. This can be vitally important if we want to gain a *full* understanding of what they know. Imagine how important it might be to find out *exactly* what had happened to a child giving evidence in a criminal trial. Attending to young children's gestures in these contexts can be extremely important. The use of video links with child witnesses is described in Chapter 2.

Gesture as a tool to enhance children's mental development?

If gesture allows children to articulate information they cannot yet put into words, it has the potential to be a useful way to gauge what children know. A number of studies have shown that when children are just about to understand a concept they are more likely to express information in their hand gestures that they do not express in words (something called gesture–speech mismatch). In other words, gesture sometimes reflects what children know *implicitly* and can't yet express explicitly. Our level of understanding of any given event or problem depends in part on the level of knowledge we have about it. Levels of knowledge can be broadly described as being either explicit or implicit (Karmiloff-Smith 1992). If you hold explicit knowledge of something typically you can verbalise that information. Implicit knowledge is embedded within procedures and we don't express it readily in speech. An example of implicit knowledge is that held by a novice piano player who has learned to play a piece of music by rote (Karmiloff-Smith 1992). The knowledge she holds about the piece is entirely implicit. She cannot verbally explain the sequence of notes, nor can she begin playing halfway through the piece – she has to start from the beginning. In order to become more creative, the pianist would have to acquire more explicit knowledge about playing; for example, through training and experience.

In order to study implicit knowledge we need to ask children to talk about things they don't yet fully understand. Children less than six years old have a number of limitations in terms of how they understand their own perceptions of physical objects. For example, if you show a child of around this age two identical glasses of juice they are usually pretty good at judging that there is the same amount of juice in both glasses. The tricky bit comes when you pour one glass into another taller and thinner glass and ask the child which glass has more juice or are they the same. Many children under six will answer that there is more juice in the tall thin glass because it 'looks more'. In the world of psychology this is called failing a 'liquid conservation task'. This is a task originally designed by Jean Piaget (1972), an important founder of modern developmental psychology.

Passing a conservation task like this involves understanding the simultaneous changing of two dimensions of the glass – the height and the width. The interesting time for us is when children are just about to understand that the amount of a substance can stay the same even if it changes its appearance. The children are in a period of changing knowledge and don't quite understand that the amount of liquid is conserved even if its appearance changes, but they're just about to. During this period, when asked to explain the reason for their answers they will often express some correct information in gesture before they express it in speech (Church and Goldin-Meadow 1986). For example, a child might say that the amount of juice has changed because 'the glass is taller' while gesturing the changing width of the glass with their hand. So on some implicit level they appreciate that the width is changing simultaneously with the height. Once they can deal explicitly with both dimensions they are likely to mention both dimensions in speech, 'because it's taller and thinner', and pass the task.

Children who *fail* such tasks and give the incorrect answer that the amount of liquid has changed will have different levels of understanding relating to it. Some will be almost ready to understand, while others will be nowhere near this point. Children's gestures can help us recognise those who are closest to understanding and hence most ready to learn. Children who produce lots of gesture–speech mismatches typically benefit more from instruction than those who express little information in their gesture. Hand gestures can therefore be incredibly useful tools when trying to

Gestures & intellectual development

teach children about different concepts. They can be used as an index of 'readiness to learn' and allow 'teachers' to adjust their instructions to fit with the children's current level of comprehension.

Initially children often learn things implicitly and can carry out various tasks without explicitly being able to verbalise how they are solving the task. With development this knowledge becomes more explicit or 'recoded' until the child understands enough to be able to reflect on their reasoning and articulate it (Karmiloff-Smith 1992). So gesture gives us a window into the implicit knowledge of a child (Alibali and Goldin-Meadow 1993). In other words, the gesture–speech mismatches found when children do not yet, but almost, understand something reflect the implicit knowledge a child holds. You can probably think of examples of your own where you have been asked to explain something you thought you fully understood. When asked to verbalise this information you then realise your own limitations and that in fact you hold the knowledge implicitly. In these sorts of situations adults too are likely to use more gesture. This is one explanation as to why adults gesture more when expressing difficult material.

Gesture can be a useful indicator of understanding in areas of school learning such as arithmetical principles. For example, the principle of arithmetical reversibility is that adding a sequence of numbers will give the same answer regardless of which way round you add them: e.g. $2 + 1 = 3$ is the same as $1 + 2 = 3$. Children can normally do both of these additions long before they understand the abstract relation between them – that they are reversals of one another. Before being able to explain this reversibility in speech, a child is likely to gesture the relationship by pointing backwards and forwards between the two sums written down (Goldin-Meadow 1999). Gesture may therefore provide an important source of information regarding a child's level of knowledge at a given point in time. If a child can do both sums and gestures the reversible relationship between them, he is closer to understanding the reversibility principle than one who can do the sums but does not articulate reversibility in either gesture or speech.

Gesture and learning

Gesture not only reflects children's understanding and knowledge but can also influence the way that children learn. Goldin-Meadow (1999) proposes that this occurs via two routes. Gesture demonstrates to teachers and parents the child's level of understanding, which may include their newest and often still implicitly understood thoughts. This can allow the adult to offer instruction or help at the most appropriate level to facilitate learning. The importance of sensitively structuring learning has been shown in a number of studies (Wood, Bruner and Ross 1976), where an adult scaffolds the child's learning by timely instructions. Further research shows that gesture provides important cues which help in this process (Goldin-Meadow 1999). So if you're trying to decide what a child understands about a given problem, make sure you look at his gestures as well as listen to what he says as he explains his reasoning to you. The information conveyed in gesture but not in speech is likely to be the information that the child is least sure of and in most need of extra help with. If some part of the reasoning is incomplete and not articulated in either gesture or speech, you may need to take a step back and give additional support to elicit this.

Second, gesture provides a different way for the child to think through problems that may be too difficult to formulate in a verbal manner. For example, it may be easier to express the dynamic and spatial relationships between the earth, sun and moon in gesture than articulating all of the information in speech. Furthermore, the use of gesture to 'think about' some aspects of the information 'frees up' verbal resources to deal with other points. In other words, encouraging children to gesture when they are thinking and reasoning about complex concepts can help them to spread the mental load of the task. In the earth, sun and moon example, it might be helpful for the child to gesture the moon orbiting the earth while saying 'at the same time the earth orbits the sun'. With a little imagination it is possible to think of similar ways to help children express almost anything, and in doing so help them to *understand*.

Gesture can help children perform better on certain tasks. For example, four-year-olds made fewer errors in counting when they were allowed to gesture than when this wasn't allowed (Saxe and Kaplan 1981). Younger children made errors regardless of whether they were allowed to gesture or not, suggesting that their gesturing behaviour did not help their processing of the task. Older children performed without error, regardless of accompanying gesturing behaviour, presumably because the counting procedure was so well learned for them and therefore less demanding. These results suggest that four-year-olds know how to count but that it is a demanding task. Performing gestures somehow decreases the 'cognitive load' of counting. The same principles will apply for an age-appropriate task at any age.

In Chapter 4 I describe how looking at children while giving them information can help them remember material better. Seeing someone gesture while giving instructions also helps children carry out those instructions accurately. Corsini (1969) studied five-year-olds' abilities to carry out instructions. The children were asked to move objects such as toy cars and boxes in particular ways in relation to one another. Some of the children listened to the instructions from an adult who did not gesture or point at the objects while speaking. Other children heard the same instructions but the adult gestured to the objects at the appropriate times. For example, if the instruction was 'Put the red bead and the blue car in the yellow cup' (Corsini 1969, p.601), the adult would point to each object in turn. The results clearly showed that children performed the task much better when they saw the gestures while listening to the instructions. Corsini proposes that non-verbal communication helps because it fits with the young child's tendency to represent information in their mind as images rather than symbolic representations like language. So pointing to materials while instructing young children helps them understand the message and remember it. This is one way of scaffolding the child's listening skills by spreading information load between the more difficult, symbolic verbal message and the easier, concrete non-verbal one.

Gesture helps you speak?

The evidence therefore seems fairly compelling. Gesture is an important external indicator of children's thinking and knowledge. Furthermore gesture can be useful in reducing the demands of expressing complex information. However, these are not the only functions of hand gestures. If gesture primarily acts as a communication cue that gives information to people who see it, why do we still gesture when speaking on the telephone, even though our listener can't see us and therefore benefit from the gesture? Are we acting like the six-year-olds doing the map task unseen? I think not. Adults are generally very skilled communicators who are good at adapting to telephone communication, adjusting their conversational style to fit the medium.

It has been proposed that the gestures we continue using even when on the telephone are of a rather special nature. It appears that one reason we gesture while speaking is not to benefit our listener but to benefit ourselves. Gesturing while speaking helps us plan what we're going to say and also to find the words to say it. Similarly, even people born blind who have never seen a gesture use it when talking to blind listeners (Iverson and Goldin-Meadow 1998). This fact is relevant to two important issues. First, our tendency to use gesture while speaking must be in part an inborn feature of human communication. Second, while gestures often affect listeners and may function to facilitate listener comprehension, this is not their only function. They also play an important role in speech production.

In fact, if you ask adults not to move their hands while speaking they end up producing an increased frequency of eyebrow and finger movements, suggesting that such movements are a necessary component of the speech production process (Rime and Schiaratura 1991). Asking people to fold their arms while speaking also influences their speech. For example, people pause more when they are not allowed to gesture, suggesting that the fluency of speech is affected. This work mirrors the research showing the beneficial impact of hand gestures in facilitating children's language development. Hand gestures therefore influence speech production both in terms of acquiring language and in using it. The fact that gesturing helps us to express ourselves makes me concerned about a trend reported to me by some teachers. In certain schools children are encouraged to sit on their hands when counting. This is to discourage them from using their fingers. It may be advisable to use such tactics carefully, ensuring that children do not get into the habit of sitting on their hands in learning situations. The research on gesture and speech suggests that in many circumstances this might impede children's abilities not only to express themselves but also to think.

Gestures, language and the development of thought

The links between gesture, language and thought have been a topic of much debate in developmental psychology. Indeed this has been central to two major theories of child development developed by Jean Piaget and Lev Vygotsky. I'll introduce you very briefly to these researchers.

Jean Piaget has been one of the most influential figures in developmental psychology and his name is one that every undergraduate student of psychology should know. His work had a huge impact on how psychologists, teachers and parents see children's developing mental abilities. Piaget's theories have not gone unquestioned, but this is not the place to debate these issues. His main concern was with how children develop their 'thinking skills' to become increasingly more adult. Piaget saw this as very much driven by the children and their experiences within their physical world. Part of mental development is of course being able to produce and understand language. Piaget saw language, and hence communication abilities, as a sort of 'side effect' of intellectual development (1951). Words therefore emerge when the infant's mental abilities have developed to a certain degree, and s/he understands that both vocal and gestural signs can be used to represent things (beginning at around one year of age). Furthermore, Piaget used non-verbal behaviour such as eye gaze and facial expression to make judgements about mental development. Piaget saw value in attending to children's non-verbal signals in order to acquire clues about their underlying knowledge. He believed, as I myself do, that facial expressions relate not only to the expression of emotion, but also to how children are representing what they know in their brains. In other words, as we have seen, what children say in their speech is only part of the story. Important clues as to their underlying knowledge representations can be derived from non-verbal channels.

Lev Vygotsky was a Russian psychologist who also saw the value of examining children's non-verbal behaviours, and in particular the social interactions of which they are part. In contrast to Piaget, who saw the child's development as 'individual discovery', Vygotsky saw development as powered by the dynamics of social interaction (Vygotsky [1934] 1962). In Vygotsky's model of child development, the child is a guided participant in knowledge acquisition. The child is guided by parents, peers and siblings, making learning dependent on the cultural setting of the child's life. These tutors 'scaffold' (or sensitively structure) the child's learning, always pushing the child just beyond what he can accomplish on his own. For example, a four-year-old wants to draw a picture. Her mother happens to be present and asks, 'What are you going to draw?' To keep the conversation going, the child answers, 'An elephant.' The child now has a plan that she didn't have before. While her mother is not deliberately instructing her, she has in fact scaffolded the little girl's limited plan making. Her mother now says, 'Yes. They have big floppy ears and a long trunk.' The child draws these features, and so the natural conversation and drawing progress. Vygotsky's idea is that these sorts of natural interactions are crucial to learning and development. With time the child will internalise such conversations and be able to come up with her own plan – 'Now what will I draw?' The argument clearly is that social interaction underpins much of children's intellectual development, including the development of language.

One example of how social interaction can facilitate intellectual growth is in how infants come to understand the use of gesture as a means of communication. Infants become involved in communicative exchanges before they have a full understanding of the symbols or words used. Furthermore, treating infants as intentional communicators, even before they actually are, makes their learning of intentional communication easier. In this vein, Vygotsky claimed that the treatment of non-intentional acts as having meaning may be instrumental in infants acquiring intentional gesture. For example, pointing develops from early attempts to grasp objects (see Figures 3.4 and 3.5). In a social context, this unsuccessful action is interpreted as being meaningful by the caregiver. In other words, it is a gesture for others before it is a gesture for the infant. The interpretations placed on the infant's actions are however crucial in driving the child's mental and communicative development.

Vygotsky considered that language was the foundation for the development of higher human thought. Children first learn words to communicate with others, but then begin using words as symbols of thinking.

Figure 3.4 How would you interpret this ten-month-old's reaching? What if she looked at her mother?

Figure 3.5 There is little doubt that this 18-month-old intends to communicate about something

Thinking is enhanced by using the symbols (or words) of language and is more powerful than earlier non-verbal thought. This is reminiscent of the mental advantages gained by language-trained chimps described later in this chapter. So using both verbal and non-verbal (e.g. gestures) symbolic expressions provides important foundations for the development of thought. Cognitive development is driven by the development of language and communication. Recent support for this comes from the work of Acredolo and Goodwyn (2000). They report a follow-up study of the babies in their study who were taught baby signs. At the end of their second year of primary school these children had higher IQs than their peers who had not been taught baby signs as infants.

Gestures and the expression of emotion

Gestures not only indicate knowledge and thinking but are also important in delivering information about the emotional state of children. Emotional information has traditionally been seen to be readily accessible through non-verbal behaviours. Indeed the link between internal *emotional* states and non-verbal behaviours has a more pervasive history than the link between *mental* states and non-verbal cues (what we've been looking at so far in this chapter).

Emotions are primarily expressed in the face. This is discussed in Chapter 5. However, there is evidence that certain gestures are also related to different feelings. One study showed that a depressed patient was able to cover up her feelings in her face but not in her other body movements (Ekman and Friesen 1969). As adults we are generally aware of the utility of covering up our facial expressions in social situations. However, we are not nearly as conscious of the emotional *gestures* we might exhibit which display our feelings. So we exert greater control over our facial expressions than other bodily expressions of emotion.

There is a valuable distinction between gestures that are linked to speech and may be intended to communicate about objects or events and those that are directed towards the self (Freedman and Hoffman 1967). Gestures directed towards the self often involve self-touching, and may be associated with 'displacement activities' that serve to reduce tension in the person carrying out the emotional gesture. These gestures include hair 'grooming', scratching and fidgeting in states of anxiety or arousal. Certainly we touch ourselves more when in negative emotional states. This is rather like the sort of displacement activities to be seen in animals which may, for example, scratch when in states of conflict or frustration.

There are many examples of studies illustrating these phenomena in adults. Similar sorts of behaviours are also evident in children. Certainly children tend to increase the amount that they fidget when excited or concentrating hard on expressing themselves. There are also a number of child-specific, self-touching gestures associated with negative emotional states; for example, thumb sucking on separation from the parent is common in two-year-olds who often cry at this time. Indeed thumb sucking is observed in many situations when children are in a state of conflict or negative emotion. Fiddling with hair or ears is often a sign of tiredness. Arms outstretched with hands rotating can be a sign of excitement in babies; the more rigorous the hand rotations, the more likely the emotion is turning to frustration. 'Auto-manipulations' such as 'ear flipping' are more frequent in aggressive interactions between children (McGrew 1972). Leaning forward with clenched fists is another common 'aggressive' signal seen in conflicts between small children (see Figure 2.2). Some displacement activities commonly found with adults, such as teeth grinding, are almost never found in children except in sleep (Blurton-Jones 1972).

Related to emotional expressions is the signalling of rapport between individuals by mirroring gestures and postures of one another. When people are getting along while having a conversation there is a natural tendency to mimic each other's non-verbal behaviours (Kendon 1970). For example, if two people are sitting opposite one another and one rests his head on his left hand, slouching over to the left, their partner will often follow suit and mirror the action. Furthermore women use mimicry like this in order to improve rapport when it is lacking in an interaction (La France and Ickes 1981). This behaviour is one way of signalling that you are in agreement or in tune with your conversational partner. Children and adults with autism or Asperger's do not engage in posture or gesture mirroring. The exception to this is when Asperger's adults consciously note and echo other people's body movements in an attempt to 'fit in better' (Attwood 1998).

Cultural differences

Gesture is a channel of non-verbal communication where there are considerable cross-cultural differences in expressions. All cultures use some gestures, both emblems and illustrators, although some use more than others, as described in Chapter 2. There are two major categories of cultures: contact and non-contact. Examples of contact cultures are Arab, southern European and South American societies. Non-contact cultures include Japanese and northern Europeans. These two types of cultures differ in terms of the intensity with which they use non-verbal channels of communication. People from contact cultures typically stand closer to one another during interaction, engaging in more eye contact and more gestures. For example, Italians are notorious for being very animated speakers who use a considerable amount of gesture. Indeed tying up the hands of Italians whilst speaking has dire effects on their speech, with a particular rise in hesitations and errors (Graham and Heywood 1976).

There are many important differences in the meanings assigned to different gestures across cultures, especially emblems (gestures that have a direct verbal translation). For example, making a circle with the thumb and forefinger is our 'OK' sign. In southern France a very similar gesture means zero or worthless. In Japan the same gesture means money and in still other societies it has an obscene meaning. In Japan people are horrified to see westerners playing the 'I've got your nose' game with children. The hand configuration used has a very obscene meaning in Japan. These sorts of cultural differences are obviously learned. So while we never give our children explicit instruction regarding the use of emblems and other gestures, they learn them through being part of the society in which they are raised.

There are only a few gestures that share meaning across all cultures, including the shrug meaning 'I don't know' and the hand up with palm facing gesture meaning 'halt'. Some researchers have suggested that these commonly shared gestures are innate and we are born with a predisposition to use them and understand their meaning. This is debatable for a number of reasons that need not concern us now. The point is that on the whole specific gestures show cultural variability that suggests a considerable amount of learning in their development. This is particularly true for the specific *forms* that gestures take. The use of gesture per se and its links with language and mental development are probably culturally universal.

Individual differences: consistent, stable traits?

The striking thing that comes across in many studies of children's and adults' gesturing is that typically around a third of people studied gesture very little or not at all. This has been shown when people are doing very different tasks: from communication tasks like the map task, to narrating stories, explaining arithmetic reasoning, and so on. The question is whether 'non-gesturers' on one task would be 'non-gesturers' on another task, or across all tasks. Alternatively, it might be the case that different sub-groups of people gesture frequently when carrying out some types of communication tasks but not others. This question is to date unresolved. We simply do not know whether gesture frequency is a stable characteristic, like certain personality traits, and if so why this should be. Certainly there could be some people whose preferred style of thinking involves using visual rather than verbal codes and who may prefer to express relatively more information in gesture. Whatever the answer, this is an important question since it will affect the way that we apply what we know about gesture. If some children consistently use very little gesture, they may not find distributing communicative effort across gesture and speech particularly beneficial.

Gesture in the animal kingdom

The occurrence of real hand gestures is very rare in the animal world. Non-human primates and other animals exhibit certain non-verbal behaviours that might be considered gestures. For example, dogs will scrape at doors when they want to get in or out and chimpanzees will rattle branches to threaten another animal or raise their arms to request grooming. Chimps also have a couple of natural hand-specific signs, such as holding their hands out, palm up, to beg for food. While we might make reasonable guesses as to what the animal 'wants', it is difficult to know whether the animal *intends* to communicate with these behaviours.

Deliberate intention is an important part of human communication. While chimps have a limited repertoire of gestures, their use is far simpler than ways in which humans use gesture. This is clearly shown when we compare the chimp begging gesture with request gestures used by human infants. Chimps will use gestures like the begging gesture to request something from another. Human children use gestures like reaching and pointing to request things, but they also use the same signs to comment on objects – something that chimps never do.

Most people are familiar with the existence of sign languages (for example, American Sign Language and British Sign Language). Sign language refers to something rather different from the natural hand gestures that I've spent most of this chapter talking about. These are languages rich, elaborate and fully grammatical *linguistic* manual systems of communication, used in place of speech by people who are deaf. They are essentially verbal forms of communication and share many properties of spoken language, but are expressed through manual signing. Sign languages have been used to study whether or not certain animals can learn some form of language. It is necessary to use sign language rather than vocal language in such studies since animals do not have the vocal apparatus to make the range of human speech sounds necessary.

Some animals (the great apes and dolphins) have been successfully taught to use limited amounts of sign language. For example, in the 1960s, a husband and wife research team raised an infant chimpanzee called Washoe in their home as one of their children and taught her American Sign Language (Gardner and Gardner 1969). After 51 months of training, Washoe had acquired 132 signs, which represents a rather small vocabulary in comparison with how many words a human child would acquire over a similar time scale. This work has made important contributions to what we know about human language. For example, there is evidence that such language training enhances intellectual abilities. Chimpanzees who have learned a sign language seem to have a better understanding of abstract relations than those who have not. For example, language-trained chimps understand analogy: 'A:A' is the same as 'B:B' (Premack 1983). Therefore if shown two apples and two bananas and asked whether the two sets are the same or different, language-trained chimps understand that they are the same because the relation between the apples is the same as that between the bananas (i.e. they are identical). It has been suggested that the benefits shown in trained chimpanzees' thinking result because the sign language they have learned gives them the necessary mental tools to think symbolically rather than just in concrete images. This illustrates the sorts of intellectual advantages that having access to symbols can have. There may be similar advantages for human babies who are taught symbolic gestures before they are able to speak.

While the research on teaching sign language to primates is fascinating, it does not change the fact that non-human primates naturally make little use of gesture. In contrast to our closest primate cousins, we are a very dextrous species. Our opposing thumb and relatively large area of brain devoted to our hands allows us to make many and fine movements with our hands. For now it appears that the extensive use of natural hand gestures is uniquely human. Furthermore these gestures play an important role in children's abilities to express themselves, feeding into their mental development, language acquisition and learning.

Gestures provide invaluable external indications of children's thoughts. For example, an infant pointing to comment shows us that she has some appreciation of the other person's mind. Symbolic rather than concrete gestures show us that symbolic thought is developing. Specific pieces of information that are just beyond a child's ability to articulate in speech 'leak out' in gesture. All these illustrations clearly show that gestures must be attended to if we are fully to appreciate what is going on in the mind of a child.

Note

1. I should include a caveat here, lest I later be blamed for an over-abundance of sleepless nights. The one exception to the respond quickly rule is when a baby is consistently and frequently wakening at night for feeding, when no longer needing to. Night-time feeding is usually necessary for very young babies who need frequent, small feeds. Some babies quickly get themselves into the routine of sleeping through the night, while others take longer.

Frequent waking for feeding and/or comforting can get out of control and lead to waking as often as every hour. This is exhausting for everyone, not least the baby. One way of dealing with it is to use a controlled crying or controlled comforting technique. This involves not lifting or feeding when the infants waken and cry, allowing them to learn to go to sleep by themselves. This is not the place for a full description of these techniques. However, they really do work and I recommend you speak to your health visitor about them. Always be vigilant for signs of illness if a baby begins wakening and crying unexpectedly.

Suggested reading

1. Goldin-Meadow, S. (1999) 'The Role of Gesture in Communication and Thinking.' *Trends in Cognitive Science 3*, 419–429.

2. McNeill, D. (1985) 'So You Think Gestures are Nonverbal?' *Psychological Review 92*, 350–371.

3. Goodwyn, S.W., Acredolo, L.P. and Brown, C.A. (2000) 'Impact of Symbolic Gesturing on Early Language Development.' *Journal of Nonverbal Behaviour 24*, 81–103.

4. Doherty-Sneddon, G. and Kent, G. (1996) 'Visual Signals in Children's Communication.' *Journal of Child Psychology and Psychiatry 37*, 949–959.

5. Wood, D., Bruner, J. and Ross, G. (1976) 'The Role of Tutoring in Problem Solving.' *Journal of Child Psychology and Psychiatry 17*, 89–100.

Key points

1. Gesture and speech are related in terms of their processing. Gesturing therefore helps us to speak but also provides another channel through which to express related information.

2. Children often express information in gesture before they can articulate the same information in speech. This has important effects on their developing sense of what it means to

communicate with other people and in their language acquisition.

3. The form of children's gestures changes with increasing age, moving from concrete to symbolic representations of information.

4. The meanings of gestures also change with age and reflect the development of cognitive abilities. For example, pointing is used first as a request and later to comment. Commenting reflects a more sophisticated appreciation of other people's minds.

5. Gesture often adds information that is not present in speech. Gesture–speech mismatches can be useful in determining transient knowledge states. Gesture therefore has a potential use in facilitating teaching and learning.

6. Very young children do not cope well communicatively when they cannot see their partners. This is partly due to their reliance on gesture as a strategy for communicating.

Things to try

1. *From birth.* Learn the emotional gestures of your child. You probably know a lot of them already. Remember it is important that other people who look after your baby when you're not there should also know her repertoire, so that they can respond sensitively and effectively to her. Many different forms of body-focused gestures are signs of emotion in children (rather like displacement activities in animals). Examples include 'hand circling' when distressed or frustrated; hair or ear twiddling when tired; thumb sucking when insecure or tired. Children also develop their own idiosyncratic gestures.

2. *From about ten months.* Babies begin 'pointing'. This will not involve a proper finger point at first, but may just be reaching towards an object. Place various objects that the baby might want out of baby's reach. If the baby points or reaches to one, always respond. You might want to comment on the baby's

behaviour before handing over the requested object; for example, while pointing at the object say, 'Is this what you want, you want the X?' Monitor the baby's response to your question, but don't wait until the baby is frustrated. This should always be fun. Around 12 months look for deictic gestures where the baby comments on rather than requests objects. These will include pointing and holding up an object for your attention.

3. *From around 11 months.* Does the baby use any symbolic signs in interactions with you? Try to notice these, write them down and talk about them to other family members and people who take care of the baby. The more often a baby is responded to appropriately as a consequence of a communication attempt, the more confident he will become with his communicative abilities.

   You might want to try teaching your baby some gestures that he can use. Make them *concrete* representations of the things they stand for. Examples to get you going: washing movements on your face as 'let's wash our faces'; hand to open mouth as 'do you want some food?'; hand to face, tilted to the side with eyes closed, as 'let's go to sleep'. Use the gestures consistently, introducing new ones gradually. Always accompany them with the speech they stand for and try to integrate them into the natural flow of your conversations with the infant.

4. *From age two years.* Have a look at what a child does and says on the phone. Try describing things to one another with a screen between you. The younger the child, the more likely they are to resort to 'peeking'.

5. *From age four years.* Show a cartoon, preferably one where there is little or no speech and lots of action. This means that much of the information a child remembers will be retained in a visual rather than a verbal code. Ask the child to retell the story to you (or to a camera – this sometimes works best as children are far less inhibited speaking in front of a video camera than most adults). Be prepared to offer prompts. Children do not easily provide open narratives. Look at the gestures the child uses. How much information does he or she gesture that is never actually

said in speech? How much information would you have missed if you had only been listening?

6. *From age five years.* If a child is stuck on a problem (for example arithmetic homework), try to encourage him to explain to you how he thinks he should solve it. Emphasise that it doesn't matter if he doesn't get it right at first. Look carefully at his gestures as he explains and listen carefully to what he says. Comment constructively on what he says both in his speech and in his gesture. Remember that children sometimes gesture information which shows a greater level of understanding than their verbal expression. Children doing this are more ready to learn than those not yet doing so.

7. *From age six years.* Try the map task with children. Copy the maps in Figure 3.2 on page 72 and photocopy to A3 size. Try doing the map task face to face and another task when you can't see one another. Does it feel different? Do you feel that either of you is compensating when you can't see one another?

8. *At any age.* Make sure you look at children's hand gestures when they are explaining things to you. For example, if they are stuck with a piece of homework get them to explain what they *do* understand. Listen to what they say and look at what they do for clues as to their level of comprehension. Try and pick up on the gestured information.

Some developmental milestones

1. Around ten months of age babies will begin to gesture. Chidren's earliest gestures are called *deictics* and thus use them to tell you about things, to direct your attention and to request things. So for example when a child wants you to look at a toy bear she has found she might hold it up to you or even offer it. Essentially this is a gesture meaning 'look at this' or 'I've got a teddy'. A further comment on the object, such as 'what a lovely teddy' or 'yes you've got a teddy', will help consolidate the original

gesture as being meaningful and help develop the child's understanding of intentional communication.

2. A little later in development these deictic gestures develop into *pointing*, again (as much as humanly possible) requiring some sort of response. Proper pointing with the index finger is normally established around 14 months of age.

3. Between one and two years of age children may also begin to use *iconic* gestures where they act out a representation of an object. For example, they might begin using gestures like flapping their arms to represent a bird. They may also use onomatopoeic expressions such as 'woof woof' for dog or 'moo' for cow. All these concrete representations are to be encouraged. Children benefit from practising communication in these ways and there is no evidence that it interferes with language development.

4. As children increase their vocabularies some of their gesturing becomes *redundant*; for example, pointing at a teddy while saying 'teddy'.

5. Children normally begin combining words into *two-word utterances* between 18 and 24 months of age. Interestingly, before this time children will often produce similar two-representation expressions, one said in speech, the other expressed in gesture. For example, they might say 'give' and point to the teddy. Furthermore the age at which they begin producing such messages predicts the age at which they will verbally produce two-word utterances (Goldin-Meadow and Butcher 2000).

6. The use of *acting out* gestures or *pantomimes* is prevalent in young children's gestures and fairly rare in older children and adults. You will see a lot of these gestures performed by pre-school children and those in the early years of primary school. As children move through primary school they will use fewer and their gestures will become more abstract.

7. During the primary school years the frequency with which children use *beat* gestures increases; for example, to add emphasis to what they're saying. Later in primary school you will start to see children using more abstract *metaphoric* gestures to refer to metaphoric concepts.

8. Between three and five years the particular form of pantomimes changes. Three-year-olds typically use body parts to represent objects whereas five-year-olds are more likely to act out an action on an invisible object. In other words, their pantomimic gestures become increasingly *symbolic*.

9. Just as children's use of gesture type changes with increasing age, so too does their ability to get by in a communicative situation without them. Young children have limited language skills. They may not know certain words or the best way of describing something in words. Therefore they often fall back on gesture when expression becomes difficult for them. If they can't be seen by their listener (for example, if talking on the phone), a considerable amount of information is likely to be lost. Children's abilities to adapt to unseen communication increase considerably from pre-school through to primary school.

10. At any age knowledge that is held only implicitly is more likely to be gestured than verbalised. This can be a particularly useful source of information when assessing a child's knowledge and deciding on when to provide help and instruction while something new is being learned.

Chapter 4

Eye Gaze

For humans as well as many other animals the eyes are a very significant part of the face. We are inherently interested in other people's eyes and deeply influenced by them. As beings that reflect upon the minds of others, we often treat them as 'windows to the soul'. This folk saying reflects the importance of eyes in mediating social relationships in almost all cultures across the world. Eye gaze serves many functions in human communication and social relationships, ranging from the social and emotional to the intellectual. Amongst the messages eyes send are love, hate, dominance, empathy, and even whether we are concentrating. Furthermore, gaze behaviour plays an important role in many aspects of child development. This chapter will describe the developmental and evolutionary significance of gaze, in particular in relation to mental development. I will then describe some social functions of eye gaze, finishing off by looking at contemporary work investigating links between children's patterns of gazing behaviour and their thought processes.

When we look at something or someone we gain information; for example, where that person is in relation to us, what they look like and whether they are looking at us. However, the very fact that we are looking at the person provides a potential source of information for others. Looking at someone is interpreted in a number of ways depending on the circumstances: as interest, threat, liking, attention and wanting. So the very act of gazing, whether we intend it or not, sends information to other people, giving them valuable information about our focus of attention, thoughts, wishes and desires. This sort of information plays a critical role the mental and social development of children, including language acquisition. Furthermore, as we will see, our observations of where and when children look provide valuable clues as to their underlying intellectual state.

The ways in which we interpret gaze behaviour develop over the early pre-school and primary school years. Only recently have researchers begun to understand this fully. Further back in the history of gaze research, greater understanding of gaze was attributed to both babies and other animals. It is only now that we appreciate the gaze-reading limitations of both these groups. For example, children do not fully understand that other people can and often do use eye gaze deliberately to communicate until they are about three or four years old (Doherty and Anderson in press). Similarly, while adults tend to interpret a lot of mutual gazing between people as a sign of liking, this is not understood by children until around five or six years of age (Abramovitch and Daly 1978). So while children are fascinated by eyes almost from birth, there is much they have to learn as to the underlying meaning of gaze and the rules governing its occurrence. This does not diminish the immense role that eye gaze plays in early human development. Quite the contrary, gaze has a particular importance in children's mental development right from birth.

Types of eye signals

In order to study eye gaze we need to decide what we are looking for. In other words how do we measure it? A common measure of eye gaze is simply the percentage of time spent (of any given conversation) looking in the direction of a scene; for example, another person's face. This looking typically does not involve steady fixation on one location on the face. Our gaze tends to flit around the face in brief fixations primarily of the eyes and mouth (Yarbus 1967). We can track these movements using eye-tracking equipment that allows even very brief and minute movements of the eyes to be measured and recorded.

If you look carefully at a video recording of people having a conversation it is clear that they do not look at one another all the time. A useful measure of eye gaze in communication is the proportion of time a person spends gazing while listening versus speaking. This can be a good indicator of the relative status between pairs of adults. In general terms, the more gaze while talking and the less gaze while listening, the higher status a person has relative to the person they are talking with. The opposite is true of more subordinate individuals who generally look less while speaking and more while listening. This is partly influenced by whether or not there is an established hierarchy between the individuals. When the hierarchy is uncertain you see more of the 'staring down' behaviour we associate with asserting dominance. However, when the dominant person is sure of their position, their style of gaze is typically relaxed. Interestingly we observe very similar patterns of gaze relating to dominance in non-human primates. For example, gorillas use staring as a threat signal. However, normally within a social group the dominant male silverback will look relatively infrequently at his subordinates. In contrast they will glance frequently at him to check on his location and demeanour. Patterns of gaze as dominance cues are less clear with children, although even toddlers will use 'staring down' in conflict situations. Part of the reason that it is harder to decipher children's cues to dominance from their gazing behaviour is because they haven't yet learned and don't understand many of the rules about gazing.

The feeling is mutual

Another type of eye signal is seen when two people look simultaneously at one another's eyes or face. This is called mutual gaze. Extended mutual gaze between adults is actually quite rare and, as we will see, has considerable emotional and physiological correlates. While we make eye contact with people we don't know well, the duration of these glances is usually quite short (about 1.5 seconds). Extended mutual gaze is generally reserved for very close social relationships. It is most frequent in adult couples who report being in love (Rubin 1970) and mutual gaze is an important signal of emotional attachment.

Looking into someone's eyes has significant physiological effects. For babies and adults, making mutual eye contact with another person increases heart and breathing rates and galvanic skin response – sweating to you and me (Field 1981; Gale et al. 1972). This can be experienced as pleasant in some circumstances; for example in a close friendship. However, the experience is distinctly negative if it is interpreted as threatening or intimidating.

Mutual gaze has social and even cognitive influences from very early in life – almost as soon as babies begin to establish mutual eye contact with their caregivers. While babies look at faces from birth they don't sustain mutual eye contact until about two or three weeks old. Delay in beginning to make mutual eye contact can sometimes be indicative of social and/or intellectual delay. One study found that babies who did not make mutual eye contact with their caregivers in their first month of life had rather different patterns of subsequent development compared with those who did. For example, early 'non-gazers' generally showed developmental delay and had more behavioural problems at age six years than those who did engage in early mutual gaze (Keller and Zach 1993). It is difficult to tell whether the non-gazing reflected an underlying problem that was also associated with the problems that emerged later. Alternatively dysfunctional gazing behaviour may have got these infants off to the wrong start with their caregivers, resulting in less than optimal patterns of interactions and potential learning experiences.

Mutual gaze is experienced as very rewarding by caregivers and the special feeling it evokes plays an important part in early parent–infant bonding. For many parents making mutual eye contact with their baby is their first 'meeting of minds'. Interestingly the same emotive import is not given to early mutual gaze in all cultures. In some societies the infants are not attributed mental states until they are much older and little significance is placed on their early non-verbal behaviours. Indeed there are individual differences within any culture in terms of what sort of mental abilities are assumed in infants. This has been called maternal 'mind-mindedness' (Meins 1998). Mothers who are high on mind-mindedness consider their infants to be intentional, thinking people from very early and treat them as such. This influences a number of aspects of development. For example, mothers who are 'mind-minded' typically have babies who are securely attached to them.

So mutual gaze has important social effects. It can be a sign of affiliation and liking but can also be a signal of threat. The meaning given depends on the situation and the individuals involved. In turn gaze influences and signals intellectual functioning. I will discuss evidence for this later in the chapter. While the physiological effects of mutual gaze occur very early in life as do some of the social effects, the full understanding of mutual gaze as a social and cognitive cue is not evident until the primary school years.

Pupil dilation

Clues about our cognitive, physiological or emotional state are found not only in the direction of our gaze, but also in the degree of pupil dilation. All these types of internal states affect pupil dilation or constriction. Furthermore what our pupils are doing can have profound effects upon people looking at our eyes, influencing how they respond to us and even whether they like us or not. This is something of which we are not conscious.

Pupil dilation occurs as a result of a number of factors including: low light levels, physiological arousal, sexual attraction, and other types of affiliative feelings. Indeed dilated pupils are generally attractive to adult humans. In a classic study, researchers showed men two photographs of a young woman. The two photographs were identical except that in one the pupils had been touched up artificially to look wider. Although the men were unaware of this manipulation they found the 'dilated pupils photograph' more attractive (Hess 1965). Wider pupils also indicate interest, so potentially romantic couples give the 'illusion' of being mutually interested in each other. This is probably why candlelit dinners are such popular choices for romantic encounters; the low light levels ensure nice wide pupils even if the interpersonal attraction isn't there initially. Pupil dilation has been used quite effectively in television adverts where a close-up shot of an eye dilating is used to reflect physiological arousal or attraction.

Dilated pupils are not always preferred and there are understandable reasons for this. One study showed adults some photographs of a baby's face either with dilated or constricted pupils, and with or without highlighting (used to make the eyes look brighter). In fact the photograph of the baby with *constricted* pupils plus highlighting was found more attractive than the others (Kirkland and Smith 1978). The researchers suggest that small, bright pupils are attractive because they are characteristic of infants in a state of alert inactivity. We may associate this state with calm, happy babies. An aroused infant is more likely to mean trouble.

We also seem to prefer constricted pupils in certain animals. Researchers asked children aged four to six years, nine to eleven years and young adults to look at two photographs of a young cat looking straight at the camera (Millot, Brand and Schmitt 1996). The photographs showed the cat with either constricted or enlarged pupils. The younger group of children did not show a clear preference for either photograph; around half of them liked the cat with constricted pupils while the others preferred the cat with enlarged pupils. Around two-thirds of the nine- to eleven-year-olds preferred the constricted pupils, and almost all of the young adults shared this preference. Again this might be because constricted pupils were associated with a lack of arousal and state of calm. This is preferable with cats, as highly aroused cats are more unpredictable and certainly more dangerous.

The fact that the younger children showed no preference between pupil sizes is rather interesting, suggesting there is a degree of learning involved in our responses to pupil dilation. Indeed there is some evidence that pupil size only becomes relevant to how we perceive other people when we reach puberty. There is some controversy about this and the absolute age at which pupil size becomes a salient interpersonal cue is partly culturally determined (Tarrahian and Hicks 1979). So our responses to pupils are, at least in part, shaped by social experiences. Young children respond less to changes in pupil size because they are less experienced.

Blinking marvellous

One other source of information that the eyes give is found in the frequency of blinking. Blinking serves various functions relating to the health and well-being of the eyes and therefore blink rate is influenced by factors such as surrounding air quality. It is also affected by other less obvious things that relate to intellectual factors. We tend to blink less when we are concentrating on something. Research from Japan suggests that blinking behaviour relates to attention, concentration and task pleasantness for eight- to twelve-year-old children in similar ways to adults, and that children blink less when they enjoy the tasks they're doing (Yamada

1998). Therefore in both adults and children blinking indicates concentration. Indeed this is one hazard of computer use. We tend to stare at screens. Combine this with the reduced blinking when we are concentrating on a computer task and the blink rate reduces to a level resulting in dry, tired eyes. Children should be encouraged to 'rest' their eyes regularly during computer use by staring into the distance for a short time and blinking.

I mention in Chapter 5 that highly motivated adult liars tend to over-control their blinking rate. This is because increased blinking is a sign of anxiety. If this is detected by an observer, the deception is more likely to be noticed. People determined to deceive realise this and therefore control their blinking. It is not clear when children begin to master this deception tactic. I don't know of any research that has looked at whether children blink more or less while they are lying. It is unlikely that children younger than around eight years of age will have the social awareness to make an association between blinking and anxiety. So children's blinking rate is likely to be high when they are lying because they will be anxious and not yet have 'learned' to control it. Pupil dilation is an eye cue of deception that is harder to control for both adults and children alike. Because we are usually anxious when we lie, pupil dilation can be an indicator of deception. Remember however that simply confronting a child about something will be anxiety evoking in itself, whether the child tells the truth or not.

We can therefore measure gaze behaviour in a number of ways. Furthermore the different types of measure tap different levels of physiological, emotional, social and cognitive functions of eye gaze. These functions are closely interrelated; for example, pupil dilation is a sign of physiological arousal that is influenced by emotional states. This in turn has significant social influences on other people. Before describing some of the functions of gaze in more detail, I'll address when children learn the rules about gazing.

Rules ought to be obeyed

Gazing behaviour is governed by rules. The explicit meanings of gaze are determined by these rules. For example, it is only acceptable to engage in high amounts of mutual gaze in certain types of social relationships. If these rules are violated, the behaviour takes on a whole new meaning. If I look at you to the extent that you feel uncomfortable, you may interpret this as a threat or that I am rather strange. Very young children often seem blissfully unaware that there are any rules and might stare strangers out or gaze inappropriately at unusual looking people. Indeed big 'vacant' eyes in young infants of many species are attractive to adults. Gazing behaviour is one channel of non-verbal behaviour for which we actually give our children some explicit instruction; for example, most pre-school children are used to being told 'it's rude to stare'.

Children's understanding of the social rules of gaze changes with increasing age (Ashear and Snortum 1971). One study looked at the response of pre-school to eighth grade children to a constantly staring adult. They found that simply staring back decreased with age. It was concluded that in this situation the older children were more self-conscious when talking to adults and responded to this by averting their gaze. Similar effects have been found across a narrower age range. Children of three to four and a half years stared back at an unfamiliar, staring adult more than four and a half- to five-year-olds, especially when the adult was a woman rather than a man (Harris 1968). Staring at men is generally less likely. What these studies have measured is how children behave in response to an adult who is violating social norms of expected levels of gaze. The decrease in gaze with increasing age may reflect children's increased awareness of such norms.

It appears that children do not learn to avoid gaze until after they are four or five years old. However, even at this age children have some understanding of the rules about gaze. One study (described in Chapter 2) clearly shows this. An experimenter stared at children in a public shopping mall. Whether the children stared back or averted their gaze was noted. The youngest children typically stared back. One of them, a boy, stared at the staring adult and on his way past punched the adult in the arm, clearly indicating he had noticed the 'deviant' behaviour (Scheman and Lockard 1979).

Adults interpret people looking at one another a lot to mean that they like each other (Mehrabian 1969). So as long as it is not interpreted as threatening or domineering, lots of gaze is typically seen as positive.

Children do not link high frequency of gaze with feelings of affiliation or liking until they are around five or six years of age. At this age they start to form the association between looking and liking. Children's understanding about what is appropriate gazing behaviour and what different amounts of gaze mean is therefore still developing even when they begin formal schooling.

Many of these studies have examined how children behave with adults. What about when the other person is another child? When we look at this a slightly different pattern of results emerge. One study found increasing amounts of mutual gaze between pairs of children as their age increased. Six- to nine-year-olds gazed more at one another than four- to five-year-olds. The increase in the older group probably reflects a more competent interactive style. In other words the older children were better at engaging one another in extended conversation and using gaze to manage these interactions. This trend reversed however in ten- to twelve-year-olds. It appears that the oldest children were more self-conscious and therefore looked less at one another (Levine and Sutton-Smith 1973). So with the onset of puberty and all the physical and social changes this brings, levels of mutual eye gaze reduce, of course depending on the situation. For example, teenagers talking with close friends about topics that are socially easy will behave differently compared with when they are with a relative stranger in a potentially embarrassing situation.

Eye gaze as a sign of knowledge

In Chapter 3 I described how children's hand gestures could sometimes give an unspoken account of children's understanding. To an extent the same is true for eye gaze. We see this if we give babies a problem that they are almost but not quite ready to solve. One such problem that ten-month-old infants tend to fail but begin to master when they're around a year old is known as the A-not-B problem. The baby is shown a toy that is hidden under one of two cloths (cloth A) in full view. He is allowed to search for the toy and typically find it. However, when the toy is then hidden under the second, adjacent cloth (cloth B, again in full view), babies typically continue to search under the cloth where they previously found the toy. In other words, although they've seen the toy being put under cloth B they continue to search under A. The cause of the infant's mistake seems to be due to an inability to suppress previously performed dominant responses (the action of lifting cloth A and finding the toy). The suppression of dominant responses requires maturation of certain structures in the brain that occurs around one year of age. Prior to this, however, babies who fail the task often *look* at the correct location as if they *know* where it is but can't help searching for the toy where they were previously successful.

Figure 4.1 shows a ten-month-old girl failing the A-not-B task. She is searching for the little yellow truck. Initially her mum hides it under the yellow cloth. She finds it there. Then her mum hides it under the brown cloth. The baby looks at the brown cloth while her mum is placing the truck (still 2). She continues to look at the correct location while her mum withdraws (still 3), but then searches under the yellow cloth again. The baby therefore knows where the toy is, but is simply not good at searching yet. The fact that she looked at B tells us that the infant has some idea where the toy is. So at ten months the baby's gazing behaviour gives us a clue as to her 'hidden' understanding.

Gazing behaviour of course gives us clues to what babies understand all the time. For example, if you say 'where's the pussycat?' and your child looks towards a cat, this indicates she understands something of your question. Perhaps she is beginning to associate the phrase 'pussycat' with cats. Or perhaps she is learning that when you say things with a certain intonation in your voice there is normally something interesting to look at, and the most obvious thing currently is the cat. Whichever interpretation we choose, it is important to respond to this in a positive way and reinforce that she is right – you were trying to direct her attention.

Similarly, if a baby is looking at an object this provides an excellent opportunity to name and talk about it since you know it has the baby's attention. This is referred to as joint visual attention. Mothers often use this in encounters with their infants and typically allow their own attention to be dictated by that of their baby. They follow the child's line of regard and attend to and comment on the child's focus of interest. Joint visual attention is one way that gaze facilitates language development. I describe this more fully later in this chapter.

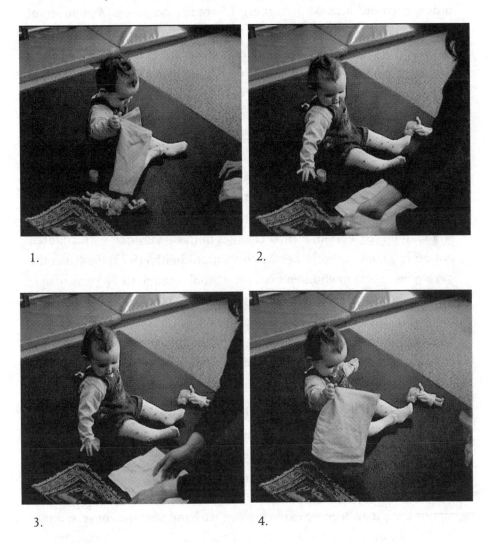

Figure 4.1 A ten-month-old fails the A-not-B task

Regulating conversation

Listeners are more likely to look at the face of a speaker than the other way round. Furthermore gazing behaviour in face-to-face conversation helps both to synchronise and regulate interaction. If you enter a room full of people, you are far more likely to begin speaking to someone who looks at you than someone who avoids eye contact with you. Once you're having a conversation, eye gaze will provide some of the cues you both require in order to co-ordinate who is going to speak and when. A number of researchers propose that adults use prolonged gaze at the end of utterances as turn-yielding cues to their listeners (Duncan 1972; Kendon 1967). When we're ready to let the other speak, we look at them letting them know it's their turn. So exactly when we look is predictable. We typically look away while in the middle of saying something but look back at the listener just when we're about to finish. When listening we tend to monitor the speaker's face and look away when we're ready to take a turn speaking. Observations of people behaving like this have led some researchers to claim that gaze plays an important part in helping conversational turn taking to occur smoothly. However, while adults use gaze skilfully for turn taking, there are developmental changes in this behaviour, with children not using gaze so adeptly. Levine and Sutton-Smith (1973) looked at the gazing behaviour of children from pre-school through to 12 years of age. They found that even at 12 years children did not look at their listeners at the end of their utterances to signal they had finished speaking. Using gaze in this sophisticated way to regulate conversation is something children have to learn over time and through practice.

Conversational structure without visual cues

This then begs the question: what happens when people have to communicate without seeing one another; for example, over the phone? One important effect is that turn taking typically becomes more formalised. So we tend to speak in longer turns, avoiding interjections that might cause interruptions. We may be more explicit when we hand over the conversational floor to the other person, using verbal markers like 'what do you think?' more often. In fact the whole style of interaction changes when we can't see one another.

As part of my PhD studies I worked on a way of describing how adults and children structure their dialogues. I don't need to go into this in any detail here, but suffice to say that the system assigns each spoken utterance a communicative function. So a speaker might use an utterance to give someone an instruction, to ask a question, to offer information, and so on (Kowtko, Isard and Doherty-Sneddon 1991). Looking at conversations in this way was very useful. It allowed me to quantify how people change their communicative style when they can't see one another while speaking.

Essentially, adults change their communication style in two important ways when they can't see one another. First, they tend to check more often that their listeners have understood or heard them. They do this by asking questions like: 'Okay, you know what I mean?' Adults ask about 50 per cent more questions of this nature when they can't see their communicative partner. Second, adults increase the frequency with which they check their own understanding of the other person's messages, questions like: 'So you mean you want me to...?' There are on average 28 per cent more questions like this in unseen interactions (Doherty-Sneddon *et al.* 1997). If you try thinking about this either when you are on the telephone or if you eavesdrop on someone else on the phone, you will hear these sorts of questions occurring a lot, particularly if it matters to the speakers that they get their message across accurately.

An important function of non-verbal communication in face-to-face encounters is therefore to allow people to gauge one another's understanding. If you are describing directions to someone face to face, you can glance at them and very quickly tell whether or not they look as though they're following what you are saying or whether they look puzzled. If you are doing the same task over the telephone this isn't possible, so every now and then you will verbally check they have understood you. Furthermore, because you can't see the person you're speaking to, you will be less confident that *you've* understood *them*. This will result in you rephrasing their speech more often in order to check your own comprehension, using questions like: 'You mean...?'

Furthermore, at points in the conversation where people ask checking questions on the telephone, they look at one another when face to face. So one factor that influences the occurrence of eye gaze in adult conversations is the confidence of speakers that their listeners have understood them. It is not clear whether the same rules apply for children. In the sample of six-year-olds that I looked at in my thesis, I could find little evidence of this sort of patterning of gaze. In fact young children generally looked much more at one another than adults did anyway, making it harder to distinguish particular points of conversation where gaze was important for them. It appears that the fine-tuned use of gaze for particular functions like feedback is another expertise that has to develop as other conversational skills are acquired.

Children of this age also did not adjust their conversational style in the way that adults did when they couldn't see one another. At this age they were typically fixated on visual cues and found it hard to cope with unseen communication. Generally speaking young children do not cope very well with telephone conversations. Without a shared visual context (being able to see what you're talking about) and access to non-verbal communication, the likelihood of them being misunderstood or of misunderstanding is high. Telephones can suffice for limited social exchanges, but trying to instruct a two- or three-year-old to carry out a particular task is a very different problem.

Eye gaze and mental development

Evidence for the evolutionary significance of eye gaze comes from studies of human infants. When looking at faces, babies during the first month of life concentrate on the outer contour of the face and spend relatively little time looking at the internal features. By only two to three months of age, infants show a preference in their scanning of human faces for the eye region and the mouth (Maurer and Salapatek 1976). Babies therefore begin attending to eyes from a very early age, suggesting that the processing of eye information may be at least partly inborn. Very young babies are not interested in the eyes per se but in the sorts of visual pattern that eyes make; that is, a pair of high contrast dark dots on a white background (the pupil, iris and sclera of the eye). I describe this in more detail in Chapter 5.

What do infants get out of attending to eyes? Why should mother nature make them so interesting to small children? Babies' responses to eyes provide a very important foundation for many aspects of development. Eye contact between mother and infant is important in developing the emotional bond between them. This in itself provides crucial foundations for social and emotional development. But the role of eye gaze in development goes far beyond this. As we will see in the next section, children's tendencies to attend to other people's gaze provide a useful platform for mental development.

Joint attention

The direction of another person's line of regard is one important source of information we get from eyes. If we can tell where someone is looking, this gives us a reliable clue as to what is taking their attention and even what they might be thinking. Visual co-orientation occurs when one person or animal looks in the same direction as another (Butterworth and Cochrane 1980). Even adults find it almost impossible not to have their attention drawn in the direction of another person's gaze (see Figure 4.2). It appears that this is an important part of social living for many primates (Anderson, Sallaberry and Barbier 1995). For example, if one monkey has seen a source of food or a predator, it makes sense for other members of the group to look in the same direction to pick up the relevant information. Indeed, there is evidence that the ability to detect where another animal is looking is 'hard wired' into monkey brains. Cells have been identified in monkey brains that respond selectively to the direction of another's gaze (Perrett *et al.* 1992).

In addition, some researchers (but not all) suggest that the great apes (in particular chimpanzees and gorillas) understand the relation between seeing something and knowing about it (Gomez 1991). In other words, if an ape sees another ape or a human looking at a banana, they act as though they know the other individual knows where the fruit is. If you see me looking at the banana you will make all sorts of assumptions about what I'm thinking; for example, 'she knows where it is'; 'she wants to eat it'. In contrast, while monkeys will follow another individual's gaze they appear less able to translate this into knowing what the other knows. The distinction between having a 'mentalistic' understanding of gaze or not is an important one. Reading gaze as a sign of mental state is something acquired by degrees over the first three years of infancy. As we will see, children become good at following other people's direction of gaze fairly quickly. It takes them longer to master what gaze means.

Figure 4.2 Seeing someone turn their head automatically makes us look where they are looking

Gaze following is automatic

Looking where another person looks is an important part of non-verbal behaviour. A number of recent studies have indicated that gaze and head turning can trigger reflexive shifts of an observer's visual attention (Langton and Bruce 1999). For example, in some studies carried out at Stirling, adult participants were asked to press the space bar on a computer keyboard as quickly as possible when a target letter appeared at one of four locations on a computer screen. Just prior to the appearance of the target, one of the possible target locations was 'cued' by a head that appeared in the centre of the display looking at it. Participants were asked to keep their eyes fixed on the centre of the screen and were told that the cue would only provide correct information regarding the likely location of the target 25 per cent of the time and that because of this fact, it should be ignored. Despite this, the results indicated that adults could not ignore the head orientation and their attention was automatically drawn to the side of the computer screen which the head had been looking at. Even though they were trying to ignore the head, if they saw it facing to the right their attention was drawn to that side of the screen.

Are children similarly influenced by head turns and shifts in gaze direction? In fact gaze cues trigger reflexive shifts of attention in infants as young as three months (Hood, Willen and Driver 1998). In these studies, infants turned their eyes to a target picture on a screen faster if the location of that target had just been cued by a picture of another person looking in that direction. At this age we typically don't see them tracking the other person's gaze; nevertheless their attention is drawn in that direction. Later in development we observe children's *overt* gaze-following response. In experiments on this response, the child sits in front of her mother who attempts to engage her in eye contact. Having done so, the mother shifts her eyes and/or turns her head away from the child and looks towards a given location in the room. The baby's gaze-following behaviour is observed. Using this procedure, studies have shown that infants as young as three to six months will follow a combination of head and eye cues (Butterworth and Jarrett 1991; Scaife and Bruner 1975), but it is not until between 14 and 18 months that they show any indication of following eye cues alone (Moore and Corkum 1998). Prior to this it seems as though children actually ignore the orientation of the eyes and simply use the position of the head as an attention following cue (Corkum and Moore 1995). All of these early onset, automatic responses allow for the establishment of joint visual attention.

Joint attention and language

The emergence of joint attention is seen by many psychologists as an important step in mental development. For example, it has been shown to play an important role in the development of language ability (Baldwin 1991). The mechanism behind the benefit is obvious. If a baby can see what you're looking at, looks at it too, and you say 'what a nice doggie', the baby will be attending to the correct object with which to associate your speech. This 'social referencing' is an important part of learning through social interaction. For example, babies from about 12 months are able to associate facial expressions of either disgust or pleasure with the object at which you are looking. So if you look disgusted and are looking at an object, a 12-month-old will be more likely to show a negative reaction to that object at a later time (Baldwin and Moses 1996). Indeed this mechanism may be at the origin of some strong dislikes and even phobias. It is unlikely that the infant reflects upon the meaning of your gaze. Instead your gaze serves as one automatic and highly efficient way of getting the baby to attend to the right object at the right time.

Joint attention therefore helps direct both parties' attention during infant–carer interactions. Might this mean that infants born with a visual impairment will be at a disadvantage in learning language? In certain ways they are. While such children end up equally skilled in language as their sighted peers, they have to bring various adaptive strategies to their language learning to compensate for the lost shared visual context (Andersen, Dunlea and Kekelis 1984). One way of buffering the effects of visual impairment is the establishment of a healthy, close mother–child relationship that motivates learning – particularly learning to use language as a tool for acting upon the environment (Willis 1979). Again this suggests that a sensitive, responsive interaction style is central to encouraging optimal development. If a shared visual context is not available, parents have to develop other ways of producing a shared *communicative* context.

It is therefore important to find accessible ways to communicate with children, taking into account the special needs they may have. The importance of inclusion in social interaction is also evident when we look at deaf children born to hearing parents. Here there is a shared visual context, but the children cannot hear the language around them. As discussed in Chapter 3, these children adapt quickly to the predicament by developing their own gestural languages. However, these children miss out on a lot of conversation and the social understanding that this brings, especially prior to their parents' learning of sign language. This can result in particular delays in some aspects of development; for example, their understanding of other people's minds (Woolfe, Want and Siegal 2002).

Eye gaze and theories of mind

Simon Baron-Cohen is a psychologist who has contributed importantly to the study of intellectual development. He has a particular interest in the role of eye gaze in normal development and also developmental disorders such as autism. He proposes a very direct link between children's experience of eye gaze and a particular part of mental development: what has been called 'theory of mind'. I will briefly describe this concept to make what follows clearer. The concept and the name in fact originate in studies of animal behaviour. The notion of theory of mind has been useful in distinguishing between species that appear to have certain higher mental functions, in some ways akin to some human ones, and those that do not. For example, monkey species are not generally attributed with theory of mind whereas the great apes often are (although this is controversial).

Theory of mind (ToM) refers to a set of interrelated concepts that we use to try to make sense of our own mental processes and those of other people (Premack and Woodruff 1978). In other words having a theory of mind means that you hold theories about your own mind and those of other people, and these theories allow us to understand our own behaviour and that of others. So we are able to reflect on situations like: 'if I am hungry I will look for and eat some food'; 'if another person is hungry they will look for and eat some food'. A theory of mind allows us to understand that our beliefs and those of others can be different, and that beliefs can be incorrect and do not always accurately represent reality.

Theory of mind is not something we are born with, but it develops over the first few years of life. In fact a crucial milestone in its development typically occurs in most normally developing children around three and a half to four years of age. At this time children begin to understand that other people can hold beliefs different from their own and that these beliefs can be false. Prior to this age children seem only able to understand other people's beliefs from their own perspective. If they know something, they expect other people to know it too.

Given the general uniformity of the age at which children seem to acquire something like ToM, it is tempting to think that the ability develops primarily as a result of the unfolding of genetic pre-programming. However, what the child experiences during the early years influences the speed with which ToM is acquired and the fullness of its development. One type of experience that influences development of ToM is the child's experience with other people's eye gaze. This is a central part of Simon Baron-Cohen's theory of how children develop ToM. He proposes that the setting up of shared visual attention (or understanding that another person is attending to the same object) sets an important stage for learning and development.

Baron-Cohen and Cross (1992) suggest that babies are born with an evolutionary and developmentally primitive 'eye direction detector' (EDD). This means that babies' brains are tuned into picking up moving eyes and their direction of movement. Perhaps like monkey brains they are 'hard wired' to pick up this important social signal. Babies' brains are therefore built to notice things like eye direction. This means that other people's eye direction is a useful cue that babies use in order to detect where other people are looking. Baron-Cohen goes on to propose that at around nine to ten months of age another mechanism begins to function. He calls this the shared attention mechanism (SAM). Once a baby's SAM is functioning, the child can appreciate that if they look where someone else is looking they are both looking at the same thing. In other words they understand that they share attention. This understanding of 'you're looking at X and so am I' may be important in many of the learning experiences that a young child is likely to come across. I already described how this might help the child learn the meaning of words and how to respond to unfamiliar objects. In addition Baron-Cohen suggests that together the EDD and SAM feed into a ToM module within the brain, allowing the child to begin to understand their own minds and those of other people.

So eye direction may function as one cue guiding toddlers to attribute mental states and abilities to certain classes of objects; in other words those with eyes as opposed to those without. Toddlers should therefore be more likely to think that objects with eyes have feelings, thoughts and desires than those without. Cartoonists of course exploit this. Many popular children's fiction characters are inanimate objects such as trains, helicopters and the like. They always have faces, and especially moving eyes. Johnson, Slaughter and Carey (1998) found that one-year-olds would turn to look in the direction that a toy moved its head only if it responded to the world in an intentional way (like turning and beeping in response to speech). If the toy didn't seem 'smart', the babies didn't bother looking where it looked.

Normal development of eye gaze understanding

Baron-Cohen suggests that there are a number of different levels of knowledge regarding gaze. One of the basic 'laws of vision' is that someone has to have their eyes open in order to see. Related to this is being able to judge when someone is looking at you. Even very young infants (three months of age) show a preference for faces looking at them rather than away from them (Caron et al. 1992). Normal children have a good understanding of 'being seen' by the time they are around 30 months of age, and indeed autistic children are also good at telling when someone is or is not looking at them.

Some types of knowledge about seeing and being seen are more complex. Ingenious experiments with chimpanzees have shown this. Chimps are extremely good at tracking another animal's or human's line of gaze. For example, if you look over a chimp's shoulder he will look behind himself in that direction. At first this was thought to reflect some comprehension of 'looking at the same thing'. In fact studies have shown that there is little evidence that chimps have any real *understanding* of seeing and looking. For example, if they approach a blindfolded trainer who has food, they will beg for the food (chimps naturally use a begging gesture, involving a palm up, outstretched hand) even though the trainer cannot see the begging gesture. So while the knowledge that eyes are for seeing is a basic form of human knowledge about gaze, this may not extend to our close primate cousins (Povinelli and Eddy 1994). Of course this begs the question, how would human children behave under similar circumstances? What is the youngest age we can be sure that children understand that eyes are for seeing and that seeing leads to knowing about what you see? In other words when do children develop an explicit understanding of eye gaze?

Understanding gaze as communication

Part of understanding explicitly what gaze means is being able to understand eye gaze as a communication cue. At Stirling we have done some work to test whether infants understand about gaze as a communication signal. The idea for the study came from studies of primates. I'll describe these briefly before going on to the infancy work. As I've already discussed, monkeys make use of others' gazing behaviours without reflecting on their meaning. Anderson *et al.* (1995) did a study to see whether monkeys would use a human's gaze as a clue to the location of some hidden food. Two wells were placed in front of the monkey's cage, one baited with some food out of sight of the monkey. An experimenter then approached the cage and either looked or pointed at the baited location. The monkey was then allowed to choose one well to look in and, it was hoped, retrieve the food from it (which it was allowed to eat). The monkeys seemed to be able to make use of pointing but, regardless of how many times they got to practise, never benefited from the human's eye gaze. The results of the experiment showed that the monkeys did not understand that eye gaze could be used to communicate where the food was.

There is some evidence that chimpanzees and orangutans are good at using head and eye gaze cues in similar tasks, suggesting that the great apes have some understanding of gaze as a communication cue (Ikatura and Tanaka 1998). In contrast, while gorillas are able to do the task very well when given pointing cues, they do not respond to eye gaze alone (Peignot and Anderson 1999). In fact when an experimenter tries to make eye contact with them and to glance at the food's location, they often become agitated and even throw food at the human. This aversion to eye gaze may occur because mutual gaze is something which gorillas do not naturally engage in and are averse to. In contrast chimpanzees are far more willing to attend to other faces.

At what age are human infants able to do this sort of task based on eye glance cues alone? We set up an analogous situation only this time human infants had to choose between one of two cups under which a desired toy (e.g. a small panda) was hidden. Babies sat in a highchair at a table on which the cups were placed on a sliding tray. An adult researcher sat opposite them. The toys were shown to the child and then hidden under a cup while a screen obscured the baby's view of the materials. The screen was then raised and the adult said, for example, 'Where is the panda?' While saying this, the adult made mutual eye contact with the baby and then alternated their gaze towards the correct cup and back to the baby. Our babies were in two age groups, the youngest an average age of 18 months old, the older children on average 34 months old.

We found that when the children tracked the adult's glance they typically selected the correct cup, suggesting that the adult's looking behaviour was a useful cue for these young children even well before their second birthday. However, the older and younger children differed in terms of how likely it was that they would in fact track the adult's gaze. The younger children did this on only about 20 per cent of the trials, while the older children did it on around a third of trials. So children who are closer to three years of age were more likely to take notice of the adult's gaze. This suggests that they are more aware of the communicative benefits that are available from these sorts of non-verbal cues.

We think that these results are telling us that children between one and two years still lack an explicit understanding of gaze as a tool for communication. They respond to eye and head movements of a caregiver and this often leads them to attend to the same object as the person they are watching. What they don't seem to be doing at that age is thinking anything like 'Mummy's trying to show me the thing she's looking at' or 'watching where Mummy is looking will help me guess what she's thinking about'. By three years of age children are apparently *beginning* to understand that gaze can be used almost to replace words and direct people's attention to things. Notice that this seems rather surprising given that 12-month-old infants will use alternate gazes between an object and another person to 'request' the object and a little later to 'comment' on it. They are also adept at directing an adult's attention to an object by pointing at it. Fully understanding *other people's* gaze appears to be far more complicated and only beginning to be mastered around three years of age.

There are numerous other tasks that young children 'fail', illustrating the prolonged development of gaze comprehension skills. In one study children were presented with a picture of a face (named Sam) on a page gazing at one of four objects, located at each corner of the page. Sometimes Sam's whole head was turned in the direction of what he was looking at, sometimes only his eyes (with his head facing forward). The children were asked 'which one is Sam looking at?' (Doherty and Anderson in press). Children were unable to determine which object the face was looking at based on eye direction alone until around four years of age. However, even two- to three-year-olds could do this task if the gaze cues were presented in concert with cues from the orientation of the head, or replaced by pointing gestures. Children therefore make use of information from the orientation of the head and the direction of pointing before using cues provided by the eyes. This shows us that while gaze cues are inevitably useful in many respects for young children, it is not until they are around four years of age that they begin to understand the meaning of gaze *explicity*. Directing toddlers' and pre-schoolers' attention is more effectively done using pointing and head turning. While children at this age respond to gaze cues alone on some level, they do not reliably appreciate other people's gaze as a communication cue.

Autism and eye gaze

The significance of eye gaze monitoring in the development of theory of mind is clearly illustrated in certain developmental disorders. Perhaps the best known example is the developmental disorder of autism. In its most extreme form this disorder is relatively rare. It is characterised by a withdrawn state and a lack of social responsiveness or interest in other people. Individuals often have serious communication and linguistic impairments and fail to develop normal attachments to other people. Autistic children are often preoccupied with inanimate objects like toy cars, but typically do not use them for pretend play. Instead they will engage in repetitive and ritualistic activities and may focus on mechanistic attributes such as the way the wheels move. Some psychologists propose that many of the characteristics of autism reflect the individuals having flawed theories of mind or failing to attribute minds to other people, or inanimate objects in the case of pretend play (Baron-Cohen *et al.* 1995). If this is true, and gaze reading plays an important role in normal development of theory of mind, we would expect autistic children to have problems with eye gaze.

Problems in understanding and a lack of use of non-verbal communication in general is indeed a pervasive characteristic of autism. Autistic infants and children typically do not engage in joint attention (looking where someone else is looking). Furthermore there is evidence that autistic children do not use social gaze declaratively; in other words to tell someone something. If we are in a room with a number of other people and I want to tell you that I plan to leave, I might look towards the door and back at you again. This is using gaze declaratively. Most normally developing infants begin using gaze declaratively, accompanied by pointing gestures and head orientation, around 18 months, but autistic children do not (Charman *et al.* 2000). In Chapter 3, on hand gestures, I described the difference between proto-imperative (used for requesting) and proto-declarative (used for commenting) pointing. Remember that pointing to request occurs earlier in development than pointing to comment. While autistic children use pointing to request, they do not use it declaratively. They do not use non-verbal cues such as gaze or gesture to comment on objects or deliberately to show interest. Autism differs in this respect from other forms of learning disability such as Down's syndrome, where the use of gaze and gesture typically follows a normal if delayed pattern. While many infant responses such as gaze, gesture and vocalisation are delayed in babies born with Downs syndrome, they do develop quite normal social communication patterns eventually.

It used to be thought that autistic children avoided eye contact with other people. However, recent work suggests that this is not the case. It appears that autistic children make normal amounts of eye contact with other people but not at the usual points within interactions (Volkmar and Mayes 1991). Normal children use gaze to establish joint attention, whereas autistic children do not; in other words it is their use of eye contact that deviates from the norm rather than the absolute amount of social gaze that they engage in (Baron-Cohen 1988). This suggests that the problem autistic children have with eyes is that they fail to *understand* them in the way that non-autistic children and adults do. They fail to see the significance of eyes for understanding people's mental states and for communication. In particular they don't appreciate that eyes provide useful clues as to people's desires, intentions and thoughts (Baron-Cohen *et al.* 1995). For example, if there is a plate of cakes and a plate of biscuits on a table and an autistic child sees another child looking at the cakes, this will not help him predict which treat the other child plans to take.

This is not to say that autistic children have no awareness of eye gaze. They know, as most typically developing 30-month-olds do, that to see an object you have to have your eyes open and an unobstructed view of it. Children with autism can also tell when someone is looking at them and are good at judging the direction of another person's gaze (Phillips, Baron-Cohen and Rutter 1992). What they fail to do is then to use gaze cues to extrapolate what is behind the gazer's behaviour. If someone looks at us we register this and then begin to think of reasons why they're looking at us. We might think they are interested in us, want to talk to us or even are angry with us. This reasoning about gaze is what children with autism don't do.

Research in Sweden has attempted to identify early signs of autism in two- to three-year-olds. Such signs include: 'appears isolated from surroundings'; 'doesn't try to attract adult's attention to own activity'; 'doesn't play like other children'. However, in addition there were some signs relating specifically to the children's gazing behaviours. Parents of children with autism reported: difficulties getting eye contact; empty gaze; and 'something strange about his/her gaze' (Dahlgren and Gillberg 1989; Gillberg 1989). Indeed, based on this work, a checklist was developed for early screening for autism between ten and eighteen months to be done by nurses in well-baby clinics. A number of items on this list relate to eye gaze; for example, ask the mother if she considers her child's eye contact to be normal; look for gaze avoidance during the examination; and watch for stiff, staring gaze (Gillberg 1989).

Problems with gazing behaviour do not on their own predict autistic development. However, they typically accompany other symptoms of the disorder. Baron-Cohen *et al.* (1992) looked at a sample of 41 toddlers who were classed as having a heightened risk of developing autism because they had an older autistic sibling. At 18 months four of these children displayed at least two of the following three deficits:

1. They did not engage in pretend play.

2. They showed no proto-declarative pointing.

3. They did not monitor other people's gaze.

All four of these children were later diagnosed as having autism, but none of the others were. This triad of problems seems to be crucial in the development of autism. Children who don't point or don't pretend at 18 months may have developmental delay but not autism. In a child who exhibits all three deficits and does not monitor other people's gaze, autism is likely.

A related developmental disorder is Asperger's syndrome (AS). This is now recognised as being on the same continuum of deficits as autism. Many features of the two overlap. Having said this, people with Asperger's generally have average to high IQs and do not have the language impairments associated with autism. In common with autism is the poor use of non-verbal cues. This includes a limited use of gestures and facial expressions and a peculiar, stiff gaze. For example, Asperger's syndrome children do not use gaze for turn taking or in acknowledgement during conversation (Attwood 1998). Furthermore, while normal adults usually gaze most when they are listening to other people speaking, people with AS report that this is difficult and interferes with their abilities to concentrate on what is being said. In other words, looking at another person's face is demanding and distracting. Therefore they typically avoid looking while they're listening. This can make them seem uninterested in what is being said.

Baron-Cohen *et al.* (1997) found that normal adults are good at judging whether someone is feeling perhaps ashamed, bewildered, reflective or playful from seeing only their eyes. So we can use the eye region to read other people's minds. In contrast, while adults with Asperger's syndrome can tell the gender of a person from seeing only their eyes, they are not good at detecting how the person is feeling.

Eye gaze and learning

Monitoring other people's eye gaze plays a part in children's learning (and adults' for that matter) in a number of ways. First, it has very specific repercussions, such as its effect on language development, as I've already described. Second, it has more generic influences on learning as a whole. I'll put forward a few points to support this claim.

A number of studies have shown that when teachers look often at their students, the students learn more. Young adult students remembered more about instructions they had been given when their tutor looked at them while giving the instructions compared with students whose instructor had not gazed (Fry and Smith 1975). Similar effects have been found with primary school children. In one study a teacher sometimes looked at her pupils while telling them a story and sometimes didn't look at all. The children remembered much more about the story when their teacher had looked at them while reading (Otteson and Otteson 1980).

Chris Fullwood, a postgraduate student of mine, has been investigating how people might be trained to make better use of video-mediated communication technologies. In one of his studies he looked at whether eye gaze would have similar effects on recall of information when it was done by an instructor speaking across a video link (Fullwood and Doherty-Sneddon in prep.). He trained an actor to recite a script describing a fictitious soap product and video recorded him doing so in two different ways. First, the actor described the product while looking forward but not directly at the camera. The effect of this on video was that it looked as though the actor was looking slightly down but not 'looking right at you' when you watched the tape. In the other condition the actor was instructed to gaze directly at the camera at key points in the script, at which times it looked on the video recording as though he was looking straight at the person watching the tape. This is essentially what newsreaders do to increase the feeling that they are speaking to you.

Chris then showed these recordings to different groups of 'listeners'. They were told that they would see a salesperson giving them the lowdown on a product and that the experimenter was interested in their responses to the salesperson and the product. One of the findings was particularly interesting and relevant to our current discussion. The listeners who watched the video in which the actor looked directly at the camera (and therefore appeared to look directly at them) remembered more information about the product when they were asked to recall it than listeners who had heard the same script and seen the same actor, but did not experience 'mutual gaze' with the actor. This is strong evidence that a speaker's gazing behaviour can influence our mental processing of information and subsequent memory for it. All of these studies suggest that looking at your listener can increase recall. Why is this so? There are a number of possible explanations.

One account is based on what has already been discussed in this chapter. Eyes are a very salient part of human faces. People looking at us make our hearts beat faster, increase our breathing rate and make us sweat. In other words our bodies get ready for something to happen. So gazing at someone is one way of saying 'something important is about to happen, prepare yourself and take notice'. Perhaps we remember information that is accompanied with eye gaze better because we take more notice of it; in other words gaze is a cue for emphasis. This is similar to the way that words or phrases can be emphasised by our tone of voice. If you are telling someone something you might gaze at the listener at the particularly important or relevant bits. Your listener benefits from this since your gaze draws attention to the key points in your statement. In this way gaze helps to break the flow of speech into meaningful chunks that are easier to remember than the statement given as a continuous whole. This is potentially important and suggests that we should ensure appropriate levels of gazing when telling children important information.

Furthermore, physiological arousal, within reasonable limits, enhances mental functioning. In other words our brains tend to work better when our bodies are in a moderately aroused, though not over-aroused, condition. Compare your own mental agility when you are alert and maybe slightly nervous with when you are sluggish and relaxed. Generally you will respond more quickly and more accurately in the aroused state. I should say that this only holds in medium levels of arousal. In highly arousing, stressful conditions mental functioning is often impaired. Under normal sorts of eye contact, the looking behaviour itself should only cause a little arousal, and it may be this that increases our memory for information imparted under these conditions.

So at certain points within an interaction eye gaze from a speaker can help consolidate information we are receiving. While most of the work has been done on adults, there is some evidence for similar benefits for children. Furthermore the mechanisms proposed to underlie the benefits – for example, increased arousal caused by gaze – operate from an early age. This has important implications for facilitating children's learning. Not only does gaze help to direct their attention appropriately, but even simply looking at them may help them remember information.

Don't look now!

Making eye contact with others and looking at faces can have cognitive benefits. Are there any circumstances when looking at another person is distracting rather than helpful? We do not look at one another continuously and we avert our gaze regularly, suggesting that it is just as crucial to avoid eye contact during certain events and particular parts of conversations.

During difficult mental activity (for example, remembering information or planning what we are going to say), we often close our eyes, look up at the sky, or away from the person we are in conversation with. This phenomenon is known as gaze aversion. The perceived importance of gaze aversion for accurate memory recall is exemplified in the recommendation that eyes should be closed as part of cognitive interviews used for eye witness testimony (Fisher and Geiselman 1992). Why do we do this and does it actually help us to remember or think about things? This whole book is about the informativeness of visual cues. It is not surprising that we try to *avoid* this potentially distracting information when we're trying to concentrate on other things. In other words, communicators need to know when to 'switch off' from the flow of visual information. A number of studies, described below, report ways in which adults switch off from environmental stimulation in order to concentrate better.

Glenberg, Shroeder and Robertson (1998) found that when asked moderately difficult questions adults often avert their gaze. In this American study adults were asked questions of variable difficulty, including general knowledge and mental arithmetic problems. The frequency of gaze aversion was related to the difficulty of the questions, but more importantly averting gaze away from the questioner improved accuracy of responses. Averting eye gaze helped people to disengage from their visual environment and thereby helped them concentrate on what they were thinking about. So certain mental tasks (those not involved with engaging with the outside world but internally driven, e.g. mental imaging, remembering) are facilitated by 'shutting off' from the external environment, leaving us better able to focus on our internal thought processes. Furthermore it seems that faces are a typically demanding source of visual stimulation. They are very engaging and difficult to ignore if we do look at them.

While gaze aversion in adult interactions can be seen as a strategy for avoiding cognitive overload, no research has yet addressed whether this phenomenon occurs in children. This is an unfortunate omission in the developmental literature since the efficiency with which children process information influences many aspects of their development; for example, how well they learn in school. As we see time and again in this book, children are particularly dependent on non-verbal signals in their communication, relying on visual communication to support their limited language abilities. So will children look away from their communicative partners or will they be even more drawn to attending to them?

It may be that disengaging from environmental stimulation is a skill that is learned (Glenberg *et al.* 1998). In support of this, my own doctoral work found that, while communicating, pairs of six- and eleven-year-olds gazed at one another more than pairs of adults. In other words they averted their gaze less often. In that particular study the increased gazing reflected a greater reliance on visual signals to complete the communication task in hand and was not detrimental to performance. It is possible however that for certain types of tasks increased gazing (and therefore access to visual information) may be detrimental to performance.

In a recent study we found just this. Children's communication abilities in face-to-face and audio-only interaction were studied using a communication task called the shape description task (Doherty-Sneddon *et al.* 2000). See Figure 4.3 for an example of one set of blocks used. In the shape description task, children attempted to describe and understand descriptions of complex, abstract shapes. The task was done in pairs with one child acting as the information sender and the other as information receiver. The sender described the blocks on the left of the dotted line, one at a time, to the receiver. The receiver had to choose matching blocks from their set (on the right of the dotted line) based on these descriptions. The task required that the information sender scrutinise the shapes for distinctive visual properties and the receiver gradually build a visual mental representation of the described shape, sufficient to select the correct target shape from distractors.

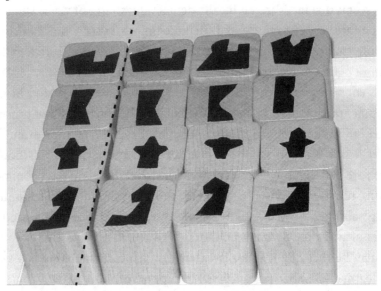

Figure 4.3 A set of shape description blocks: the four in the left-hand column are the information sender's; the others are the information receiver's

Perhaps surprisingly the results revealed that children performed *less well* when they could see one another than when they could not. This was in direct contrast to all of our previous studies which had always shown that visual cues helped children communicate better (Doherty-Sneddon and Kent 1996). After much deliberation we concluded that the task involves considerable visual/spatial demands for both partners because it requires the use of processes such as mental imagery or seeing pictures in your 'mind's eye'. We know from studies of human memory that many types of visual information are processed initially in a short-term memory store that has a limited capacity. This visual 'sketch pad' is employed not only when we use our 'mind's eye', but also when we process other visual information. Visual signals in the face-to-face context therefore interfered with performance of the task because they were taking up 'space' in this short-term memory store.

If this interpretation is correct, the results also suggest that the children were not 'switching off' effectively from their partner's visual signals at the appropriate times. Attending to a face can sometimes make it harder to concentrate on other kinds of tasks. Gaze aversion is one way of cutting down on visual load. Other studies with adults suggest that it is not just visual load that is saved, but mental load in general. Is it the case that children don't avert their gaze in the way that adults do in order to avoid cognitive overload?

Certain gaze aversion behaviours develop from a very early age. Young infants often break mutual gaze with their caregivers during face-to-face encounters (Bruner 1977). It has been suggested that this allows them to control physiological arousal. As mentioned earlier, mutual gaze with another person produces an increase in heart and breathing rate in infants. The suggestion is that they break mutual gaze in order to reduce arousal to an optimal level (Stern 1977). This gaze aversion is an automatic response and doesn't involve the baby reasoning about the behaviour. It suggests that we might expect to see some gaze aversion in fairly young children.

We designed a study to investigate specifically whether or not children avert their gaze in the way that adults do when questioned about difficult material. We have found that children from six years of age increased the frequency with which they averted their gaze from a questioner's face as questions became harder (see Figure 4.4). The children were asked different types of questions ranging from verbal reasoning to mental arithmetic. They averted their gaze during all question types. We concluded that children of this age use gaze aversion to control their cognitive load in a similar way to adults. This however was not the case with pre-school children. When we did the same tests with three- and five-year-olds we found that they did not consistently look away from the questioner as questions got harder. Therefore averting gaze as an attention shifting strategy seems to be something that is not yet fully developed in the pre-school years (Doherty-Sneddon *et al.* 2002).

Figure 4.4 A six-year-old averts her gaze when asked a difficult question

Indeed, when questions were difficult these young children were more likely to look at the questioner, perhaps for clues or feedback. For example, when thinking about arithmetic questions nine-year-olds looked away on average 82 per cent; eight-year-olds 78 per cent; and three-year-olds only 40 per cent of the time. This may be advantageous for the youngest kids in normal circumstances; after all, adults often provide extra feedback and scaffold children's attempts to solve such problems. Thus, very young children are more likely to maintain eye contact with a questioner when they are finding things difficult. Perhaps this reflects that they have simply given up and are no longer engaged in thinking about the problem. Alternatively maintaining gaze with the adult may signal that they need more assistance. Conceivably, both explanations are correct.

Gaze aversion is a rather good cue as to whether a child is actually trying to answer a question or not. When doing homework with my own six-year-old, I can tell whether we are likely to make progress on something based on her gaze patterns. If she averts her gaze I know she is thinking about the problem. If she maintains gaze with me for any length of time without giving an answer, she is not. However, while children of this age do avert their gaze while thinking, I'm not convinced they are consciously aware of doing this. In fact I don't think adults are particularly aware of this until it is pointed out. When trying to take some photographs for an exhibition where I was presenting some of this work, I asked a six-year-old boy to 'look away, you know, how you do when you're trying to work out the answer to a difficult question'. He assured me that he did not do this and 'just looked normally'. We set up the camera, I asked the question and, much to his own amazement, he immediately and automatically did a classic look to the side and up.

Preliminary work I've done recently has investigated whether gaze aversion can be used as an indicator of children's readiness to learn something new. From one developmental perspective children learn and are motivated to continue with learning when this occurs in their zone of proximal development (ZPD). They are in this zone when they can accomplish a task with guidance from a more able other, but not on their own. Children typically go through different stages when they are learning something. They go from not understanding at all, to being able to deal with the concept with help from another person (ZPD), to being able to understand and complete the problem on their own. Furthermore, children working within their ZPD are much more likely to benefit from instruction compared with those who are not (Peters 1996).

One challenge for teachers and parents is to recognise when children are in this mental state. Preliminary work shows us that patterns of gaze aversion may be one clue that can be used for this. A student of mine found that six-year-olds' gaze aversion increased substantially from when they did not understand at all, to when they were just beginning to understand various arithmetic concepts she was teaching them. Once they fully understood (shown by consistently responding correctly to new problems) their gaze aversion levels reduced again but not to their pre-understanding state (Longbotham 2001). This suggests that there may be a peak in gaze aversion when children are in a critical learning 'zone'. Gaze aversion is a reliable external cue that tells us if a child is thinking about something. Relatively high amounts are likely to signal a readiness to learn, while maintaining eye contact during difficult tasks may well indicate that the child is disengaged and has given up.

Children (at least from six years old) and adults use gaze aversion to switch off from the distraction of perceiving faces while concentrating hard. More work is planned in order to pinpoint accurately the feasibility of using gaze aversion as a cue in learning situations. Gaze aversion can be used in teaching and promoting learning and indeed is a useful cue in any situation where a child's knowledge is being assessed. Some preliminary suggestions are as follows:

1. If a child does not respond to a question but does avert her gaze she is likely to be thinking about her response or trying to work out an answer. She may still answer incorrectly, but the gaze aversion indicates that she has thought about the answer.

2. If a child averts his gaze relatively frequently (compared to his normal 'resting rate') he may well be in a state of 'readiness to learn'.

3. If a child does not respond to a question and maintains eye contact with the questioner it is likely that he has given up and is not trying to work out the answer. It may be that he needs extra help with the question.

Following a seminar on these ideas, someone asked me whether I thought that the relationship between gaze aversion and cognitive load might be related to the dysfunctional patterns of gaze exhibited in autism. This is a very interesting question that needs to be addressed. Autistic people have a problem focusing their attention on one thing at a time and switching their attention to new tasks. It may be that because of this they are in a state of cognitive overload more of the time and this is one reason why they avert their gaze. This idea is backed up by Tony Attwood's (1998) reports of people with Asperger's syndrome finding it difficult to concentrate on what someone is saying if they look at them while listening.

Gaze aversion is a way of controlling cognitive demands that develops through the pre-school years. When do children begin to understand that gaze aversion is a sign of *someone else's* thinking? A developmental mile-stone in this understanding of eye gaze comes between three and four years of age (round about when children are developing a definite theory of mind). Most adults judge that another person is thinking if they see them gazing up and/or to the side 'into space'. Some three-year-olds understand this sign, but it is not until children are nearer four years of age that most of them interpret this gaze to mean someone is thinking (Baron-Cohen and Cross 1992). While four-year-olds read gaze aversion as an outward sign of other people thinking, they are not aware explicitly of their own gaze aversion. It is difficult to be sure when children gain this level of awareness. Certainly, even for adults, gaze aversion is difficult to control consciously and most people are not aware that they avert their gaze while thinking about difficult material.

This chapter has described how gaze behaviour changes with age and plays an integral role in children's social and mental development. It can be a useful cue to many different things:

- what a child is attending to
- whether children are thinking about something
- how likely it is that they have understood
- how they are feeling
- whether they are being deceptive.

Furthermore the dysfunctional use of gaze by children with certain developmental disorders can help us gain insight into the underlying cognitive and social deficits involved. Even in normal development the explicit understanding of gaze patterns is something that cannot be taken for granted in the early years. Although children's eye gaze is a useful indicator of their internal emotional and cognitive states and while they respond to other people's gaze in a variety of ways, their own knowledge of what gaze means and the rules surrounding its use develop well beyond the pre-school years and into primary school.

Suggested reading

1. Gomez, J.C. (1991) 'Visual Behaviour as a Window for Reading Minds of Others in Primates.' In A. Whitem (ed) *Natural Theories of Minds: Evolution, Development and Simulation of Everyday Mindreading.* Oxford: Blackwell.

2. Baldwin, D.A. and Moses, L.J. (1996) 'The Ontogeny of Social Information Gathering.' *Child Development 67*, 1915–1935.

3. Andersen, E.S., Dunlea, A. and Kekelis, L.S. (1984) 'Blind Children's Language: Resolving Some Differences.' *Journal of Child Language 11*, 645–664.

4. Doherty-Sneddon, G., McAuley, S., Bruce, V., Langton, S., Blokland, A. and Anderson, A. (2000) 'Visual Signals and Children's Communication: Negative Effects on Task Outcome.' *British Journal of Developmental Psychology 18*, 595–608.

Key points

1. Eye gaze plays an important part in children's emotional, social and cognitive development.

2. Mutual gaze has significant physiological and emotional effects for children and adults.

3. Joint visual attention and social referencing are important in language acquisition and in children's development of theory of mind.

4. Many functions of gaze are initially automatic. An explicit understanding of other people's gazing behaviour is not evident until children are at least four to five years old.

5. Eye gaze is an important way of providing emphasis and can facilitate memory for information.

6. One reason for averting gaze is to concentrate. Gaze aversion is therefore a useful external indicator of thinking and may help determine when children are working within their ZPD. This seems to be true from six years onwards and so far has not been established for younger children.

Things to try

1. *From birth.* For those of you who have just had or are expecting a new baby, watch for when your baby first makes mutual eye contact with you. This normally happens around the second to third week after birth. There is however much individual variation in this, so don't be concerned if it takes a little longer. When it does happen think about the way it affects you. Does it, for example, make you feel closer to your infant?

2. *From around eight months.* With babies from about eight months, try seeing whether they will track your gaze when you look at something to your left or right. You can try this from four months but don't be surprised if your little one fails to do anything with any consistency. Also remember to move your head when you look. As the baby gets older you can make the tracking games a little more difficult. So, for example, by around 18 months babies may turn their head, to see what you're looking at over their shoulder.

3. *Babies of any age.* Play peek-a-boo. Babies love this. They find it very stimulating and it may help them begin to understand about taking turns in games.

4. *Babies of any age.* Play 'interaction games'. Pop the child on his or her back and face them. Talk playfully while maintaining eye contact. Baby will respond by vocalising, smiling and looking back at you. He will often become increasingly excited and will then break his gaze with you and look away, looking back at you when you get his attention again.

5. *From around 12 months.* Make sure you look for signals that older babies and toddlers might give you in their gaze. Are they trying to ask for something? Show you something? Remember the more you respond to the child's early signs as intentional and communicative, the easier it will be for the baby to begin to understand about communication.

6. *Child of any age.* When confronting a child about an issue, does the child look you right in the eye or away and down? Being able to look you in the eye is often a sign of self-assertion and confidence. It can also mean that whatever you're discussing has real importance for the child. Listen to his side of the story. If the child is embarrassed or feeling bad about himself, he might look away. This does not necessarily mean that he is trying to deceive you. Try to gently coax him into discussing what's on his mind and/or yours.

7. *Any age.* Try asking children (or any unsuspecting adult) moderately difficult (age appropriate) questions. You will soon see how prevalent gaze aversion is when people think about and answer questions. You may not see this with pre-school children. We haven't yet found this consistent pattern of gaze aversion in children below the age of six years.

8. *Child of any age.* If a child is having difficulty with her homework or schoolwork, it can be helpful to encourage her to look at a blank surface (the floor or wall) while working out problems.

This is likely to be particularly useful when the problem she's trying to solve involves the use of working things out in her mind's eye. For example, children learning to count might be encouraged to see number lines in their heads, or to visualise a word when trying to spell it. Certainly, staring blankly at you is unlikely to help.

9. *Any age.* When reading to children, try looking at them at important or interesting points. This will help maintain interest, add emphasis to what you're saying and increase the chance that they will 'get the point' and remember it.

Some developmental milestones

1. From birth, babies track moving objects and look about their environment. They are quite short sighted so don't see things at a distance with any clarity.

2. When newborns look at your face they mostly look around the perimeter; for example, at your hairline.

3. From about two and a half weeks, infants begin to make mutual eye contact with other people.

4. Some research suggests that babies from four months might track head movements.

5. Certainly from 12 months babies will track whole head movements to the left or right.

6. Try the A-not-B task with babies around ten months. Before they get it right you may see them looking towards the correct location but searching in the incorrect one.

7. By 18 months toddlers will track your gaze over their shoulder.

8. Between the ages of three and four children acquire an elementary theory of mind. At this time they also begin to understand that looking away can be a sign of thinking.

9. By six years children begin to understand some of the rules about gazing behaviours – for example, that it's rude to stare, or that staring can mean hostility – and that mutual gaze can be a sign of friendship and liking.

10. By the time children are at school they will be fairly adept at averting their gaze when they need to think about something.

Chapter 5

Facial Expressions

In this chapter we will look at evidence that suggests human facial expressions are innate skills, but are at the same time strongly influenced by children's experiences. The argument about whether human behaviour is innate or learned is pervasive across psychology. In my opinion the study of facial expressions gives one of the clearest illustrations of both these sources of behaviour and how they interact to produce an end result. I will describe how and when babies develop their abilities to both produce and understand facial expressions. In addition, we will consider the cultural universality of human use of faces. I will also look at the evolutionary significance of expressions in the social behaviour of non-human primates like monkeys and chimps. Finally I will discuss the development of other types of facial cues, like those used in lip-reading and recognition of others.

Types of information faces give us

Faces are particularly important for the expression of emotion. Other non-verbal channels give information about the intensity of the emotion rather than defining specific emotions. However, faces also provide other types of very important information. For example, there are a number of facial gestures like looks of 'disbelief' or the 'eyebrow flash' used as a greeting or acknowledgement. Some of these are recognised across all cultures, and many have meaning without needing the accompaniment of words. Another source of information we get from faces comes from the configuration of the lips, teeth and tongue while we speak. This aspect of face processing is something that develops very early and seems to occur independently from children's understanding of emotional expressions. Finally, an incredibly important ability that faces give us is a visual way of identifying other people. The ways in which children and adults use facial configurations to do this differ considerably. This chapter will consider each of these types of face processing in turn.

Neurology and physiology behind facial expressions

The face is the most finely tuned non-verbal channel. We have evolved the ability to produce very subtle and also very dramatic facial expressions that are carefully monitored by those with whom we interact. Relatively speaking there is a disproportionately large part of our motor cortex, the part of our brain that allows us to produce voluntary movements (see Figure 5.1), allocated to the face. This allows for the variety of controlled movements of our faces that we are familiar with. Indeed we are generally very good at controlling our facial movements, when we set our minds to it, and even masking our true feelings. This is a skill learned during childhood. Babies and young children are really not very good at hiding their feelings. However, as we will see, voluntary control of our faces is only one way that facial expressions are produced. There is an evolutionarily much older source of facial expressions that is spontaneous and involuntary.

There are two main types of facial expressions differing in terms of their brain origin: *spontaneous* (involuntary) expressions and *posed* (deliberate) expressions. Essentially we describe deliberate voluntary facial movements as 'posed expressions' because they are in fact posed. These do not necessarily reflect how we feel, but instead are what we want to tell the outside world we feel. In contrast, spontaneous expressions, the evolutionarily older of the two, occur as a direct consequence of an emotional experience or feeling. So when we feel sad or happy our faces mirror this (unless we try to mask these expressions by posing others). These expressions are called spontaneous because they occur automatically with no voluntary attempt to produce them. These are essentially natural and the sort we see first in human babies. They are also the only sort of expressions we see in non-human primates. For adult humans facial expressions are typically a mixture of the two.

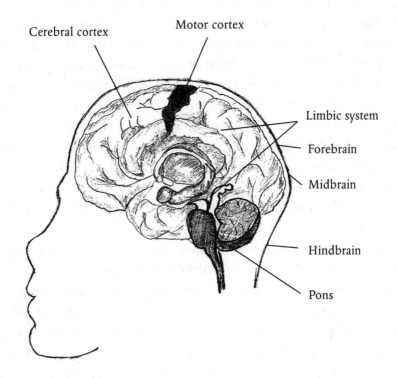

Figure 5.1 An artist's impression of a human brain showing the important structures involved in the production of facial expressions
Source: picture by Stuart Doherty (2002)

I want now to consider the neurological underpinnings of posed and spontaneous expressions. This neurological distinction demonstrates very nicely the interplay between inborn and learned mechanisms underlying the production of facial expressions. It also helps us explain children's development of spontaneous facial expressions, and the development of display rules (rules about the appropriateness of expressions).

Before going on I need to give you a whirlwind tour of the anatomy of the human brain, so that what I say about this makes sense. Essentially the human brain consists of three main parts: the hindbrain, the midbrain and the forebrain (see Figure 5.1). In very general terms, the higher up the evolutionary scale a species is, the more it has in common with the human brain in terms of these three areas. The hindbrain begins just above the spinal cord. It controls many basic biological functions, like breathing, circulation and reflexes such as swallowing and coughing. Even the most primitive creatures, birds and reptiles, have hindbrains. One region of the hindbrain is the pons, which plays an important role in integrating movements of and sensations from the facial muscles, eyes, ears and tongue.

The midbrain is located between the hindbrain and forebrain (as you might have guessed from its name). It is important for targeting sound and vision and is, for example, the part of the brain that makes dogs prick up their ears in response to a novel event. Birds have relatively large midbrains while mammals have comparatively small midbrains. Mammals have shifted much of their control of vision and hearing to higher areas of their forebrains.

The forebrain contains everything that lies above the midbrain. In lower animals like fish and reptiles the forebrain is very small. In mammals, especially the primates, the forebrain is very large. Indeed humans have such a large forebrain that it surrounds and hides all of our midbrain and half of our hindbrain. In mammals, the most obvious part of the forebrain is the cerebral cortex. Only primates and other complex mammals have this level of development of the forebrain. The cortex is the rather wrinkled outer part of the brain that encases the rest – the bit you see if you were to look immediately under the skull. The name cortex comes from the Latin for 'bark'. In humans the cortex accounts for around 80 per cent of the brain's volume. It is this part of the brain that is generally associated with intelligence and consciousness, and flexibility and voluntary control of behaviour.

The cortex can be divided up into different regions associated with different functions. The one you need to know about in this chapter is the part called the motor cortex (see Figure 5.1). This part of the cortex allows us to make voluntary movements. When we deliberately move our muscles it is activation from this part of the brain that allows us to do so. There are also important forebrain structures that lie beneath the cortex. A group of these, called the limbic system, is important in the production of facial expressions. These subcortical structures are older in evolutionary terms than the cerebral cortex.

Facial expressions are made by movements of the facial muscles that lie beneath the skin. These movements are controlled by the facial nerve nucleus in the pons of the hindbrain. This nucleus is like a relay station, bringing together messages from different parts of the brain that influence the movements of our faces. From the nucleus come the five main facial nerves, each influencing different parts of the face. The facial nerve nucleus gets 'instructions' from two distinct parts of the brain, one more primitive in evolutionary terms than the other (Argyle 1996). First, as a result of emotional arousal, activity comes from the limbic system, in the subcortical forebrain. When we feel an emotion (for example, happiness), activation from the emotion centre is transmitted to the facial nerve nucleus that in turn causes a spontaneous (or automatic) expression of happiness. This contrasts with the facial expressions that occur when activation comes from the motor cortex, which results in posed, socially controlled facial expressions. So when we deliberately try to look happy we use our motor cortex to produce a 'happy face'.

As we will see, the time courses of development of spontaneous and posed expressions are very different. There are other important differences between the two types of facial expressions. The first is due to the different parts of the brain in which they originate. Our cerebral cortex is essentially spilt into two parts, the left and right cerebral hemispheres. The left hemisphere controls movement on the *right* side of the body, while the right hemisphere controls movement on the *left*. In addition some brain functions are more controlled by the right hemisphere (e.g. processing of spatial information) and some are controlled more by the left (e.g. language). It appears that the right hemisphere is dominant for faces. This means that movements on the left-hand side of the face are stronger or more pronounced than those on the right-hand side (controlled by the less dominant left hemisphere). Posed expressions therefore are slightly asymmetric (or unequally distributed across the face) because they originate in the cerebral cortex. In contrast, subcortical areas of the brain are far less lateralised so that spontaneous expressions originating in the emotion centre of the brain are more equally portrayed on both sides of the face.

Other differences between the features of spontaneous and posed expressions are that they often involve slightly different regions of the face. For example, a posed smile usually involves only the mouth region, whereas a spontaneous smile involves the mouth and eye regions. You will be familiar with terms like 'smiling eyes'. Controlling the lower half of the face is generally easier than the top half. We see this especially in children when they are asked to pose facial expressions. Figure 5.6 shows a four-year-old posing an angry face. She has an angry looking mouth but her eyebrows do not show any of the muscle movements associated with real anger. Finally, the timing of the onset of the two types of expressions is different. Posed expressions generally begin quickly and end abruptly, whereas the onset of spontaneous expressions is typically slower and smoother. These sorts of differences are important, as you will see when we consider detecting deception from facial information.

Inborn or learned expression?

Paul Ekman, a famous scientist who has contributed a huge amount of influential work on facial expressions, argues that there are at least six neurophysiological programmes for the production of emotion that we are born with and which quickly unfold over the first few months of life (Ekman 1982). He concludes this from his own work and a review of other studies that find there are considerable cross-cultural similarities in both the expression (encoding) and comprehension (decoding) of emotional expressions. There are six types of expressions that seem to be universally found across societies: happiness, sadness, surprise, fear, anger and disgust. Figure 5.2 shows a ten-year-old posing these six expressions. Some are quite clear, while others are less so since she does not always use all the facial movements typically associated with the expression. For example, she fails to include wide staring eyes in her fear expression. As she gets older and more practised she will become better at posing facial expressions.

Figure 5.2 A nine-year-old poses the six universal face expressions. Can you tell which is which? Are some better representations than others?

It appears that we are born with the potential to produce these six basic emotional expressions spontaneously and do not have to learn them. Babies do not make all of these expressions from birth (although they make some). Over the first few months of life, brain maturation causes them all to appear. Normally children begin producing the six basic expressions within the first few months of life without any explicit instruction. Fine tuning the expressions via voluntary control occurs later.

Children who are born blind produce similar expressions even though they have never seen them. Research has shown that observers of facial expressions by blind and sighted children made equally accurate judgements of the children's emotions regardless of the children's sightedness. The portrayals of emotions by the sighted children were however judged as more adequate (Thompson 1941). Blind children cannot have learned these facial configurations by observing and imitating other people; therefore the six main expressions must at least in part be inborn. Other work has shown that while the *spontaneous* facial expressions of blind and sighted individuals do not differ, the same blind people were unable to *act out* or pose facial expressions (Dumas 1932). This suggests that spontaneous facial expressions are largely controlled by innate mechanisms, whereas posed expressions result from learning from others within our social environment.

Monkeys and other primates make considerable use of facial expressions in their social encounters. Chimpanzees have the most extensive range of facial expressions among the primates even compared with human beings. Humans have around nine main emotional expressions (including the six I've just described) while chimpanzees have about twenty. For primates, facial expressions are very important for group cohesion and relationship management. They are used to express many meanings, such as dominance, affiliation, fear and submission. Some unpublished work reports that cutting the facial nerves of monkeys (essentially making their faces inert) results in the disintegration of the social structures within their groups (Izard unpub.). Monkeys reared in isolation (and therefore unable to learn expression by observation) show the same emotional expressions as those brought up in normal social groups, although their onset tends to be a bit delayed. Therefore monkey facial expressions also appear to be inborn.

It has been suggested that some chimpanzee facial expressions give us clues as to the origins of certain human expressions. For example, chimps have a 'play face' which may relate to the human laugh and pleasurable smile. Eyebrow 'flashes' are used by a number of primate species to show friendliness and affiliation. The eyebrow flash is also claimed to be a universally recognised human expression of greeting or friendly attention. The pervasiveness of this facial emblem across cultures and its apparent predecessor in primate eyebrow flashes has led some researchers to propose that it is innate.

There appear to be universal, inborn mechanisms that determine facial configuration relating to emotions (we will see more evidence of this when we consider the development of expressions in human infants in detail). However, cultural learning influences certain aspects of expressions. There are culture-specific differences in particular facial configurations that are used to express certain emotions. For example, in many cultures raised eyebrows are used as part of the expression of happiness. However, in Thailand a raised brow is used to express unhappiness.

As well as cultural differences in specific configurations used to portray certain expressions, there are considerable differences in the rules about public expression of emotion and attitudes. These rules are called display rules and refer to cultural norms about where and when emotional expressions are acceptable and to what intensity. For example, the public expression of intense unhappiness is quite acceptable in contact cultures like Italy and Greece, but extremely unacceptable in non-contact cultures such as Japan. These kinds of rules have to be learned by children and are part of socialisation into their culture.

Measuring facial expressions

In order to study facial expressions you need some way of measuring them. For example, when is a happy face a happy face and how does it differ from a sad face or a fear face? One way of doing this is to get the opinion of a number of people about what a particular facial expression means. If there is enough agreement you can be fairly sure that the interpretation is correct. However, this doesn't really answer my question as to what specific movements of the face characterise some expressions and not others.

Facial expressions are produced by the network of superficial facial muscles that lie beneath the facial skin (these are independent from the muscles associated with chewing and other movements of the jaw). These superficial muscles are activated by the branches of the facial nerve. Each of these muscles produces very definite movements, visible to the outside world as movement of the skin that lies on top of them. For example, the corrugator muscle runs across our brows and is the muscle responsible for making us frown. Contraction of the zygomatic muscles pulls back our lips and mouth regions to make us smile.

One obvious way of describing facial expressions is to characterise them in terms of the muscle movements involved in producing them. Ekman and Friesen (1978) did just that and came up with an elaborate muscle-based way of coding (or describing) facial expressions – the Facial Affect Coding Scheme (FACS). This coding scheme is based on small but observable facial movements or action units. There are 33 different action units made by human faces and 44 combinations of them. They are mostly due to single muscle movements. The important thing about this form of measurement is that it is based on observable movements. It is carried out by doing frame-by-frame video analysis of people performing facial expressions. Figure 5.3 shows the action units involved in eyebrow movements and their associated meanings (in western cultures).

Eyebrows are actually a really interesting part of the human face (and indeed many species of primates). They are associated with a number of emotional expressions such as surprise and anger. In addition they are also used to transmit facial emblems. Emblems are gestures that have a direct verbal translation, or can replace a word or phrase without any accompanying speech (see Chapter 3). There are a number of emblems transmitted by the face. For example, an American emblem for disbelief or withholding belief is a combination of the following action units: eyebrow movements 1 + 2 + the corners of the mouth down + relaxing the upper eyelid, pushing up the top lip and rocking the head. This little mosaic of movements sounds complicated when you write it down. In fact when done in a natural setting, particularly by individuals raised in a culture who use it frequently, it is very easy. (Watch the film actor Robert De Niro). These types of facial movements, like the acquisition of display rules, will develop over a much longer time course than the development of spontaneous emotional expressions. In fact it is unclear just when children begin to understand these sorts of cues.

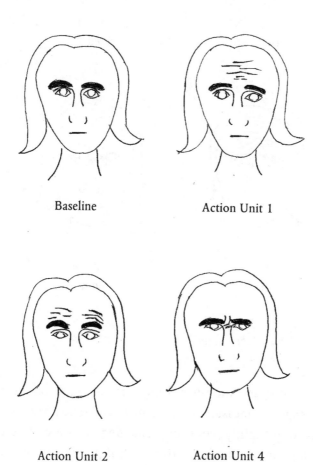

Baseline Action Unit 1

Action Unit 2 Action Unit 4

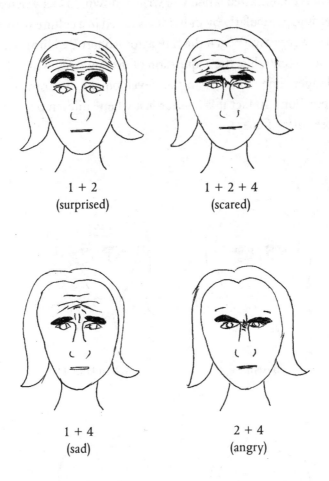

1 + 2
(surprised)

1 + 2 + 4
(scared)

1 + 4
(sad)

2 + 4
(angry)

Figure 5.3 Action units of the eyebrows
Source: adapted from Ekman (1979)

An alternative to observation-based measures of facial expressions is to take electromagnetic measurements of muscle activity. Muscles that are moving even very slightly will show some degree of increased electrical activity. When used on faces this technique is known as facial electromyography (EMG) and can be used for measuring unobservable movements. This is not going to be of much use to most of us in everyday life, but it has been useful in a number of clinical studies. For example, it is sometimes possible to pick up a tiny amount of positive mood improvement in people who are clinically depressed in response to antidepressant drugs (Schwartz *et al.* 1976).

First expressions

Right from birth babies have a repertoire of facial movements which expands rapidly over the first few months of life. Newborn babies make a number of different facial expressions while awake. They make a 'crying face' when crying and distressed; they have a startle expression; and they even look disgusted in response to bitter or novel tastes (Steiner 1977). All of these expressions are entirely automatic and reflect fairly directly the infant's internal state. They are essentially reflexive behaviours and derive from primitive reflex programmes within the brain.

Another reflexive expression that newborns have is non-social smiling. This early form of smiling is called 'non-social' because it occurs without any external social cause. These smiles typically involve the mouth and cheeks but don't get as far up the face as the eyes or forehead. They don't carry the emotional tone of a true smile. The smiles only happen when the infant is drowsy or in a rapid eye movement (REM) sleep state. The baby will be sound asleep and his eyes will move rapidly underneath their sockets as he sleeps. In adults this type of sleep is associated with dreaming. While in REM sleep, newborn babies will often smile spontaneously. This used to be called 'hives' and was thought to be due to the infant releasing trapped wind. In fact it is nothing to do with wind but results from reflexive brain activity associated with this type of sleep. These reflexive facial expressions are the first way that a baby's face gives us a clue as to his cognitive state; they show us that certain brain mechanisms are functioning. The smiles are also very engaging for caregivers and may play a part in the 'cuteness' factor of young infants. Figure 5.4 shows a newborn reflexively smiling during REM sleep. In some ways, these smiles are similar to other reflexes that the infant has from birth. These include grasping – babies will automatically grasp anything placed in the palm of their hands – and rooting – a baby will turn his head towards the source of a light stroke on the cheek. As the baby gets older these reflexive behaviours are replaced by more voluntary ones. For example, the grasp reflex is all but gone by three or four months of age. However, by five months the baby is able to reach for and voluntarily grasp objects.

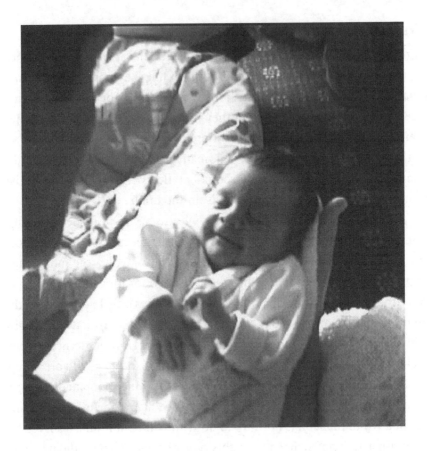

Figure 5.4 A newborn girl performs a reflexive smile while in REM sleep

Human babies do not smile while fully awake until they are around three weeks old. They begin to smile in response to people or objects around them and smiling often occurs in response to the range of expressive signals that caregivers exhibit in face-to-face interactions with babies. This is immensely important in developing social relationships with their caregivers and other people. It is extremely rewarding for caregivers to see the baby smiling and some psychologists suggest that early infant smiling plays an important role in caregiver–infant bonding. These early real smiles therefore occur in response to things in the outside world – typically the presence of other people. In fact the most likely thing to elicit a smile at this age is the sound of a human voice. Seeing a face has little effect over and above the sound of a voice.

During the fifth week of a baby's life this changes. By six weeks he is smiling at human faces. Now faces supersede the importance of voices. This developmental sequence of smiling is due to the unfolding of the human genetic code. We can tell that this is the case since the time course of smile development is closely related to an infant's conceptual age. Conceptual age is measured from conception, with a full-term baby arriving at around 40 weeks gestation. Babies can of course be born several weeks earlier than this or a couple of weeks later. A number of studies have shown that babies start to smile in response to faces at the conceptual age of 46 weeks (Dittrichova 1969). If a baby is eight weeks premature then his chronological age at this time would be 14 weeks compared with a full-term baby who would be six weeks old. The increased length of time in the outside world (and therefore exposure to faces and so on) makes no difference to the onset of this type of smiling. Both babies will start smiling in response to faces at 46 weeks gestational age.

This smiling is often interpreted by onlookers as true social smiling, and treated as such. However, we have good reason to believe that this account is not entirely accurate (Bower 1977). One reason we know that these smiles are not as social as we once thought is that they are just as effectively brought about by a mask with two blobs on it as they are by a real face. In fact one of the best ways of getting a 'six-week' smile is by showing the baby a white card with three pairs of black dots on it – indeed this is even better than a human face (Bower 1977). In other words this stage of smiling is not really social at all but occurs in response to high-contrast images, especially pairs of black dots on a white background.

So human faces are good at eliciting these smiles partly because they contain a pair of eyes, which are essentially two dark areas (the pupils and irises) surrounded by a white background – the sclera (Schaffer 1971). This sort of response to dot patterns only lasts until three or four months of age when babies begin to smile specifically at human faces. This is not to say that human faces aren't incredibly important for social interaction and development before this. Of course they are. It may be that babies learn to smile at human faces because of the extremely positive reactions given to them when they smile at the two dots that happen to be human eyes. Caregivers react very positively to such 'social' smiles, which leads the infant to experience these exchanges as highly pleasurable. So certain visual stimuli are very attractive to babies (e.g. high-contrast dots). This keeps infants attentive to human faces, which in turn provide the baby with one of her most important sources of social information during these early months.

Early smiling is also linked with other types of baby experiences. In particular it is related to the infant's ability to learn from his environment. From very early on babies can learn to control events in their environment if given the opportunities. In other words they learn that their own behaviour has a predictable effect on external events. Studies have been made where babies are taught a contingency relationship between one of their own behaviours and something else happening. For example, babies from a few weeks old can learn to kick their legs in order to move a mobile that is attached to a string connected to the leg. They will learn to suck more rapidly on a dummy/pacifier if the sucking brings about a rewarding experience like hearing a tape recording of their mother's voice (De Casper and Spence 1986). The external event is rewarding in itself but babies also seem to get pleasure from discovering the contingency – that they can control what happens.

So babies find the discovery of ways they can influence their environment very rewarding, and often smile vigorously upon the discovery (Watson 1973). One reason that babies smile at faces may be that they are likely to come across contingencies in face-to-face play situations. For example, if every time a baby blows a raspberry his mother laughs and blows one back, a contingency relationship becomes established between these two events. The infant finds this pleasurable and will smile and laugh. Furthermore, the baby begins to associate the pleasure of solving contingency problems with the presence of responsive adults. Here again we see the importance of being responsive to infants. If a baby does not experience responsive care he has fewer opportunities to discover contingencies.

Young babies have other facial expressions. They show 'intent interest' with fixed eye gaze, knit brows and general immobility. When distressed they lower their brows and curl the corners of their mouths down and pout. This is often the warning sign that crying is about to ensue. Another expression is the 'stranger face': when meeting a stranger babies stare at the new person in a very serious way. So by only six weeks human babies have quite a repertoire of facial expressions, all reflecting different internal states. Generally expressions associated with positive affect are accompanied by eye gaze at the caregiver, while signals of negative affect are associated with gaze being averted away from the direction of the other person.

Other expressions quickly follow. By four months babies make angry faces and by six months they make fear faces (Izard 1978). In fact by six months babies have, for the most part, acquired the main set of inborn expressions of emotions made by adult humans. This is achieved primarily because of the natural unfolding of behavioural knowledge held in their human genetic code. One exception to this is in the full development of surprise expressions. From seven or eight months infants may give surprise-like expressions in response to unexpected events, but many features of the classic surprise expression shown in adults – for example, raising the eyebrows – are typically not observed during the first year of life. Over the second half of the first year babies begin fine-tuning their facial expressions for display to others. Figure 5.5 shows some of the variety of smiles made by an eight-month-old boy.

As well as inborn expressions of emotion, young babies have a reflexive ability to imitate other people's facial expressions. Babies as young as 12 to 21 days old will imitate expressions like the mouthing of 'oo', tongue rolling and eyebrow movements (Meltzoff and Moore 1977). This imitation is not due to any intention to imitate and therefore does not require the baby to appreciate the adult's expressions, or indeed that they are copying the adult face. Early imitation is therefore not true imitation. It occurs because the infant's movement sensations and responses are integrally linked to the baby's visual sensory system. In other words, for certain types of behaviour (that is, certain facial movements), what the baby sees the baby does. As the baby's brain matures, these different brain functions become more distinct and independent. When this happens reflexive imitation no longer occurs. It is not until twelve months that babies can engage in true imitation of faces. At this time the infant has some knowledge that 'he looks like the other person' (Meltzoff and Moore 1977).

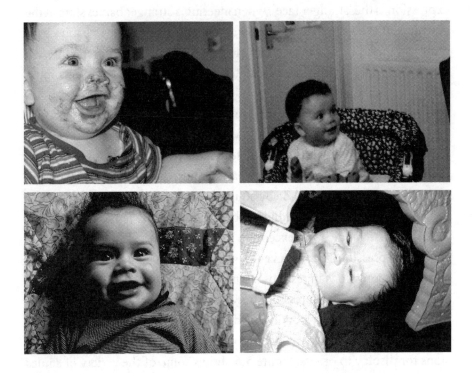

Figure 5.5 There's no doubt that this eight-month-old baby is pleased with himself and showing it to his carer. Each picture depicts a slightly different smile

By six months of age infants are on their way to proper imitation of facial expressions. (Figure 6.1, in the next chapter, shows a 10-month-old copying an adult facial expression.) We also see pseudo-imitation when babies are unsure how to react to, say, a novel object or event. Imagine a scene where six-month-old Lucy is visiting relatives with her mum. As they enter the relatives' house the rather large family dog (whom Lucy has never met) bounds up and jumps to greet Lucy's mother. Will Lucy react with fear, excitement or pleasure at this unexpected welcome? What happens is that Lucy looks uncertainly to her mother to see how she reacts.

She reads her mother's expression and behaves in a similar way. In this case Lucy's mother laughs and pats the dog. Lucy, previously unsure, smiles too. Note that this is not Lucy imitating her mother in a deliberate way. Instead her mother's emotional *expression* influences Lucy's emotional *state*. If the emotional reaction had been negative, a different outcome would have ensued. Indeed babies who see other people showing fear faces to objects such as spiders are more likely also to develop a fear of those things.

A related phenomenon is when babies mirror adult emotions in more subtle ways. Two-month-old infants scan the eyes and mouth of someone who is talking to them and perceive and react to the expressions of feeling on the other's face. Indeed, even at this young age babies are capable of transmitting (contingent on the behaviour of others) feelings of liking, disliking, shyness, sadness, annoyance, inattention and sleepiness. They often react with distress if their mothers face them with a blank and static face. They seem naturally geared up to interact with other people and find non-interactive behaviour disturbing. By three or four months this tendency reduces and babies are more likely to look around their environment should this happen.

Not all automatic facial signs begin so early. Blushing while experiencing shyness or shame develops later. Blushing is a uniquely human phenomenon which does not occur in non-human primates, even the great apes, and does not occur in human children who are less than two or three years of age. This is somewhat surprising since blushing is a direct result of physiological arousal that produces a dilation of blood capillaries in the skin. Furthermore it is something over which we have little control. The reason blushing does not appear before two or three years of age is because the *causes* of blushing do not appear until then. These causes are related to two phenomena. First, the child is increasingly aware of self-attention, or a realisation of being observed. This awareness requires a certain level of cognitive development and appears not to be an issue for children less than two or three years old. The second phenomenon is the lower sensitivity of younger children to approach-avoidance forces in their interactions with others. As mentioned in Chapter 2, these forces can be used to explain many adult social behaviours. Furthermore the knowledge about appropriate approach-avoidance strategies is acquired throughout childhood.

For example, two-year-olds are less aware of the taboos about disclosing personal information and less likely to feel difficult about socially embarrassing events – hence their lack of blushing. I could recite many stories of parental embarrassment that resulted from statements produced by innocent offspring. To save blushes I won't share them with you here.

What a yawn!

In adults yawning is contagious. When adults see someone else yawning they typically yawn too. In fact this even happens when we read about or think about someone else yawning (Provine 1989). This is reminiscent of the reflexive imitation of facial expressions shown by newborn infants. While this is a commonly experienced phenomenon in adults we do not yet know much about how it develops in children. The physical act of yawning is evolutionarily ancient, beginning in the human foetus just 11 weeks after conception (De Vries, Visser and Prechtl 1982). However, we know little about the development of yawning in response to another person's yawn. Only one researcher has written about this and he suggests that the socially related aspect of yawns does not occur until some time during the second year of life (Piaget 1951). A case study of a baby boy is being carried out in Stirling. We began testing his response to yawning at six months of age. He is now nine months and we still have little evidence that other people's yawns are infectious to him.

Posed facial expressions

The development of spontaneous expressions therefore appears to be largely inborn, as we might expect since they originate in subcortical brain regions. As mentioned, there are exceptions to this and experience certainly matters. From about six months of age cultural learning commences and the infant starts to learn: to use facial expressions intentionally and in culturally specific ways; and the display rules of the culture. Figure 5.5 shows an eight-month-old boy displaying happiness. Each of the smiles shown is slightly different. These differences reflect subtle variations in the underlying emotional states and are not intentionally made at this point in time. Babies begin to be able to fine-tune their use of facial expressions by using *voluntary* movements of the face originating in the cerebral cortex. Learning to do this takes time and experience. Indeed, voluntary expressions take considerably longer to master compared with the production of spontaneous expressions and develop throughout the primary school years.

One study that showed the development of display rules investigated how well children aged between six and ten years of age could cover up negative emotional states such as anger and disappointment (Saarni 1979). In order to do this the researchers had to make their young participants disappointed and then monitor what their faces did. The children were asked to take part in a study and promised a good 'prize' for participating (in today's world this might be something equivalent to the latest Harry Potter book). In fact the children were given a 'baby's toy' and were understandably not best pleased. The interesting thing was that the older children showed their disappointment much less than the younger ones. So it appears that the older children had a much better notion of the inappropriateness of appearing negative. Among the reasons given for hiding their disappointment were things like 'avoiding trouble' and 'not hurting the experimenter's feelings'. Interestingly, the girls who took part showed less negative emotion than the boys. The reason behind this gender difference is probably that girls generally socialise faster than boys. Becoming familiar with the display rules for facial expressions of their culture is simply part of that socialisation.

The ways that children cover up their emotions change as they get older. If you ask children how they would pretend not to be angry, most will say that they would try to cover it up. However, the older children are much more likely to try more elaborate strategies; for example, trying to change the emotion they feel (Harris, Olthof and Terwogt 1981). This is rather like method acting, something that would-be actors strive to perfect. Children typically don't use the 'method acting' strategy until they are in their teens.

Judging children's understanding

So facial cues provide us with information about children's internal emotional states. Faces are also useful indicators of mental states like comprehension. This is a crucial cue when we are trying to teach children or assess what they know. Children less than nine years of age are notorious for giving non-verbal indicators of comprehension and non-comprehension without saying whether or not they understand (Cosgrove and Patterson 1977). For example, if they have not understood an instruction they typically do not say 'hang on I don't understand'. It is left very much up to the instructor to check whether they've got the message. Furthermore youngsters are not always very good at realising whether they have understood something or not (Markman 1981). So it is important that parents and teachers can accurately pick up on the non-verbal cues of incomprehension in order to sensitively gauge how much help a child requires in order to progress.

Clues that a child has understood something are varied and range from the frequency of body movements to particular hand gestures (see Chapter 3) and facial expressions such as puzzlement. However, there is a significant degree of ambiguity in reading these clues. In one study new teachers were asked to view short films of children being taught. They were then asked to judge whether or not the children had understood the lesson. Initially the teachers found it difficult to judge children's comprehension accurately (Jecker, Maccoby and Breitrose 1965). Perhaps this is accentuated by the emphasis on what children say in speech to the cost of attending to their non-verbal behaviours. However, following training in recognising non-verbal cues of understanding, their accuracy increased. The cues used in that study included the amount of blinking and the duration of lowering and raising eyebrows.

The facial clues of when children are just about to understand something are particularly interesting to me in my ongoing research. So far it appears that judging when children are about to understand involves attending to a variety of cues, including facial expressions of concentration and thoughtfulness and temporal patterns of eye gaze. (The particular features of this type of eye gaze are discussed fully in Chapter 4.) But essentially looking away from the face of a questioner while thinking about and making a response is normally indicative that the child is actively engaged in working out a problem. If children maintain mutual gaze while unable to answer a question it often means that they have given up. Some of my most recent research suggests that very high levels of gaze aversion may be a signal that the child is just about to understand something and is therefore amenable to assistance. (Also see Chapter 3 for a discussion of the clues that hand gestures give us to children's thoughts and understanding.)

Liar, liar

One important application of studying comprehension of faces is in the area of deception detection. Deception involves a conflict between spontaneous and posed expressions. You feel one way, but don't want the rest of the world to know it. Obviously children only become adept at deception when they have acquired the relevant skills to use posed facial expressions and mask their true feelings. Furthermore highly motivated liars generally do certain things that derive from their knowledge of the folk psychology surrounding deception; something we would not expect very young children to have great expertise in.

There are a number of cues which most people consider indicate that someone is lying: 'looking shifty' (avoiding eye gaze and/or frequent posture shifts), speech errors and less smiling. The problem is that people who try to deceive others are only too well aware of this folklore and therefore try to over-control such behaviours. Someone who is highly motivated to lie will therefore generally try to maintain eye gaze and control the frequency with which he moves his head and body (Zuckerman and Driver 1985). Other more valid cues to deception include pupil dilation, reduced blinking (see Chapter 4), skin pallor, raised voice pitch and speech hesitations. When we lie to other people we typically feel anxious about it. We also have to concentrate hard to avoid tripping ourselves up. So some of the reliable cues reflect anxiety, while others reflect mental concentration. Another important cue to deception is the occurrence of asymmetric, stilted facial expressions that do not seem to fit well with what the person is saying or their other body movements. This is a sure indication that they are deliberately posing their facial expression rather than it being a spontaneous indication of their true feelings. You may also see very brief momentary flashes of spontaneous expressions of anxiety.

Adults are good at picking up some cues to deception (like speech hesitations), but quite naive about a significant number (such as reduced blinking). On the whole it is much harder than is generally assumed to tell when someone is lying. One study showed that customs officers were no better than laypeople at detecting smugglers because of the tendency to misread non-verbal cues of deception (Kraut and Poe 1980).

Lying by children aged six to eight years appears to be quite common (Gervais *et al.* 2000). Research is often based on parental and teacher reporting of lying. The behaviour can be problematic and is generally more common in boys than girls. It can also be associated with other disruptive behaviours, although most children will lie in certain situations at some point. However, it appears that while we are fairly good at judging when children are telling the truth, we are less able to judge when they are being untruthful. This is probably related to the problems adults have decifering untruthfulness in adults – like using the wrong cues. For example, introverted or socially anxious children are more likely to be mistakenly accused of deception, partly because they make less eye contact (Vrij 2002).

A common belief in the psychology world was that children were not capable of intentional deception (where they actually mean to deceive another person) until they had an established theory of mind at around four years of age (see Chapter 4). Prior to this age it was thought that if children used deceptive behaviours these reflected no more than the 'blind' use of strategies to get what they want rather than wilful deception. For example, children might learn by trial and error that if asked whether they had done something, saying 'it wasn't me' generally had a more favourable outcome than saying 'I did it'. This could occur without any reflection on the part of the children that they were deliberately trying to deceive other people. However, more recent work suggests that this may underestimate younger children's abilities. Indeed, two-and-a-half-year-olds have been shown to produce varied, flexible and complex deceptions that are hard to imagine are a result of 'blind' learning (Newton, Reddy and Bull 2000).

Nevertheless older children are better than younger children both at being deceptive and at recognising deception in others. I know that my own daughter got the idea that maintaining eye contact while telling a lie was a good idea sometime between her fifth and sixth birthday. Between the ages of three and eight years the abilities improve to deceive a 'hunter' about the location of a 'bear cub' during a game (La Frenier 1999). The oldest children were the most efficient at doing this. Children aged seven-plus were also much better at detecting when an adult was trying to trick them in a card game than pre-school children, who were easily fooled.

Children older than six years should be more aware of the sorts of cues that observers will be looking for if they are lying since they have a better ability to 'take the role' of other people than younger children (Flavell *et al.* 1968). At this age they are also beginning to understand some of the nuances of non-verbal communication. We would therefore expect them to be better at covering up their deceptions. In contrast younger children typically look nervous when lying because they are less likely to try and suppress cues of anxiety. Children's abilities to control the muscle movements of their faces also increase with age. One study compared five-, nine-, and thirteen-year-olds and found that the older children were much better at deliberate production of different facial expressions than younger ones (Ekman, Roper and Hager 1980). Figure 5.2 shows that there are still subtle differences at nine years of age in the deliberate portrayal of emotional expressions.

Figure 5.6 shows a four-year-old deliberately showing anger. This face differs significantly from spontaneous (or felt anger) expressions of anger in a number of ways. One is the lack of eyebrow frown (see figure 5.3). Young children pick up on certain facial cues that they think of as being 'good portrayals of emotion' and use them in their deliberate expressions. This child has noted a jaw thrust but is not yet making frowning eyebrows. Children's abilities to control accurately their faces are still developing and lower parts of the face are easier to control than upper.

So being a good liar, at least in part, requires a certain skill in controlling our faces; for example, controlling eye gaze and looking sincere and relaxed. On the whole we find it easier to control our facial expressions than other more body-focused signs of emotion. Ekman and Friesen (1969) carried out a study where a depressed psychiatric patient was video recorded while she met with her panel of doctors and psychiatrists. The woman was attempting to persuade them that she was feeling better and ready to leave hospital and return home. The researchers then showed this video to other people who were asked to judge her emotional state based only on what they saw and heard on the tape. Some people watched a tape showing only the woman's face, while others saw her whole body. They found that the emotional state of the woman was judged more accurately from the video of her body than from the video showing only her face. Furthermore, those seeing the body shot judged her to be emotional, tense and not ready to go home. In contrast, those seeing just her face thought

Figure 5.6 A four-year-old poses an angry expression. Notice her eyebrows are not involved in the expression as they would be in a spontaneous angry face

she was warm, friendly and ready to leave hospital. The whole body video showed her doing a number of body-focused gestures that are generally associated with emotional arousal and upset. In contrast her face was far more controlled and appeared calm.

So detecting deception involves looking at both facial and bodily cues. Furthermore the best indicators of deception change with the age of the child. Once children reach a certain age they know, like adult deceivers, how to control certain aspects of their behaviour. Read the following example and see which child you think is guilty of the misdemeanour described:

> Two girls, one eight years old, the other four years of age, have been playing. The younger girl has come downstairs with a section of her hair cut off. She claims the older child did it. Either this is the case or she did it herself. Later in the day the two children are confronted. The older girl denies all knowledge. She maintains eye contact, holds her back straight and her arms are loose and relaxed. Her facial expression is one of surprise and there are no indicators of anxiety such as increased blinking. She leans forward and gestures while having her say – her speech is fluent and does not contain hesitation. The young child had entered the room at a cheerful run. As soon as the topic is raised her behaviour changes dramatically. She says very little, glances briefly at the adult and then hangs her head. Her shoulders are rounded and she stands absolutely still throughout the whole encounter.

Given these patterns of behaviour, I would believe the older child. The younger one is the picture of guilt. She has not yet mastered covering up her obvious anxiety and instead withdraws in order to avoid giving clues away. Her posture, gaze avoidance and stillness are all signs of submission. It could be argued that the older child is just better at controlling her cues to deception. However, this is unlikely, given the set of behaviours she is exhibiting. If guilty, she would try to control her eye gaze and facial expression. However, she would be unlikely to be aware of her blinking, gesture, posture or speech fluency.

Learning to understand faces

As well as learning to express emotions and other messages using our faces, an extremely important skill we have to acquire is being able to interpret accurately the expressions of other people. We typically think of ourselves as being very good at this. However, if we take away contextual and movement cues that are available in face-to-face conversation, we find that even adults can struggle to understand facial expressions. People are surprisingly poor at judging facial expressions from still photographs. Happiness is generally the easiest expression, with people correctly identifying it around 79 per cent of the time. Other expressions are remarkably difficult. For example, disgust is typically identified only around 54 per cent of the time (Argyle 1996). These figures are found even when the people posing the expression and those trying to guess what it means are from the same cultural background. Things can get even worse when judges are from different cultures. For example, fear faces made by people from New Guinea were only identified 18 per cent of the time by Americans (Ekman 1972). This clearly demonstrates that faces are more ambiguous to us than we think. If this is true then the task that children face when learning to interpret faces is difficult – human faces are a far from straightforward affair.

Having said this we have certain reasons for believing that at least some of our skills in interpreting faces are innate. We are born with the necessary mechanisms to produce spontaneous expressions and these originate in an evolutionarily early part of our forebrain. We might therefore expect that we have analogous in-built abilities to decode facial expressions. This makes sense if we consider the use of faces in monkey social groups. Monkeys are not normally attributed the sorts of higher mental functions we associate with human intellectual abilities. Nevertheless their use of facial expressions is extensive. Furthermore there is little evidence that they use posed expressions. Their repertoire of facial movements is produced spontaneously and originates in the precortical structures associated with our own spontaneous expressions. Similarly, monkey comprehension of monkey expressions is also automatic. This would lead us to believe that, at least for monkeys, understanding faces is an innate ability. The suggestion is supported by other animal work showing that baby monkeys reared in isolation (and therefore with no opportunity to learn facial expressions from other monkeys) are equally able to discriminate certain monkey facial expressions at two months of age as normally reared youngsters (Sackett 1966).

So do human infants show a similar in-built sensitivity to understanding faces? Certainly human babies are extremely interested in human faces and seem drawn to things that look like faces. When babies are only minutes old they prefer to look at face-like masks (with the eyes, mouth and nose in the correct locations) rather than masks that have the same features but are jumbled up (Morton and Johnston 1991). These results suggest that babies have an inborn interest in things that look like faces. As described before, the evidence for a strong claim that newborns are naturally attracted to faces per se is disputable. What we can be sure of is that newborn infants orient to visual images of *face-like* stimuli that share the sorts of contrasts and shapes found in human faces.

Between three and five months of age babies can discriminate happy faces, then surprise, fear and sadness (Ekman 1982). Happiness is the first and easiest, fear the most difficult. Given this early discrimination of different facial expressions, it is tempting to think that at least some of our abilities to understand faces are inborn. Furthermore, babies as young as 12 months are adept at using information from people's faces in order to determine whether different objects are likely to be pleasurable or not. For example, babies seeing their mothers look with disgust at object A and with pleasure at object B are more likely to want to approach object B.

Experiences to which babies are exposed influence the speed at which they come to understand the distinction between different expressions. Babies whose mothers are depressed learn to discriminate sad faces faster than babies of mothers who are not depressed (Field *et al.* 1998). This also helps explain why happiness is the earliest expression that is discriminated. Babies generally see a lot of smiling. Smiling and high voice pitch come naturally when we converse with young infants (both features of motherese – the communication style used with infants and toddlers). In contrast, we seldom show infants fear faces, and perhaps this is one reason why fear is the last expression that babies come to terms with.

Being able to discriminate between facial expressions involves implicitly knowing that one expression looks different from another. By two years of age children recognise the six innate expressions of emotion (Ekman 1982). This is rather different from explicitly understanding facial expressions. Not until age five years do children have a reasonably good *understanding* of the main adult facial stereotypes (Bradshaw and McKenzie 1971). Children younger than this have limited comprehension in two main ways. First, they might judge only one feature to indicate a given expression, rather than a combination of features. For example, children often focus more on the eyes of a face than on other features which can lead them to misinterpret expressions. Sad eyes with a sad mouth will look like a sad face to most people, including pre-school children. However the same sad eyes with a smiling mouth can look like a happily sleepy person. This subtle difference, caused by the *combination* of features, might be missed by younger children. In fact three-, four- and five-year-old children are extremely proficient at identifying happy and sad faces, but less likely to identify correctly surprised or angry faces (Walden and Field 1982).

This research also showed that the pre-schoolers' 'disadvantage' with these more difficult expressions could be eliminated by prompting the children to consider the different features of the face that were relevant to the expressions: for example, encouraging children to look for a lowered brow *and* inverted mouth for 'angry'. This suggests that explicitly pointing out features of expressions and talking about them can effectively improve children's understanding of faces. Children and young adults with learning disabilities who find identifying facial expressions difficult also benefit from training. Instructions include providing verbal labels for expressions and parts of expressions, showing many examples, getting participants to trace with their fingers the features of expressions on photographs and providing positive feedback for correct identification (e.g. Stewart and Singh 1995).

Understanding facial expressions involves not just the perceiving of different configurations of facial movements, but also knowledge of how facial expressions should be applied to real life. This is the second area of comprehension where pre-schoolers have a lack of knowledge. An important milestone comes between four and five years, when children begin understanding mixed emotions where, for example, someone looks both happy and surprised at the same time. Four-year-olds can identify mixed emotions (for example, a face showing angry and sad features simulta-neously), but do not consistently match the facial expression to the appro-priate situation (e.g. a child being forced to clean up her room [angry] and then discovering that she can't find her favourite toy [sad]). In contrast, five-year-olds show a deeper understanding and ability to disentangle the different emotions that are exhibited together, and which situations they fit (Kestenbaum and Gelman 1995). It has yet to be established why four-year-olds fail to match mixed expressions with appropriate situations. One interpretation is that they have a limited world knowledge with which to interpret the situations and hence link the mixed facial expres-sions explicitly to them.

So, clearly, although babies very quickly learn to use and recognise the main expressions of emotions, a deeper understanding of emotional expressions continues to develop throughout the pre-school years and cannot be taken for granted in very young children. There are a number of developmental disorders that are characterised by a deficit in some aspect or other of face processing. These sorts of problems have been linked to a number of particular brain dysfunctions. Children with autism and Asperger's syndrome have particular problems with both producing and understanding emotional facial expressions (Attwood 1998). Parents may report having to exaggerate their expressions of anger, happiness, and sadness before their children recognise the underlying emotion. As well as comprehension difficulties, people with autism generally lack normal, non-verbal *expressivity*. In other words, they generally do not use facial expressions or hand gestures for communicative meaning. A pervasive problem for children with autism and Asperger's is a difficulty in under-standing social behaviour and intentions of others. Their difficulties with facial expressions are linked to this. The child's own expressions are often inappropriate or imprecise. For example, a common trait shown by Asperger's syndrome children is to express mild distress with giggling.

Williams syndrome is a developmental disorder that contrasts with autism. Its cause has been associated with a chromosomal defect, specifi-cally part of chromosome seven is missing. It has some characteristic features. For example, all the children have a facial similarity, sometimes called an 'elfin' face. This includes a wide mouth and a flat-bridged nose.

Psychological characteristics include hyperactivity in the early years and exaggerated displays of emotion. These children are characterised by having good language skills (particularly in production of language and not always in its comprehension) alongside general mental retardation. They have particular difficulties in visuo-spatial tasks; for example, drawing pictures of objects. However, these children (and adults with the syndrome) are very good at processing faces. In particular they are at near normal levels for recognising, discriminating and remembering both faces they know and those of strangers (Bellugi *et al.* 1990).

Other types of facial information

Facial expressions of emotion are of course only one type of information that we use our faces for. I've already mentioned that many cultures also have a repertoire of facial emblems that add meaning to face-to-face encounters. However, there is still more to how faces influence our communication and social interactions. The human face provides a very important way by which we can identify individuals. Other channels of non-verbal information can also help to distinguish one person from another; for example, their walking style. However, faces are the main way in which we identify people visually.

The work on face recognition shows that there are certain aspects of face processing acquired over a considerable length of time and indeed throughout childhood and into early adulthood. While recognising facial expressions comes fairly early in development, our abilities to recognise individual faces take a lot longer to develop. This makes sense since the possible variability in facial construction of the human face is immense – we seldom see two individuals who look exactly alike. In contrast the number of facial expression categories (e.g. happy, sad, surprise) is more finite. It appears that face recognition involves rather different processing mechanisms in the brain than other types of facial information to allow for this.

The way that children recognise other people's faces is something that changes with age. Children up until around ten years of age typically rely on specific distinctive features (for example, nose shape, moustache). So in an analogous way to their processing of facial expressions, children rely on a feature analysis to identify individuals (Diamond and Carey 1977). Children are very susceptible to focusing on distinctive features of unfamiliar faces such as whether they are wearing glasses. One problem with this approach to recognition is that these features often change. For example, men shave their moustaches, so relying on them to recognise people may prove unreliable. Diamond and Carey (1977) found that six- and eight-year-old children made a lot of mistakes when trying to recognise *unfamiliar* people who wore different 'disguises' like hats, scarves or glasses. However, when the faces were of people they already knew, even young children were able to ignore these paraphernalia. There is a clear improvement from pre-school until children are around ten or eleven years old in identification skills, where abilities typically are at adult levels.

Older children and adults depend more on the overall configuration and combination of features rather than individual facial features. Adults use a more holistic approach, recognising individuals by looking at the spatial relationships between individual features. This kind of information is more constant and relatively uninfluenced by changes in visual angle of viewing, lighting, etc.

In addition adults tend to rely on internal features of the face (such as the spatial relationship between eyes, mouth and nose). However, this partly depends on whether they are identifying a person who is familiar compared with one who has only been seen once or twice. When recognising faces of people they already know, adults rely primarily on internal features. This contrasts with trying to recognise an unfamiliar face when external features become more important. For example, if you witness a robbery and are subsequently asked to identify the robber from an array of photographs, you will be attempting to identify an unfamiliar face. In this situation you typically look at the internal features (as with familiar faces), but now your attention will also be significantly drawn to the external features of the face you remember and those in the identity line-up (Ellis, Shepherd and Davies 1979). People are often swayed by things such as hairstyles and colour. A change in hairstyle can make a considerable impact on the likelihood you will recognise someone you're not familiar with. These issues have important implications for children and adults who, as eye-witnesses to crimes, are asked to identify an unfamiliar defendant. In contrast, once you really know a face, hair matters far less. We recognise our friends and family even if they change their hair dramatically.

Babies as young as four days old recognise their mothers' faces and discriminate between it from other unfamiliar women (Pascales *et al.* 1995). Infants accomplish this on the basis of the outer features of the mother's face – her hair, hairline, chin and ears. Indeed when the outer features are masked babies less than 35 days old do not recognise their mothers' faces (Bartrip, Morton and de Schonen 2001) – certainly an argument for avoiding dramatic hairstyle changes during the first month or so of a baby's life.

Even at five to six years of age children are better at recognising their classmates from seeing their hair, chin or ears than when seeing only their eyes, noses or mouths (Campbell, Walker and Baron-Cohen 1995). Even by the time they start school children still generally focus more on external features. Furthermore, in contrast to adults, this happens whether the face is familiar or not (Campbell *et al.* 1999). In the mid-1990s Campbell *et al.* (1995) showed that children do not rely on internal features to identify faces until they are around nine or ten years of age. Her more recent work suggests that the ability to use internal features for recognising faces develops even later, at around 14 to 15 years of age. The change in attention from external to internal features during recognition may be related to the change from a feature-analysis to a configural approach when processing faces. As children become more expert at processing faces, they become more likely to rely on configural aspects and this may drive the move to a greater reliance on internal features.

What we do not yet know is *how* children learn to rely on internal features of familiar faces. Lesley Bonner, a researcher at the University of Glasgow, is investigating precisely this part of child development. She is interested not only in the time course of development of internal feature use, but also in which internal features of faces are most useful to children when identifying faces. For example, the eyes may be the most obvious and therefore the first internal features that children use.

Certain types of learning disability may influence the parts of the face that are attended to. Autistic children pay more attention to the lower part of the face than the upper. They do not develop the tendency to recognise faces in the configural way that older children and adults do. Instead they maintain a more feature-analysis approach typical of younger children (Carey and Diamond 1994). Interestingly this does not always result in a decrement in their abilities to recognise faces and they seem to make the feature analysis work rather well.

Another type of information that we gain from faces is lip-reading. Although we generally associate lip-reading with people who have impaired hearing, even in the normal hearing population lip movements influence what listeners hear. An example of this is a phenomenon known as the 'McGurk effect' – an illusion caused when what you hear someone say doesn't match the lip configuration that you see. You can achieve this effect by playing an audio track that does not match the facial movements on a video. For example, if the audio track is saying the syllable 'ba' over and over again and is synchronised with the video of a person mouthing 'da', what you 'hear' while watching and listening is usually something like 'ga' (McGurk and MacDonald 1976). This is a robust and striking effect: if you close your eyes you hear 'ba' and if you open them looking at the video immediately your perception changes. This is probably why watching dubbed movies is a strange experience. As a child in the 1970s I remember being fascinated by a dubbed version of *The Three Musketeers* – it's only now that I understand why.

Lip-reading is important from a very young age. When babies, as young as three months are shown video recordings of people speaking where the lips are not synchronised with the audible speech they quickly lose interest. Their attention is re-established when the synchronisation is returned to normal. So even at this tender age infants make the connection between what they're hearing and lip movements. This helps them to decipher particular sounds from the stream of speech spoken to them and plays an important role in developing language (Dodd 1984). By the age of 19 months toddlers can lip-read familiar words. In contrast, autistic children are impaired in terms of their lip-reading skills. The way that they combine the visual and auditory signals differ and they do not, for example, experience the McGurk illusion (Dodd 1987).

At Stirling we have carried out a large study of face-processing abilities with children from four to eleven years of age. My colleagues produced a battery of tests designed to tap a range of skills including recognition of identity, eye gaze perception, lip-reading and facial expressions (Bruce *et al.* 2000). We found clear improvement in all these aspects of face processing across the age range we tested. So ability to recognise another person's face or to judge where they are looking, what they are saying or how they are feeling all continue to develop until children are at least 11 years old. On most of our tests normal 11-year-olds were almost 100 per cent accurate. The only exception to this was on our hardest identity recognition test. Here children were asked to identify a target face from a pair of faces (one the target, the other a distracter). The distracter in this case was similar to the target face (for example, same gender and hair colour) and therefore more likely to cause confusion. This again shows that children's abilities to recognise faces are skills that continue developing over a longer period of time and into the teenage years.

Helping children get the most out of faces

A considerable amount of production and comprehension of facial expression, particularly of emotion, is derived from the maturation of inborn systems. Certain culture-specific rules about particular facial configurations, and, more importantly, the knowledge of display rules, has to be learned. Furthermore, in all cultures children develop increasingly sophisticated strategies for dealing with information from faces; for example, the move from external to internal features in face identification. Nevertheless it is a rare occurrence to find parents or teachers engaging in any explicit instruction about expressing facial information or in interpreting other people's faces.

An important question is whether all children develop the same aptitude in using and understanding faces. Of course the majority of children develop to a high standard that we consider within the normal range. I have described briefly a couple of developmental disorders, autism and Asperger's syndrome, that are characterised by problems in processing facial information. What about children who to all intents and purposes are developing normally? Is there a subgroup of children who have problems dealing with facial cues? Does this result in particular difficulties for them?

The answer to both questions is 'yes'. Some children fail to use or understand faces properly and in turn often experience a variety of problems, including being rejected by their peers. Walden and Field (1990) found that children's abilities to understand other people's facial expressions predicted social competence. Production of expressions is also important. Typically, children who show fewer expressions of positive emotions are more likely to be rejected by their friends and judged to be less socially competent by their teachers. At Stirling we recently carried out a study investigating this (Day 2001). We found that children who were unpopular with their peers understood photographs of facial expressions just as accurately as popular children. The problem for the 'peer rejected' children was that they failed to produce appropriate facial expressions in response to a variety of situations. Furthermore such children can experience very real benefits from explicit teaching about facial information.

One study trained children with learning disabilities how to understand the emotional expressions of others and also how best to express their own emotions. After training, the children's peers thought they were more acceptable and 'played nice' more often than 'played mean' (Straub and Roberts 1983). It is therefore important that children's skills with faces are monitored as this develops. Talking about emotions and feelings within different contexts and looking at different facial expressions and discussing their features seems to help hone abilities.

Facial attractiveness

What our faces look like is important. Few of us would like to admit it, but we make all sorts of judgements about other people based on how attractive they appear to us. Adults consider attractive men and women to be more socially competent, have better personalities and better jobs (Dion, Berscheid and Walster 1972). This is sometimes called the 'halo' effect of physical attractiveness whereby beautiful people are seen generally in a more positive light. The attractiveness stereotype is not always positive. For example, attractive women are often expected to be unfaithful, materialistic and vain (Dermer and Thiel 1975). Whether the effects are positive or negative, it is striking that physical characteristics of people make such an impression upon us. These sorts of stereotypes are also used by children and about children. For example, even at the young age of four years children will expect attractive kids to play better and be less aggressive. Furthermore attractive children are generally dealt with more leniently and judged to be less culpable for their transgressions than unattractive kids (Hatfield and Sprecher 1986). These effects are primarily subconscious. As adults dealing with children we must be vigilant that we treat them equivocally, regardless of their physical looks.

So our faces influence our social lives and are important in many different ways. They help us to communicate thoughts and feelings and recognise one another. We configure our faces in a wide variety of ways; some of them universal across cultures, others not. Some help us hear speech spoken to us while others allow us to communicate without words. Children are born with at least the foundations of these skills. However, many of them unfold as children develop and gain experience in their social world. Good understanding and use of faces is a central part of social competence. Many children acquire these skills naturally, but some may need a little more help. If a child is having problems with making or maintaining friendships, *one possibility* is that he is having trouble reading and transmitting non-verbal cues. Social skills training can be very useful if this is the case.

Suggested reading

1. Ekman, P. (1982) *Emotion in the Human Face.* Cambridge: Cambridge University Press.

2. Meltzoff, A.N. and Moore, M.K. (1977) 'Imitation of Facial and Manual Gestures by Human Neonates.' *Developmental Psychology 198*, 75–78.

3. Kestenbaum, R. and Gelman, S.A. (1995) 'Preschool Children's Identification and Understanding of Mixed Emotions.' *Cognitive Development 10*, 443–458.

4. Attwood, T. (1998) *Asperger's Syndrome: A Guide for Parents and Professionals.* London: Jessica Kingsley Pulishers.

5. Saarni, C. (1979) 'Children's Understanding of Display Rules for Expressive Behaviour.' *Developmental Psychology 15*, 424–429.

6. Campbell, R., Coleman, M., Walker, J., Benson, P.J., Wallace, S., Michelotti, J. and Baron-Cohen, S. (1999) 'When Does the Inner-Face Advantage in Familiar Face Recognition Arise and Why?' *Visual Cognition 6*, 197–216.

7. Diamond, R. and Carey, S. (1977) 'Developmental Changes in the Representation of Faces.' *Journal of Experimental Child Psychology 23*, 1–22.

8. Zuckerman, M. and Driver, R.E. (1985) 'Telling Lies: Verbal and Nonverbal Correlates of Deception.' In A.W. Seigman and S. Fledstein (eds) *Multichannel Integrations of Nonverbal Behaviour.* Hillsdale, NJ: Lawrence Erlbaum.

9. Vrij, A. (2002) 'Deception in Children: A Literature Review and Implications for Children's Testimony.' In H. L. Westcott, G.M. Davies and R.H.C. Bull *Children's Testimony.* Chichester: Wiley.

10. Dodd, B. (1987) 'The Acquisition of Lip-Reading Skills by Normally Hearing Children.' In B. Dodd and R. Campbell (eds) *Hearing by Eye.* London: Lawrence Erlbaum.

Key points

1. Faces give us a variety of types of information ranging from facial expressions of emotion, to facial gestures, visual speech and person identification.

2. The study of facial expressions gives a clear example of the interplay between inborn behaviours and those that are learned.

3. Facial expressions originate in two distinct parts of the brain. Innate, spontaneous expressions are a result of activation in the

precortical emotion centre. Deliberate, posed expressions originate in the motor cortex.

4. Every culture has a set of *display rules*. Children learn these and to control their facial expressions accordingly. The fine-tuning of facial expressions begins around six months of age. Children continue learning strategies to control their faces throughout primary school.

5. Monitoring and reacting to other people's facial expressions towards objects or events is an important part of social referencing and feeds into the development of attitudes to these things.

6. It takes until around five years of age for children to acquire a reasonable understanding of the relationship between features of expressions (such as a smiling mouth or sad eyes) and the underlying emotion. Children can be taught to be better at reading faces through practice.

7. Reliable facial cues of deception are: dilated pupils; reduced blinking; skin pallor; asymmetric, stilted facial expressions; momentary flashes of anxiety. Other more obvious cues such as gaze aversion or expressions of anxiety may occur in young children who are lying simply because they are less able to control their behaviour.

8. Skills at identifying people from their faces improve until children are at least 10 or 11 years old. Young children are far more susceptible to being fooled by disguises and are more likely to remember individual features of faces. Older children's and adults' memory for faces is more resilient in that they are more likely to process faces configurally, remembering the spatial layout of features. Even adults are prone to the effects of changes in external features such as hair colour or style when trying to identify a face they don't know well.

9. Lip-reading is important, even for people who do not have a hearing impairment. This is true from infancy where lip movements help decipher speech.

Things to try

1. *Newborn.* Watch your newborn sleeping. When she is in rapid eye movement sleep she will often smile reflexively.

2. *Newborn.* Try seeing whether you can get a newborn baby to imitate your facial expressions. Do 'tongue rolling', 'open mouth' and saying 'aah' or 'ooh'. Be patient and keep the infant interested in what you're doing. You may have to repeat the expression several times.

3. *From three months.* If you have a baby of three months or older, try showing him faces (perhaps your own) with different expressions. Look at his reaction. You may see his facial expression change in response to your changing face. You can also try a habituation procedure. Habituation basically refers to 'getting bored' with something. If you show babies a picture of something they will attend to it until they are 'bored'. If you show them different pictures of essentially the same thing, (for example, a smiling face), they will eventually begin to show less and less attention to the pictures. If you then show a picture of something different they are likely to renew their interest (dishabituate) if they detect the difference. So if you start showing sad faces once they have habituated to happy faces and the infant dishabituates, this illustrates that the infant can discriminate between happy and sad faces. Be careful what you do since infants are generally quite sensitive to faces and may become distressed if you seem to be behaving in a strange way.

4. *From 18 months.* For a toddler there are many storybooks that depict different facial expressions of emotion. These are usually quite fun. Look at the pictures with your toddler, talking about

how the person in the photograph is feeling. Ask your child to make the face too.

5. *Pre-schoolers*. Look at pictures of people showing different emotions. Ask the child what it is about the face that means that the person is sad, happy, angry, and so on. Remember that children of this age will tend to focus on one particular feature of an expression; for example, mouth shape. For children who are finding identifying expressions difficult, point out the critical features of expressions, finger tracing them on photographs and getting the child to do the same. Perseverance and practice will result in improvement.

6. *With children of any age*. Try doing some face exercises in the mirror or even role play different scenarios. Look at the expressions you would both make in different social situations. Talk about the underlying emotions and why some are appropriate in some situations but not others.

7. *From about three years*. Play 'recognition' games. Take photographs of people the child knows and mask either the internal part of the face or the external. Children right up until at least ten or eleven years will rely primarily on external cues and find recognising people difficult if these cues are not available.

8. *From about three years*. Ask children from around three years onwards how they could cover up what they were feeling. With increasing age children tend to get better at doing this and develop more elaborate strategies for doing so.

9. *Any age*. Try using the 'cues to deception' when deciding if a child is telling you the truth or not. Remember that the cues will change depending on the age of the child, with older children wiser as to how best to cover their deception.

Some developmental milestones

1. From birth, babies show a number of inborn reflexive facial expressions. These include 'startle' (in response to, for example, loud noise), crying and disgust (in response to bad tastes; *please do not try this*).

2. Newborn babies will smile reflexively during rapid eye movement (REM) sleep. Newborns never smile while fully awake.

3. Sometime during the second month babies begin 'true smiling'; in other words they smile when they find something pleasurable – for example, seeing your face.

4. Babies begin showing angry faces around four months and fear faces around six months.

5. Surprise tends to come around seven or eight months of age but generally not accompanied by raised eyebrows.

6. During the second half of their first year babies become increasingly adept at using facial expressions and other expressions of emotion to 'get what they want'. You may find your infants using crying to get your attention rather than because they are actually in distress.

7. By ten months babies begin using adult facial expressions directed to objects as a source of information about the object. So if you smile at one and show disgust to another, a baby is likely to act more favourably to the first.

8. From about 12 months children begin to fine-tune their emotional expression and learn the display rules for their culture. However, it is not until they are school age that they become good at covering up their true feelings. Girls tend to master this faster than boys.

9. By two years of age children have some notion as to recognising the main expressions of emotion. However, it is not until age five years that they become really proficient at this, and even then have difficulty with surprised and angry faces.

10. During the pre-school years children are more likely to focus on only one feature of an expression, such as a smiling mouth for happy. This contrasts with older children and adults who look more at a combination of features. When we judge whether someone is really happy we tend to look not only at what the mouth is doing but also what the eyes are doing. In fact adults can judge whether someone is smiling or not even if they can only see their eyes.

11. Five-year-olds have a deeper understanding of mixed emotional expressions such as surprised plus happy than four-year-olds.

12. The ability to use internal features of faces, such as the configuration of eyes, mouth and nose, to recognise people does not happen until fairly late in childhood. Some research suggests 10 to 11 years while other research states 14 to 15 years. So up until these sorts of ages children typically rely on external features such as hairstyle to make identity judgements.

13. Children's abilities to recognise facial expressions, to lip-read and judge eye direction are generally at adult levels by around the age of 11 years. Identification is the exception to this.

Chapter 6

Touch and Social Development

Touch is the channel of non-verbal communication that is perhaps most tightly regulated in most societies. While there are implicit rules about gazing behaviours and which facial expressions are appropriate, we have particularly explicit rules about touch. People are now more than ever very much aware of ways that they touch their own and other people's children. In addition parents can be quite distrusting of child-care providers. Professionals such as teachers are now explicitly instructed about what is considered appropriate touch. No such guidelines are set down for the types of facial expressions they should show to children or how often they should look at them.

Of course the impact of touch in human interactions is entirely different when touch falls outside normal, acceptable boundaries. A worldwide increase in awareness of physical and sexual abuse has influenced how we think about touch. There has been a necessary awakening to the plight and tragedy of so many children caught in abusive situations. This is not the topic of the current chapter. I hope to show in this chapter that normal and appropriate touch has an important and very positive role to play in human social relations. This is especially true for children, where touch can be important in emotional, social and intellectual development. It would be a sad day when we teach our children to avoid all sorts of touch. Our social relationships would be much impoverished by this. What we need to do is better understand touch, what it means and the rules surrounding it. As a society and as individuals we must be vigilant with regards to abuse of children, but we must not lose sight of the importance of perhaps our most ancient form of communication.

Origins of touch

Touch is a primitive form of communication to be found even in simple animals and is involved in basic encounters such as mating, feeding of young and defending territories. For social primates the impact of touch goes even deeper. Most species of monkeys and apes live in groups. There are many advantages to this; for example, protection from predators and co-operation in finding food sources. However, living with others is associated with certain problems. Social primates need to be together (to develop affiliative relationships) and yet they fear rejection in the form of hostility and aggression. Indeed, along with co-operation in gaining resources and mates that a group brings, there is also competition for the same resources. There are therefore considerable social dynamics that have to be dealt with in these groups. One way of resolving tensions and 'binding' individuals to one another is the act of grooming. All group-living monkeys and apes spend a huge amount of time grooming one another. It appears to be immensely pleasurable for both parties involved and has been claimed by a number of authors to be the 'glue' that holds primate groups together. Interpersonal touch between monkeys and apes is therefore an integral part of social living.

Adult humans spend considerably less time per day touching one another in this way. Our language systems have given us an alternative way of sharing feelings, telling one another things and stating our intentions. We maintain friendships and relationships by talking, rather than combing one another's hair. Nevertheless, as I hope to show in this chapter, the positive effects of touch that other non-human primates appear to experience still have residuals in our own experiences when we do touch one another. Many people recognise the therapeutic value of touch, investing time and money in, for example, various massage treatments. As I will discuss later, the therapeutic value of touch is very real for both children and adults.

Table 6.1 Categories of touch	
Category of touch	*Examples*
Positive affect	Reassuring touches
Playful	Slap on back, tickle
Control	Tap on shoulder to get attention
Rituals	Greetings, christenings
Mixed	Greeting plus affection
Task related	Measuring feet in a shoe shop
Accidental	Bumping into a stranger on a train

It is useful when trying to understand the effects of touch to be able to describe and measure different *types* of touch. An extensive attempt at classifying types of touch comes from research reported in the 1980s (Jones and Yarborough 1985). This puts forward seven different categories of touch, shown in Table 6.1. As shown there are many different types of touch. Each has a different meaning and effect upon us and each has a set of rules surrounding its use. The rules about touching people change depending on the perceived motive of the toucher. For example, we are far more accepting of quite invasive forms of touch, even from strangers, when they are perceived as accidental rather than deliberate, or when they are task related. Some of the rules are discussed more fully later in the chapter.

Touch in infancy

Touch is central in day-to-day care giving and play activities with infants. Because of their nature, infants need to be lifted, moved around, fed, changed and so on by other people. All of these activities involve some form of touch. However, the importance of touch goes way beyond this. Touch plays an important role in the welfare of infants over and above its impact on physical care giving. As you will see later in the chapter, touch has the potential to impact on physical, social/emotional and intellectual well-being. There is evidence that infants who do not receive enough physical contact become distressed and suffer emotionally. A number of studies have been reported of children's development in impoverished orphanages where there is little social contact with adults (and touch is an important part of this). All report important social and intellectual deficits in children raised in these conditions. Optimistically these effects seem to be reversible if children are removed and given better quality care (Skeels 1966; Spitz 1946).

Close and continuous contact between mother and child in the first couple of weeks after birth is almost universally advocated in many cultures (Oakley 1982). In contrast, until relatively recently it was common practice in industrialised countries to separate mother and infant in the immediate period after birth. Infants would be taken away to nurseries while the mother was in hospital, only to be seen at feeding times. Recognition of the importance of touch and close contact between baby and mother is reflected in changing maternity hospital practices. Mothers are now encouraged to engage in close contact with their babies immediately. Mothers may put their babies straight to the breast following birth. Indeed skin-to-skin contact may help stabilise the newborn's heart rate and breathing.

I support this wholeheartedly, not only from the research literature but also from personal experience. My second child, Dylan, was born quite small because I had suffered pre-eclampsia towards the end of my pregnancy. In addition the cord was around his neck when he came out and he was rather blue and floppy. He was rushed off for a couple of minutes and given oxygen. When the midwife brought him back his breathing still sounded erratic. I insisted on removing his wrappings (and my own) and holding him skin to skin. The effect was amazing. His breathing immediately settled down and within a few minutes he was having his first breastfeed. I am also a firm believer in skin to skin contact helping to get breastfeeding off to a good start. Sometimes newborns need a little time to come around to feeding from the nipple. Letting them lie on the breast, smelling and feeling mum without being 'forced' to feed, can help.

Skin-to-skin contact continues to be beneficial for infants long after birth. It is often advocated by midwives and health visitors for soothing crying or restless infants in the early weeks and months, as is gentle massage. Related to these positive changes in care practices are other changes in attitudes. While it has always been the practice in more 'primitive' cultures to respond immediately to crying, in western societies considerable negative attitudes to this developed. Many of you may have been told that you will 'spoil' your baby if you respond too quickly. These attitudes are changing and important benefits of practices such as demand feeding and quick and sensitive responding to babies' crying are now recognised.

Touch changes with age

Never again do we experience the high level of physical contact that we find in infancy. Unfortunately the frequency of being tickled and cuddled is much less in adulthood. So when does touch begin to decease? Over the first year of life there is considerable touch, but after this there is a fairly steady decline in frequency throughout childhood. Generally little girls are touched more than boys and younger children touched more than older children (Cowen, Weisberg and Lotyczewski 1983). The gender difference is quite striking and seems to be largely due to different cultural attitudes towards boys and girls. From when they are only months old, little boys are expected to be more physically active and independent compared with girls. Mothers are more likely to put a baby boy on the floor and encourage him to crawl or to kick about. In contrast little girls spend more of their day being held and carried by caregivers who are also more likely to soothe and stroke them.

Most touching between pairs of children is same gender, perhaps reflecting the higher frequency of girls playing with girls and boys with boys. About 12 years of age opposite-gender touching between children becomes more prevalent (Willis and Hoffman 1975), possibly due to the increasing interest that children begin to show in the opposite sex as they reach puberty.

Both autism and Asperger's syndrome (AS) are associated with touch sensitivity and aversion. Temple Grandin (1984) has Asperger's syndrome and has written about her experiences. She reports experiencing significant tactile sensitivity and finding skin-to-skin contact unbearable.

Children with AS might avoid social contact such as cuddles, not because of a desire to avoid being sociable but because of a physiological reaction to touch (Attwood 1998). Certain areas of the body may be more sensitive than others; for example, the scalp, upper arms and palms.

Rules about touch

Different types of touch have different rules associated with them that children learn as they acquire the other rules of their society. These vary with the relationship between the toucher and the touched and with the situation. We are subconsciously familiar with these rules and notice violations when the rules are broken. We can all think of instances when someone has touched us and we noticed the touch, remembering it because it made us feel uncomfortable. For example, while same-sex adult friends in western cultures readily touch the hands and lower arms, touching of the lower trunk region is unacceptable. Obviously the absolute rules are determined by cultural differences and the specific relationships involved.

Touches that do not violate the rules are more likely to go unnoticed. This does not mean that they do not carry some influence. For example, experiments have shown that unsuspecting men are more easily coerced into giving bigger tips to female waitresses or helping strange females with a variety of tasks when the female has innoxiously and 'accidentally' touched them (Crusco and Wetzel 1984). The opposite is true however when unfamiliar men touch women. Women are far more likely to feel threatened and therefore to evaluate the man negatively in these circumstances. Great fun can be had trying some of these things out for yourself – although be careful as the effects are not always predictable or desirable.

The appropriateness of touch very much depends on the situation in which it occurs; for example, a physiotherapist massaging a footballer's leg on the field is entirely acceptable. The same might not be true if someone else does this in the pub later on. Being made to stand close to strangers on a crowded train may not always be pleasant, but it does not have the same impact as strangers brushing up against us in a non-crowd situation for no reason. So there are many situational factors that influence how we interpret touch and hence its influence on us.

Situational factors that influence touch behaviour affect children of both genders in similar ways to adults. In one study the touching behaviours between pairs of girls and pairs of boys was observed in two different situations (ages of the children ranged from around six years to high schoolers). The first was a neutral situation where no particular reason for touching one another was present. The second was where team spirit was emphasised in an athletic competition. We typically see high amounts of adult male–male touching in physical team activities. Watch any football match and you will see the sorts of antics that go on. This reflects the cultural acceptability of touch in these circumstances. In contrast, very little male–male touching typically occurs in neutral situations. The study showed that even the youngest children touched one another less in the neutral scenario than the team one (Berman and Smith 1984). This illustrates that even young children are aware of the social and cultural inhibitions surrounding touch and respond by increasing touch when situational factors alleviate the rules.

Sometimes the judgements children have to make regarding whether touch is 'good' or 'bad' are more difficult. Many instances of sexual abuse are examples of this. Research has shown that very young children are able to recognise intrusive molestation as bad, even if they have had no prior exposure to, say, a prevention programme. However, most cases of sexual abuse involve types of touch that young children find harder to understand. There may be inconsistency or ambiguity for the child. In these cases children experience an 'attribution dilemma' and are unable to assess the situation accurately (DeYoung 1988).

In touch with education

The pros and cons of appropriate touching have been addressed in recent literature directed towards professionals working with children in schools (Del Prete 1998). A study in the USA showed that teachers in pre-schools were variable in terms of how much they touched their young charges. Some used touch to offer affection and comfort, but the more frequent sorts of touch were those classed as caretaking-helpful or con-trol-punishing. Children were more likely to receive positive touch if they in turn expressed affection to their teachers. Children reported by teachers to be difficult received a greater frequency of negative-punishing touch than other children (Lawton 1998). Important factors determining how much teachers touched their charges were the implicit policies regarding touch held by pre-school directors. This study concludes that there needs to be better teacher–parent education regarding the developmental signif-icance of touch. Furthermore it advocates an increase in positive touch in early childhood education. Thoughtful, appropriate physical contact between teachers and children plays an important role in early childhood education (Mazur and Pekor 1985).

Emphasis and persuasion

Like eye gaze, touch can be an effective way of providing emphasis. As an example, think of someone offering you congratulations about something. This always feels more sincere if they combine what they say with some form of touch – perhaps a slap on the back, a gentle touch of the arm, or even a hug (depending on how well you know them). We interpret the touch as 'I really mean what I'm saying'. In addition, when people are trying to be persuasive they generally touch those they're trying to persuade more: not only that, it seems to work and they become more effective in their attempts. A number of social psychology experiments have been carried out to look at how touch affects persuasion of adults (Willis and Hamm 1980). Across these studies there is a consistent and marked effect that when someone is trying to persuade another person to help them, they are far more likely to be successful if they accompany the request with a touch. This only holds if the touch does not violate social norms.

Gender of the toucher and touched matters a lot in terms of predicting the effectiveness of touch for persuasion. For example, some researchers at the University of Missouri got actors (confederates in experimental psy-chology speak) to walk down a corridor carrying a pile of papers (Paulsell and Goldman 1984). When approached by an unsuspecting passer-by, they 'accidentally on purpose' dropped all the papers on the floor. The researchers were interested in what would determine whether the pass-ers-by would help pick up the papers. One important influence was whether or not the confederate touched the passer-by when asking for help or not. Touching increased the likelihood of helping. However, this generally only happened when the confederate was a woman and the passer-by was a man. Generally men are unphased by strange women touching them (indeed they often like it). So men were more than willing to help a woman pick up papers, especially if she touched him when asking for help. In contrast, when both confederate *and* passer-by were men, the confederate was seldom helped. Men typically do not like being touched by other men, especially strangers. Similarly the results were mixed when the passer-by was a woman. Women are very wary of strange men touching them, but are more positive when the stranger is female. This probably relates to how threatening touch is perceived to be. It is less of a threat from a woman than a man.

These results illustrate an important difference between men and women in terms of rules about acceptable touching. Men generally do not like being touched by other men, but rather like being touched by women (even if the woman is unfamiliar to them). Women on the other hand are generally more anxious about men touching them (unless they are familiar), and less concerned if a woman touches them. On the whole women typically respond more positively to touch and are more likely to interpret it as a sign of warmth and friendship. Men, in contrast, are far more likely to see a touch from another person as a sign of potential domi-nance.

Sources of anxiety about touch

So clearly touch can have positive effects but in certain circumstances it is likely to result in adverse reactions. There are two main sources of anxiety about touch which can produce problems in social encounters. First, touch can have aggressive connotations. Physical aggression is of course one type of touch that can potentially happen if you allow another person or animal close enough to touch you. Our wariness in this respect is probably something that originates in our evolutionary past. The likelihood of physical threat for our ancient ancestors was probably quite high, especially when they were meeting individuals from social groups other than their own. In this vein, touch can be a strong signal of dominance. Second, there are sexual implications for certain types of touch. This can be responsible for anxieties that women have regarding touch from men, particularly those with whom they are unfamiliar. These sources of anxiety about touch help explain some important differences in how men and women respond to touch in different situations. Concerns that men have about touch tend to focus more on it being a signal of dominance. Women worry more about its sexual implications. Care must therefore be taken when using touch as a social signal. Touch can have many positive effects, but only if the anxieties associated with it are not evoked.

Cultural differences

There are huge cultural differences in touching behaviours. In contact cultures, such as in southern Europe, Latin America, Arab societies and some African cultures, frequent touching is the norm. However, this partly depends on the gender of those involved; for example, lots of touching is the norm between Arab males but male to female touching is prohibited in public. In non-contact cultures such as northern Europe and Japan touch is far less frequent and has tighter rules associated with it (Hall 1966). This is one reason why people from contact cultures report people from non-contact cultures to be cold and stand-offish while the same people find those from contact cultures to be overbearing, with a tendency to invade their personal space. Ignorance about another culture's touching norms can lead to considerable embarrassment and offence. It is certainly worthwhile thinking about these issues before travelling or if you are meeting with adults or children from cultural groups other than your own. On the whole we tend to be rather ethnocentric and immediately assume that people from other cultures ought to behave like us and are surprised when they do not.

Rules and children

Just as we have to consider cultural differences in touching behaviours, we also have to consider how children see touch. Relationships between adults and children are typically very asymmetric, with the adult the more dominant party (see Chapter 2 for a fuller discussion of symmetry/asymmetry). Partly because of this, adults often seem to hold the belief that the sorts of rules governing touch in adult interactions do not apply when they are with a child. This leads them to behave with children in ways they would never consider with adults. On a first meeting would you pick up an adult and cuddle and kiss them? This is exactly what we often do to children, particularly very young children. Such an affectionate interactional style with children can be extremely valuable and I am not in any way suggesting that it is wrong – children thrive on affection and warmth. What I am saying is that some degree of caution is required in order to gauge children's responses to adults they are unfamiliar with, allowing them to accept (or not) the friendly gestures offered. Adults perhaps need to be less condescending and treat children as individuals with their own personal space.

We tolerate a different set of behaviours from young children than older children and adults. Adults accept both accidental and deliberate play/affectionate touches from toddlers and pre-schoolers that they would not be happy about if they came from an older child. For example, most adult house guests will accept and even enjoy a two-year-old's clamberings and cuddles. If a ten-year-old behaves in the same way it seems inappropriate and is typically rejected. We see similar patterns when children and adults are total strangers in public places. A toddler approaching a stranger in a shop queue and poking their leg is likely to receive smiles and encouragement in return. The same thing from an older child results in ignoring or even rebuking. So it seems that the rules about touch (especially between strangers) extend to children. We tolerate most behaviours until the child is of an age where they can be reasonably expected to appreciate what is appropriate and what is not.

Inappropriate touching behaviours by children can be a sign that they are anxious or upset about something; for example, older siblings who are feeling a bit jealous of a new baby might squeeze the baby when allowed to hold him or push against mum when she is feeding him. These are emotional signs showing that the older child wants/needs some attention.

Another area where different rules apply to adults and children is interpersonal aggression: for example, the controversial question of 'smacking'. This is not a debate I wish to enter into in any depth here. It does however reflect some of the differences between 'adult rules' and 'child rules' about touch. Often there is one set of rules for children and another for adults. This is a perilous path to take and often sends confusing messages to the children involved. An example will help explain this:

> Diane has three children and considers smacking to be an acceptable form of punishment and uses it regularly, sometimes severely, with them. She works as a supervisor in a department store where she is responsible for a team of seven other workers. At times she has to be involved in staff discipline. She would never dream of hitting any of her co-workers. One day she is horrified when her eldest son, Jack, is sent home from school for punching another child. Diane confronts Jack about his behaviour and he attempts to justify it by saying that the other boy started it with being horrible to him. How can Diane explain to Jack that it's all right for her to hit him, but not for him to hit anyone else?

This is one consequence of smacking. Children who are disciplined by frequent, harsh physical punishment tend to be more prone to aggression themselves and less able to deal with social relations in a mature way.

Touch, social development and attachment

Touch can have important influences on the development of relationships between babies and their caregivers. Before trying to convince you of this I need first to describe an important psychological concept in children's social-emotional development – *attachment*. Ainsworth and Bell (1970) define attachment as 'an affectional tie that one person or animal forms between himself and another specific other – a tie that binds them together in space and endures over time'. We form attachments to those we love and other important people in our lives. Being attached to someone means that we feel a need to be near them and are unhappy when we can't be.

The first human bond is the infant's attachment to its caregiver (often the mother, but not necessarily; for simplicity I will refer to 'mothers').

Signs of attachment are the baby wanting to be near his mother and, if unhappy, being comforted by her sight, sound and touch. In these respects human infants are similar to many other young animals who seek close physical contact with their mothers. As they grow older all young animals begin to venture further and further from their mother, using her as a secure home base for exploration. I will spend the next few pages describing attachment, what causes it and how it influences development. I will then go on to describe the particular role that touch plays in attachment relationships.

Why do infants show such attachment to their mothers? Much of the early work in this field was inspired by Sigmund Freud, a famous psychoanalyst of whom readers will have heard varying amounts. Freud made two major claims in relation to attachment, neither of which hold true (Freud 1926). First, a child's first social relationships are ultimately based on gratification of basic creature needs like hunger. Indeed, until about 30 years ago it was widely believed that love for the mother was a secondary consequence of the infant's association of the mother with satisfaction of hunger, thirst and pain. In other words, the suggestion was that babies get upset when their mother isn't there because they fear that their needs will no longer be met.

The second claim was that relationships between children and their parents determine all future social relationships. So if things go wrong in early childhood, negative patterns of social relations can be set for the rest of the child's life (unless of course you can afford expensive psychotherapy). While both these claims have added to the way in which we think about how children develop socially, as you are about to see neither of these claims holds water when we look at the scientific evidence against them.

John Bowlby is an influential critic of Freud's theory. Bowlby (1969) called Freud's theory the 'cupboard theory of mother love'. Two important reasons given for criticising the cupboard theory are as follows. First, it is evident that babies often show great interest in people who have never fed them or otherwise taken care of them. Babies are incredibly interested in human beings. For example, at birth babies are predisposed to hear sounds within the human voice range. Within a few months they enjoy seeing other people smile or playing peek-a-boo. It appears that infants are pre-disposed to seek social contact with other people because this contact is rewarding in itself (see Figure 6.1). Anyone used to being around babies and young children will know this. Of course babies need to be looked after physically, but if their mental, social and emotional development is to be optimal, caregiving has to involve more than physical care. Very simply, babies need social contact, love and interaction with others (Bowlby 1969, 1973).

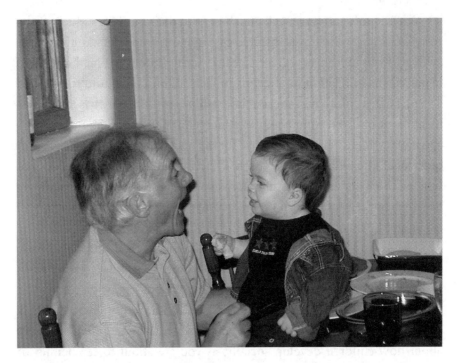

Figure 6.1 Social contact is fun, even with someone who never feeds or changes you. Babies enjoy social interaction for the sake of it

In the early months and years a significant part of love, affection and inter-action involves touch. Touch continues to play an important role through-out infancy and childhood. Rocking, cuddling and stroking are all part of good caregiving. In fact our infancy is the time of our lives when we are touched the most. In addition to this caregiving touch, babies experience a lot of social and play touch such as tickling games. This is not to say that there aren't important differences between individual babies in terms of how they respond to touch. Rudolf Schaffer, a British developmental psychologist, pointed out that some infants are what he called 'non-cuddlers' (Schaffer and Emerson 1964). These babies generally resist close physical contact and do not enjoy being held. They appear to have normal attachment relationships with their mothers and prefer instead perhaps to be able to see their mothers and remain close, rather than actually being held.

If social contact is important for development, then infants deprived of this ought to be negatively affected. There are two main sources of evidence which support this: experiments on socially isolated infant monkeys; and studies of babies raised in relative social deprivation in poorly run orphanages. Related to the first is the work done by Harry Harlow in the 1960s and 1970s, at the Wisconsin Primate Lab (Harlow and Harlow 1972). These studies are sometimes called the 'motherless monkey experiments'. He looked at the social and physical development of baby monkeys when they were raised in complete isolation from their natural mother and other monkeys. The only company for these unfortunate little creatures was a wire structure 'mother' from which they received milk and a similar wire construction covered in soft terry-towelling (where there was no milk). The results of these studies were very interesting. It was found that the infant monkeys spent far more time clinging to the terry-cloth 'mother' than to the milk 'mother'. In fact the monkeys only went to the wire milk mothers for feeding and spent very little time in contact with them in comparison to the towelling mothers. Furthermore, when frightened by mechanical toys placed in their cages, the infant monkeys ran and clung to the cloth 'mothers' for comfort. The infant monkeys got what Harlow called 'contact comfort' from the terry-cloth 'mother', which appeared far more important than food. So these monkeys loved their mothers (real or terry cloth) partly because they felt comforting rather than because they fed them.

This work made an important contribution to what we understand about early infant bonding. Young primates and possibly other types of young mammals bond with their mothers for reasons other than gratification of hunger and thirst. Babies seek and need contact comfort and this is an important type of stimulation they get from their mothers. Given these experiments, it is hardly surprising that infants and children often become attached to security blankets and soft toys. Anything soft and cuddly provides contact comfort.

In later experiments Harlow showed that complete isolation for periods of three months to a year had severe debilitating effects on infant monkeys. The animals showed many 'neurotic' and abnormal behaviours. They would huddle in the corner of their cages, perhaps rocking back and forth. When placed with normally raised monkeys the isolates showed no abilities to cope with the social encounters they experienced. For example, if another monkey lunged at them the isolates would withdraw, rock and bite themselves. The effects were long term. Once mature the monkeys did not cope with normal breeding. If the females were impregnated (often artificially) they were not adequate mothers; indeed many engaged in dreadful abuse of their infants. So early social deprivation has drastic negative consequences for baby monkeys. Would human infants react in a similar way if they experienced early isolation?

A number of researchers have looked at the effects of early social deprivation by studying children raised in inadequate orphanages. Of course, these children are deprived in many ways, but the lack of social interaction is of central importance in determining the outcome for them. Just as with infant monkeys, relative social isolation and the lack of attachment in human infants has a dramatic impact. One study compared the development of children in a foundling home (where physical care was adequate, but there was little social contact) with the development of children in a nursery home (described as a more personal type of foster home). Those brought up in the nursery home developed normally. In contrast, those in the foundling home showed deficits in physical, motor, emotional and intellectual growth. Furthermore, some studies have shown that early social deprivation can cause lasting intellectual deficits (in language development and abstract thinking) and also emotional and social deficits such as increased aggression and delinquency (Yarrow 1961). So social contact and healthy attachments are crucial to children's development. While these studies provide extreme examples, they clearly highlight the central role that quality interaction plays in all aspects of development.

Given appropriate reversal of circumstances, the effects of early deprivation can be reduced, if not eliminated. One study looked at children raised in an overcrowded orphanage and given little individual attention. When the children were around one and a half years of age, some of them were transferred to an institution for mentally disabled women. Each transferred child was 'adopted' by one of the women, allowing a special attachment relationship to form between them. Over the following years the outcomes for the transferred children were far better than those remaining in the orphanage. For example, IQs of the transferred children increased, while those of the children in the orphanage dropped. Furthermore, while only half the orphanage children finished the equivalent of three years' primary schooling, the 'adopted' children reached an occupational and educational level that was average for their country at that time (Skeels 1966). These women had little to offer the children in the way of material provisions. What they did offer was the most important thing for any child, a loving attachment relationship. Babies don't need fancy clothes or toys to thrive – all they need is love. In addition this study showed that early negative experiences do not predetermine later development, although they do provide a framework for later experiences. This argues against Freud's second assertion, that early negative experiences determine the rest of a child's life. When exactly the critical age is (if there is one) for the reversal is unclear; most probably the earlier the better.

John Bowlby's criticisms of Freud's theory therefore seem to be well justified. What does he offer as an alternative? Bowlby suggests that attachment results because infants are born with a number of built-in tendencies that make them seek direct contact with an adult. From birth the infant enjoys being with his mother and from birth he is well equipped for social interaction. For example, he quickly comes to recognise and prefer his mother's voice and smell. Furthermore, babies are very attractive to adults and in many ways draw us to them. This 'cuteness factor' is obvious when babies are contented and calm. Babies' crying also serves to bring adults into close contact with their infants. The sound of an infant's cry elicits a physiological response in those who hear it, often producing a strong urge to see what's wrong and comfort the infant. For breastfeeding mothers the crying often triggers the 'let-down reflex' that stimulates milk production.

From about six weeks of age babies start producing proper social smiles in response to seeing friendly human faces. Adults happily smile back at the infant and make mutual eye contact with the baby. Eye contact and social smiling are very rewarding for both parties and interactions between adult and child are immensely enjoyable. As discussed in Chapter 4, some babies are delayed in terms of when they begin establishing mutual eye contact, and this can have important consequences for the social relationship that develops between carer and child. Although I am not aware of any research that addresses this, it seems to me that the negative impact of delayed mutual gazing might be reduced if parents are aware of the delay and the effect that a loss of eye gaze can have on how an interaction 'feels'.

As infants get more mobile, they begin actively to seek contact by reaching and crawling towards their mother, and will use crying instrumentally to get her attention. Now we can see infants 'voting with their feet'. They typically seek to maintain a degree of physical closeness to those they are attached to. When relaxed they venture from their mother and explore their environment. If they become uneasy they will seek to be close to her again. How readily babies explore their environment and ways they maintain contact with their mothers provide indicators of the quality of mother–infant attachment. This is described shortly.

Bowlby proposes that attachment seeking has a second, more negative cause: a built-in fear of the unknown and unfamiliar. This fear has survival value. Baby animals and humans are less likely to stray and perish if they are frightened of unfamiliar places and objects. Infants do not know enough about the world and potential dangers to be fearful in an 'informed' way; therefore the built-in fear is non-specific. A mother's absence produces a fear similar to 'free-floating anxiety' where the infant is generally nervous about things around him. Even minor external threats may seem enormous to the child and lead to clinging behaviours. The suggestion is therefore that a fear of the unfamiliar produces feelings of attachment to a familiar object. This object is often the mother or father but does not have to be; other familiar people can substitute (for the baby monkeys it was a terry-towelling model). Whoever the attachment figure is, they provide a safe haven for the infant from which to explore the outside world.

Bowlby asserts that it is crucial to meet children's attachment needs. This involves being responsive to infants' demands for attention and affection. He cautions that a lack of responsiveness can have psychological and social consequences for the child. We have already seen evidence of this in the results of studies of social deprivation. Furthermore how well caregivers read their infants' non-verbal cues determines how sensitively they respond. The quality of attachment relationship between parent and child will depend partly on how parents behave with their children, and this quality can be measured by looking at how the baby behaves when separated from his mother.

Patterns of attachment

During the first few months of life babies readily accept substitutes for their primary caregivers and having other people to babysit is generally not a problem. However, this all changes around six to eight months when the infant begins to exhibit what is called 'separation anxiety'. Babies of this age typically cry and fuss when their mother leaves and do not accept strangers as temporary fill-ins. Separation anxiety occurs in babies from all cultures at around the same age and peaks in terms of its effects around 12 months of age. Essentially babies have to learn that everything is all right while their mothers are away and that they will return. Once babies know this, the anxiety experienced when she goes away reduces. Infants differ in terms of how distressed they become while separated, and how easily comforted when reunited with the parent. In other words, babies differ in terms of how secure they feel in their relationships with their mothers. Some infants are confident of their mother's availability while others are not. These differences provide the basis for measuring differences in quality of attachment relationships.

An ingenious procedure developed to measure attachment is the 'strange situation' (Ainsworth and Bell 1970). This was thought up by Mary Ainsworth, a student of John Bowlby's, in the 1970s. Originally it was designed to look at children of about one year of age, just at the peak of separation anxiety. Essentially there are eight main stages to the strange situation as follows.

1. The baby is brought to an unfamiliar room that has toys in it.

2. The child is allowed to explore and play as he wishes.

3. A stranger enters the room and talks to the mother. The stranger then approaches the child and plays with him.

4. The mother leaves room and the stranger attempts to play with the child.

5. The mother returns and the stranger leaves. The mother greets and/or comforts the baby.

6. The mother leaves again. The baby is alone.

7. The stranger returns and approaches the baby.

8. The mother returns and picks up baby. The stranger leaves.

The strange situation is designed to become increasingly stressful for the child. The baby's response and behaviour during each of these stages is used as a way of gauging whether or not he is securely attached to his mother.

Babies react to the strange situation in four main ways. Typically, around two-thirds of one-year-olds are described as *securely* attached. When their mothers are present they tend to explore and play with the toys. When she leaves they show some distress but greet her with enthusiasm when she returns and are easily comforted by her. These babies do not like their mother to be gone but are confident that she is available to them should they need her. They soon learn that she always returns and deal with short periods of separation. It is interesting that parents sometimes misread the distress shown when a parent is absent as problematic. They worry that their child will never settle with other people. In fact, although upsetting at the time, the child is showing the strong bond between parent and child by protesting at their absence.

The other third of one-year-olds fall into one of three other *insecure* categories:

- insecure/ambivalent-resistant
- insecure/avoidant
- insecure/disorganised.

The *insecure/ambivalent-resistant* babies tend not to explore the new room, even when their mother is with them. They become intensely upset when she leaves and are utterly inconsolable. However, they are emotionally ambivalent when she comes back, often reaching to be picked up and cuddled and then pushing her away when that happens. They appear distressed by her absence and almost angry with her on her return.

The *insecure/avoidant* children remain distant and aloof throughout the procedure. They show little distress when their mother leaves and typically ignore her when she returns.

The *insecure/disorganised* infants seem disorientated, confused and even fearful throughout the strange situation.

Ainsworth suggests that behaviour in the 'strange situation' reflects stable characteristics of the child's relationships at least for the first few years. Children rated securely attached at 15 months typically are more outgoing, popular and well adjusted in nursery at three and a half years (Waters, Wippman and Sroufe 1979). Securely attached infants tend to become children who interact with other adults such as teachers in a friendly and appropriate way. They are more socially competent and even show certain intellectual advantages. In contrast, insecurely attached infants show more behavioural problems. Insecure boys tend to be more aggressive and girls more emotionally dependent at age four. Effects even reach into adolescence. Anxiety problems in adolescents have been linked to ambivalent insecurity in infancy, while aggression problems have been associated with avoidant attachment (Sroufe and Warren 1999).

The claim is that the 'strange situation' is a good index of mother–child relationship and that this relationship forms an important foundation for later social and emotional adjustment. Early effects are however changeable; for example, an infant may initially be secure, but changes in family circumstances may lead to parental stress and decrease the quality of attachment. Therefore early attachment seems to bias rather than determine later social relationships. Furthermore, insecurely attached children can become more securely attached when given the right circumstances.

What causes some children to develop secure attachments and others to be insecure? Essentially, attachment is affected by the quality of care that a child receives. An important part of this is the style of interaction that the baby experiences with his caregivers. The following characteristics are displayed in parents of securely attached infants:

1. They have a general *sensitivity* to the infant's needs. In other words they are reasonably good at deciding what the baby needs if, for example, she is crying.

2. Carers are *responsive* to the baby's needs and attempt to satisfy these within a reasonable time scale.

3. Carers talk and play with the infant in ways that encourage the child's development. These sorts of behaviours probably reflect a generally warm and loving parent–child relationship.

Fulfilment of all three characteristics requires that carers communicate effectively with their children from an early age.

In contrast carers of babies who are insecurely attached treat their infants rather differently. Carers of avoidant babies tend to be unavailable or even rejecting of their infants (Cassidy and Berlin 1994). They often ignore their infants' signals and typically have little physical contact with them and may be irritable when they do interact with their babies. Perhaps these babies simply learn that carers will generally not be there for them and therefore stop seeking attention. Babies who are ambivalent/insecure often have parents who are inconsistently responsive to them (Berlin and Cassidy 2000). Sometimes they are responsive and sometimes they are not. They also tend not to be very affectionate.

Babies who are classed as disorganised/insecure often have parents who may neglect or even physically abuse them (Main and Solomon 1990).

So how parents behave towards their infants matters a great deal and influences the quality of children's earliest social relationships and their social-emotional development. Notice that warm, affectionate, close interactivity are features only of parents who foster securely attached babies. It is obvious then that what babies experience within their early social encounters influences how they will feel about those relationships. This has relevance to this book since understanding children involves being able to read their non-verbal communication. Furthermore, signalling emotional warmth towards children is done through many types of non-verbal interaction including touch.

One study that clearly shows the benefits of touch on infant attachment involved training a group of mothers with babies of eight months old or less in infant massage. Four months later the babies were evaluated in terms of their attachment relationships to their mothers. It was found that the babies who had been massaged more than once a week were significantly more securely attached than those who had been massaged less than once a week (Jump 1999). This suggests that putting some time aside for close, appropriate and affectionate touch benefits the caregiver–infant relationship. Babies enjoy the touch and will associate their mothers with feeling pleasant and relaxed. They also 'read' it as a sign of affection, reassuring them of love and attention.

Impact of touch 'therapy'

Over and above the social and emotional effects that touch has, there are even more fundamental ways in which it exerts an influence on our well-being. There is some evidence that certain types of touch can actually be good for our physical health. Female surgery patients were found to recover faster and have lower blood pressure when they were touched prior to their operations by female nurses. This may have been because the patients were reassured and calmed by the touch. The opposite was true for male patients touched by female nurses (Whittaker and Fisher 1979). Touch can be interpreted as a signal of dominance in certain situations and perhaps being touched by the nurses increased stressful feelings of helplessness in the men. The mechanisms underlying such effects and the different ways we interpret touch are poorly understood. It strikes me that hospital practice would benefit greatly if these issues were considered. For example, the practice of male nurses bed-bathing elderly women is entirely ill advised given what we know about the psychology of touch. So touch can be beneficial even for adults, but only if it is within social norms and experienced as pleasant.

The physical benefits of touch are also shown in studies of premature infants. Babies born too early (particularly those born more than eight weeks premature) often have a number of medical conditions and complications; for example, they are more likely to require tube feeding and artificial ventilation. A number of studies have investigated whether a schedule of rhythmic stroking of premature babies influences their recovery. One group of babies was stroked from head to toe for ten minutes twice a day, either by their parents or hospital staff. Another group received normal medical attention only (De Roiste and Bushnell 1996). The babies who received the touch therapy recovered faster than those who did not; for example, they were quicker to begin oral feeding and went home sooner. Such effects illustrate the very real connection between physical contact and physical well-being.

In addition there were intellectual benefits for the treated infants. At one year their IQ scores were significantly higher than the other pre-term babies who had not received touch therapy. There is a link between touch, physical well-being and cognitive development. What causes these beneficial effects? Some evidence suggests that the touch stimulates pressure receptors which in turn have a particular impact on the nervous system, causing a slowing down in physiological arousal. This makes the babies more relaxed, decreases their production of stress hormones and increases immune function (Field 1998). Whatever the cause of the effect, touch has definite physical benefits for infants who have begun with a less than an optimal start. So is there something special about infant massage over and above normal, everyday contact?

Some research has shown that a systematic schedule of massage is of particular benefit over more general physical contact. The particular benefits of massage are illustrated in a study of one- to three-month-old babies of depressed adolescent mothers. The babies were given 15 minutes a day of either massage or rocking for two days a week over a six-week period. The massaged babies did better than those who had only been rocked. The time invested in the massage resulted in those babies becoming 'easier' to deal with. They had reduced stress levels, better emotionality and sociability, and were more quickly soothed (Field *et al.* 1996).

Behavioural benefits of touch

So touch has behavioural, physical and emotional benefits in infancy: what about older children with and without special needs? Touch therapy has also been used effectively to improve communication behaviours such as joint attention and social activities in pre-school children with autism. The touch therapy consisted of rubbing the children on their heads, necks, arms, hands, torsos, legs and feet. The therapy also decreased certain negative behaviours associated with autism such as touch aversion, but by no more than experiencing sitting in a caregiver's lap and being engaged in a game. Learning to accept any close contact is therefore beneficial for children with autism, although full touch therapy seems to bring additional positive effects (Field *et al.* 1997).

Field *et al.* (1999) also found beneficial effects on normal pre-schoolers' behaviour following repeated massage treatment. The children daily received 20 minutes of massage prior to nap time for five weeks. Among the positive effects was an increase in the children's co-operation and a reduction in the amount of time it took them to fall asleep. For any caregiver or parent these sorts of effects will be very welcome.

So touch is important in social development. In particular it influences social/emotional security and impacts on the quality of relationships between parent and child. In addition there are fundamental physical, behavioural and intellectual benefits associated with therapeutic touch for both normally developing children and those at risk either physically or intellectually. It is important that we keep sight of the important role that touch plays in social relationships in general and especially those of children. Touch is a social signal deeply rooted in our evolutionary past. If it loses its place in human social interactions we will lose an important part of our heritage.

Suggested readings

1. Del Prete, T. (1998) 'Getting Back in Touch with Students: Should We Risk It?' *Professional School Counselling 1*, 62–65.

2. Mazur, S. and Pekor, C. (1985) 'Can Teachers Touch Children Anymore? Physical Contact and its Values in Child Development.' *Young Children 40* 10–12.

3. Jones, S.E. and Yarborough, A.E. (1985) 'A naturalistic study of meanings of touch.' *Communication Monographs 52*, 19–56.

4. Ainsworth, M.D.S. and Bell, S.M. (1970) 'Attachment, Exploration and Separation: Illustrated by the Behaviour of One Year Olds in the Strange Situation.' *Child Development 41*, 49–67.

5. Berlin, L. and Cassidy, J. (2000) 'Understanding Parenting: Contributions of Attachment Theory and Research.' In J.D. Osofsky and H.E. Fitzgerald (eds) *WAIMH Handbook of Infant Mental Health*, Vol. 3. New York: Wiley.

6. Field, T.M. (1998) 'Touch Therapy Effects on Development.' *International Journal of Behavioural Development 22*, 779–797.

Key points

1. Appropriate touch has important effects on many aspects of development from infancy throughout childhood. It can influence social, emotional, physical and cognitive growth. Touch therapies can be usefully employed to promote development.

2. The meaning of a touch and the impact that it has on the touched depends on many situational factors; for example, was it accidental or task related?

3. Touch is highly rule governed and these rules vary across cultures. Even fairly young children are aware of this.

4. Adults are more tolerant of rule breaking by younger rather than older children, and often apply one set of boundaries for their

interactions with other adults and another for interacting with children.

5. Touch in infancy is related to the development of an attachment relationship between child and carer. At 12 months this can be measured and infants classed as securely or insecurely attached. The quality of this attachment has important implications for the child's future development and behaviour. Secure attachment is associated with sensitive and responsive parenting.

Things to try

1. *Newborn.* Skin-to-skin contact with newborns and young babies can be very rewarding for both mother and child. It may stabilise breathing and heart rate and soothe a crying infant.

2. *Babies of any age.* Infant massage has been reported to have many positive effects. This is *not* true massage and should never involve any deep muscle stimulation or anything at all forceful. Parents can lightly stroke their infants' legs, arms, hands and feet and perhaps gently rub them with olive or grapeseed oil. Health visitors can give advice on both this and information on infant massage classes. The benefits of touch therapy for infants who are born early or have other disadvantages are clear.

3. *Pre-schoolers.* Try similar light massage with older pre-school children at nap time or bedtime and see whether it helps getting them off to sleep.

4. *Any age.* Make a list of your own attitudes to touch. When do you feel comfortable touching another person or being touched? How do your attitudes differ regarding touching other adults and touching children?

5. *Children of any age.* Watch children as they interact with others. How aware are they of rules about touching? Sometimes children touch others inappropriately and break social norms; for example, they might grab another child roughly when playing as a way of controlling. They do not necessarily mean to be

aggressive but this is how it may seem to other children; if persistent, other children might protest. At this point it may be helpful to explain what's going wrong.

6. *Any age.* Try using a brief touch on the arm when complimenting someone or asking a favour. See if your message has a greater impact.

7. *Toddlers and infants from six months.* It is important that parents understand the signs of secure and insecure attachment. Separation anxiety is a normal part of development and alongside positive reunion behaviours is a sign that the child has a good attachment relationship.

8. *Toddlers and infants from six months.* If children are showing signs of insecure attachment, parents should think carefully about how they interact with them and be given help to identify aspects of their interactional style that may be contributing to their children's insecurity.

Chapter 7

Conclusion

While language is a crucial part of human communication and even thought, non-verbal communication gives children another valuable way of expressing themselves. Children's eye gaze, hand gestures and facial expressions are all channels of interaction that can be capitalised upon before, and then alongside, speech. We see evidence of thoughts, feelings and even knowledge in these cues and by acting upon this information we can optimise what children learn from us and assist their development.

In this book I have discussed the many ways that non-verbal communication influences and reflects the development of children. Child development occurs in a number of dimensions. Childhood involves a continual change in cognitive, social/emotional as well as physical abilities. I have shown in this book that non-verbal communication provides invaluable indices of all these aspects of growth as well as feeding into the very development itself. By attending to facial expressions, eye gaze and hand gestures we can sensitively read children's needs and desires, making it possible to respond effectively and to scaffold their learning and development.

By understanding the time course of development of non-verbal communication we can understand children's communication better and watch their underlying cognitive and social growth. Making use of non-verbal cues lets us build accurate theories of the minds of children: What are they capable of? What do they understand about a topic? What are they attending to? How are they feeling? Just as children have to develop a theory of mind to allow them to function effectively in their social world, so too must we appreciate their minds as best we can.

Non-verbal behaviours provide catalysts for development in a number of ways. First, by using non-verbal communication children open a whole repertoire of skills that they can use to influence the people in their world. This drives, for example, their developing sense of self-efficacy. Second, these indices of internal development provide invaluable information to adults so that they can tailor their help and support of the child effectively. Third, the non-verbal behaviours that the child is exposed to in the social interactions they experience have a significant impact on each aspect of development; for example, emotional warmth is largely transmitted via cues such as mutual eye contact, touch and smiling. Children readily understand these signals from an early age and use them as reassurance of the affection and love felt towards them from the sender. This is the case from very early in infancy. Touch is exemplary of this and has tremendous influence in the development of secure attachments between babies and their carers. As we have seen, the impact extends beyond social and emotional benefits. Hand gestures can be used to spread the cognitive load of messages to children to facilitate their understanding of them. Even touch has positive influences on mental growth. Adults must therefore be effective users of non-verbal cues in sending children the messages they intend. Gesture, touch, facial expressions and eye gaze are positive and powerful tools for us to use in our attempts to foster good relationships with children and their development.

Babies are born into a social world. They come well equipped with innate foundations of social and communication skills. These allow them to begin discovering how to communicate with other people right from birth. There is much that they have to learn. Within the first year of life infants use many forms of gestures, facial expressions, eye gaze and touch to send signals and to gain information from others. The fine-tuning and deep understanding of these cues takes several years to acquire – dependent upon and at the same time influencing the child's increasing cognitive and social abilities. Social experiences also teach children culture-specific rules about non-verbal behaviours that are operationalised in the display rules they will later adopt.

The most important parts of a child's world are the people in it and the relationships formed with them. Child development occurs partly driven by the child's genetic endowment, but this interacts in important ways with what the child experiences. Throughout this book we have seen that there is a significant innate foundation for all channels of communication. However, what children learn and experience in their social interactions has an equally important impact on the unfolding of their communicative potential and their cognitive social and emotional development. Facial expressions exemplify this. Babies are born with the innate potential to produce a whole range of facial movements and expressions. A considerable amount of this range unfolds over the first few months of life. As infants' social awareness increases, so too does their ability to pose expressions in deliberate attempts to influence others. Throughout the primary school years children learn the display rules of their culture and become increasingly adept at controlling their facial movements.

Children gain a lot of information from other people's non-verbal behaviours and there is plenty of evidence that understanding non-verbal signals is often easier than understanding the same message articulated in speech. Furthermore in adult–child interaction careful management of the adult's non-verbal communication can help place the child at ease, provide reassurance and reduce negative feelings such as intimidation. It is important for adults to be aware of their own non-verbal behaviours, making sure that the wrong message isn't sent. Adjusting intimacy distance to a comfortable equilibrium that suits the situation is essential; if too distant, management of the conversation and engagement of the child can be difficult. However, if too close the child is likely to withdraw. Non-verbal channels of communication are not only central to the portrayal of affiliation and liking, but also in signalling dominance. Careful consideration of these behaviours will help to project the right message; careless use may mean that you come across in a way that was not intended. Getting the balance right is always important, whether it is a police officer interviewing a child, a doctor treating a sick youngster, a teacher instructing a pupil, or even a parent dealing with a problematic situation.

This book could never give an exhaustive account of every possible non-verbal cue. What I hope to have done is provide some principles and frameworks within which to understand children's communication. By applying these principles we can communicate with and understand children better, making us more able to judge their needs, knowledge and development accurately. Your theory of children's minds will benefit from asking yourself the sorts of questions begged by the principles of communication I describe in Chapter 1 whenever you interact with a child:

- Is the non-verbal cue automatic or intentional?
- Is it innate or has she learned to use it instrumentally?
- What information about the child's knowledge does it offer?
- What is the emotional content?
- How should I respond?
- Can I offer instruction or help that will scaffold his thinking or communication?

There are many professional applications of this knowledge. An exemplary one is the teaching profession. Teachers have to be able to judge children's understanding all the time. Accurately determining when a child is ready to learn or requiring extra instruction is crucial to effective teaching. There are a number of non-verbal cues that can be used in this respect. Hand gestures are a rich source of information. We process some of this automatically without being aware of it. Thinking about the content of gestures can tell us a lot about the level and state of a child's knowledge and what they do not yet understand. This is an important source of information in deciding whether to offer additional instruction when a child is learning something new. It has yet to be determined whether even experienced teachers consciously use these cues or not. Eye gaze also promises to be a valuable way of judging whether children are thinking and engaged in a task and therefore ready to learn. If children look away a lot while being asked a difficult question, this typically indicates that they are concentrating hard on working out the answer.

Social workers and other legal professionals must take children's non-verbal communication into account when listening to children's accounts of events. Non-verbal signals provide information that may not be articulated in speech. In addition there are significant issues relating to the perception of credibility and deception. There is much folklore about signs of deception. It is important that professionals familiarise themselves with reliable cues of deception and truth. These are not foolproof and indeed there are ways of checking for truth and deception in the verbal message (Vrij 2002). We should however make the most of the visual information available. Children and adults using live video links in court should be made aware of the effect that mediating interaction has on communication and the accessibility of potentially important visual cues. Training and practice with live links will help accustom users to them. Jurors also need to be made aware of the potential effects; for example, the increased social distance experienced between them and the child can alter the emotional impact of the testimony.

Doctors, midwives, psychologists and health visitors are health professionals who not only have to assess young children's physical, cognitive and emotional development but also have to advise parents on what to expect of their children and how best to deal with the problems that parenthood brings. Making full use of the channels of communication through which you obtain as well as send information will optimise your communicative effectiveness. For example, you may find ways of using your non-verbal behaviours to get across messages that are important for the child to fully understand, perhaps using gesture to back up what you say and eye gaze as emphasis.

Last but not least, parents can also benefit from a better understanding of children's non-verbal communication. Thinking about the principles of communication that I have described will help you see things from your child's viewpoint. You can help teach your children fundamentally important social skills by modelling good non-verbal practices. Think about how you greet people and interact with them. In what circumstances do you project affiliation or dominance? What is your style of interaction with your children? Parents can provide some of the most important learning experiences which children encounter. Try to optimise what you teach them by making use of their non-verbal signals of knowledge and understanding.

Whatever your involvement with children, remember that communication is a two-way process. When we communicate effectively with young people our minds meet with theirs; it is then that we can learn from one another. Non-verbal signals and language are the ways that we bridge our thoughts with others. If we do not attend to the non-verbal aspects of communication we simply weaken the link, making misinterpretation more likely and losing valuable sources of information.

References

Abramovitch, R. and Daly, E.M. (1978) 'Children's Use of Head Orientation and Eye Contact in Making Attributions of Affiliation.' *Child Development 49*, 519–522.

Acredolo, L.P. And Goodwyn, S.W. (2000) 'The Long-Term Impact of Symbolic Gesturing during Infancy on IQ at Age 8.' Paper presented at the Biennial Meetings of the International Society for Infant Studies, Brighton, UK.

Aiello, J.R. And Jones, S.E. (1971) 'Field Study of the Proxemic Behaviour of Young Children in Three Subcultural Groups.' *Journal of Personality And Social Psychology 19*, 351–356.

Aiello, J.R., Nicosia, G. and Thompson, D.E. (1979) 'Physiological, Social and Behavioural Consequences of Crowding on Children and Adolescents.' *Child Development 50*, 195–202.

Ainsworth, M.D.S. and Bell, S.M. (1970) 'Attachment, Exploration and Separation: Illustrated by the Behaviour of One Year Olds in the Strange Situation.' *Child Development 41*, 49–67.

Alibali, M.W. and Goldin-Meadow, S. (1993) 'Transitions in Learning: What the Hands Reveal about a Child's State of Mind.' *Cognitive Psychology 25*, 468–523.

Andersen, E.S., Dunlea, A. and Kekelis, L.S. (1984) 'Blind Children's Language: Resolving Some Differences.' *Journal of Child Language 11*, 645–664.

Anderson, J.R., Sallaberry, P. and Barbier, H. (1995) 'Use of Experimenter-Given Cues during Object-Choice Tasks by Capuchin Monkeys.' *Animal Behaviour 49*, 201-208.

Argyle, M. (1996) *Bodily Communication.* London: Routledge.

Argyle, M. and Dean, J. (1965) 'Eye-Contact, Distance and Affiliation.' *Sociometry 28*, 289–304.

Argyle, M. Alkema, F. and Gilmour, R. (1972) 'The Communication of Friendly and Hostile Attitudes by Verbal and Non-Verbal Signals.' *European Journal of Social Psychology 1*, 385–402.

Ashear, V. and Snortum, J.R. (1971) 'Eye Contact in Children as a Function of Age, Sex, Social and Intellective Variables.' *Developmental Psychology 4*, 479.

Attwood, T. (1998) *Asperger's Syndrome: A Guide for Parents and Professionals.* London: Jessica Kingsley Publishers.

Baldwin, D.A. (1991) 'Infants' Contribution to the Achievement of Joint Reference.' *Child Development 62*, 875–890.

Baldwin, D.A. and Moses, L.J. (1996) 'The Ontogeny of Social Information Gathering.' *Child Development 67*, 1915–1935.

Baron-Cohen, S. (1988) 'Social and Pragmatic Deficits in Autism: Cognitive or Affective?' *Journal of Autism and Developmental Disorders 18*, 379–402.

Baron-Cohen, S. (1989) 'Perceptual Role-Taking and Proto-Declarative Pointing in Autism.' *British Journal of Developmental Psychology 7*, 113–127.

Baron-Cohen, S. and Cross, P. (1992) 'Reading the Eyes: Evidence for the Role of Perception in the Development of Theory of Mind.' *Mind and Language 7*, 172–186.

Baron-Cohen, S., Allen, J. and Gillberg, C. (1992) 'Can Autism be Detected at 18-Months? The Needle, the Haystack, and the CHAT.' *British Journal of Psychiatry 161*, 839–843.

Baron-Cohen, S., Campbell, R., Karmiloff-Smith, A., Grant, J. and Walker, J. (1995) 'Are Children with Autism Blind to the Mentalistic Significance of the Eyes?' *British Journal of Developmental Psychology 13*, 379–398.

Baron-Cohen, S., Jolliffe, T., Mortimore, C. and Robertson, M. (1997) 'Another Advanced Test of Theory of Mind: Evidence from Very High Functioning Adults with Autism or Asperger Syndrome.' *Journal of Child Psychology and Psychiatry and Allied Disciplines 38*, 813–822.

Bartrip, J., Morton, J. and de Schonen, S. (2001) 'Responses to Mother's Face in 3-Week to 5-Month-Old Infants.' *British Journal of Developmental Psychology 19*, 219–232.

Bates, E., Benigi, L., Bretherton, I., Camaioni, L. and Volterra, V. (1979) In E. Bates (ed) *The Emergence of Symbols: Cognition and Communication in Infancy.* New York and London: Academic Press.

Bates, E., Camaioni, L. and Volterra, V. (1975) 'The Acquisition of Performatives Prior to Speech.' *Merrill-Palmer Quarterly 21*, 205–226.

Baum, A., Aiello, J.R. and Calesnick, L.E. (1978) 'Crowding and Personal Control: Social Density and the Development of Learned Helplessness.' *Journal of Personality and Social Psychology 36*, 1000–1011.

Baumrind, D. (1967) 'Child Care Practices Anteceding Three Patterns of Preschool Behaviour.' *Genetic Psychology Monographs 75*, 43–88.

Baxter, J.S. (1990) 'The Suggestibility of Child Witnesses: A Review.' *Applied Cognitive Psychology 4*, 393–407.

Beier, E.G. and Sterberg, D.P. (1977) 'Marital Communication.' *Journal of Communication 27*, 92–97.

Bellugi, U., Bihrle, A., Jernigan, T., Trauner, D. and Doherty, S. (1990) 'Neuropsychological, Neurological and Neuroanatomical Profile of Williams Syndrome.' *American Journal of Genetics 56*, 115–125.

Berlin, L. and Cassidy, J. (2000) 'Understanding Parenting: Contributions of Attachment Theory and Research.' In J.D. Osofsky and H.E. Fitzgerald (eds) *WAIMH Handbook of Infant Mental Health*, Vol. 3. New York: Wiley.

Berman, P.W. and Smith, V.L. (1984) 'Gender and Situational Differences in Children's Smiles, Touch, and Proxemics.' *Sex Roles 10*, 347–356.

Blank, M., Gessner, M. and Esposito, A. (1978) 'Language without Communication: A Case Study.' *Journal of Child Language 6*, 329–352.

Blurton-Jones, N. (1972) *Ethological Studies of Child Behaviour.* Cambridge: Cambridge University Press.

Bower, J. (1977) *Infant Development.* San Francisco: Freeman.

Bowlby, J. (1969) *Attachment and Loss. Vol 1: Attachment.* New York: Basic Books.

Bowlby, J. (1973) *Separation and Loss.* New York: Basic Books.

Boyle, E.A., Anderson, A.H. and Newlands, A. (1994) 'The Effects of Visibility on Dialogue and Performance in a Cooperative Problem Solving Task.' *Language and Speech 37*, 1, 1–20.

Bradshaw, J. and McKenzie, B. (1971) 'Judging Outline Faces: A Developmental Study.' *Child Development 32*, 929–937.

Bruce, V., Campbell, R., Doherty-Sneddon, G., Import, A., Langton, S., McAuley, S. and Wright, R. (2000) 'Testing Face Processing Skills in Children.' *British Journal of Developmental Psychology 18*, 319–333.

Bruner, J.S. (1975) 'From Communication to Language: A Psychological Perspective.' *Cognition 3*, 259–287.

Bruner, J.S. (1977) 'Early Social Interaction and Language Acquisition.' In H.R. Schaffer (ed) *Studies in Mother–Infant Interaction*. London: Academic Press.

Butterworth, G. and Cochrane, E. (1980) 'Towards a Mechanism of Joint Visual Attention in Human Infancy.' *International Journal of Behavioural Development 3*, 253–272.

Butterworth, G. and Jarrett, N. (1991) 'What Minds Have in Common is Space: Spatial Mechanisms Serving Joint Visual Attention in Infancy.' *British Journal of Developmental Psychology 9*, 55–72.

Campbell, R., Coleman, M., Walker, J., Benson, P.J., Wallace, S., Michelotti, J. and Baron-Cohen, S. (1999) 'When Does the Inner-Face Advantage in Familiar Face Recognition Arise and Why?' *Visual Cognition 6*, 197–216.

Campbell, R., Walker, J. and Baron-Cohen, S. (1995) 'Development of Differential Use of Inner and Outer Face Features in Familiar Face Identification.' *Journal of Experimental Child Psychology 59*, 196–210.

Carey, S. and Diamond, R. (1994) 'Are Faces Perceived as Configurations More by Adults than by Children?' *Visual Cognition 1*, 253–274.

Caron, A., Caron, R., Mustelin, C. and Roberts, J. (1992) 'Infant Responding to Aberrant Social Stimuli.' *Infant Behaviour and Development 15*, 335.

Carter, C.A., Bottoms, B.L. and Levine, M. (1996) 'Linguistic and Socioemotional Influences on the Accuracy of Children's Reports.' *Law and Human Behavior 20*, 579.

Cassidy, J. and Berlin, L. (1994) 'The insecure/ambivalent pattern of attachment: theory and research.' *Child Development 65*, 971–997.

Charman, T., Swettenham, J., Baron-Cohen, S., Cox, A., Baird, G. and Drew, A. (2000) 'An Experimental Investigation of Social-Cognitive Abilities in Infants with Autism: Clinical Implications.' In D. Muir and A. Slater (eds) *Infant Development: The Essential Readings*. Malden, MA: Blackwell.

Church, R.B. and Goldin-Meadow, S. (1986) 'The Mismatch between Gestures and Speech as an Index of Transitional Knowledge.' *Cognition 23*, 43–71.

Corkum, V. and Moore, C. (1995) 'Development of Joint Visual Attention in Infants.' In C. Moore and P.J. Dunham (eds) *Joint Attention: Its Origins and Role in Development*. Hillsdale, NJ: Lawrence Erlbaum.

Corsini, D. (1969) 'The Effect of Nonverbal Cues on the Retention of Kindergarten Children.' *Child Development 40*, 599–607.

Cosgrove, J.M and Patterson, C.J. (1977) 'Plans and the Development of Listener Skills.' *Developmental Psychology 13*, 557–564.

Cowen, E.L., Weisberg, R.P. and Lotyczewski, B.S. (1983) 'Physical Contacts in Interactions between Clinicians and Young Children.' *Journal of Consulting and Clinical Psychology 51*, 132–138.

Crusco, A.H. and Wetzel, C.G. (1984) 'The Midas Touch: The Effects of Interpersonal Touch on Restaurant Tipping.' *Personality and Social Psychology Bulletin 10*, 512–517.

Dahlgren, S.O. and Gillberg, C. (1989) 'Symptoms in the First Two Years of Life. A Preliminary Population Study of Infantile Autism.' *European Archives of Psychiatric and Neurological Sciences 386*, 1–6.

Davies, G.M. and Noon, E. (1991) 'An Evaluation of the Live Link for Child Witnesses.' Home Office report. London: HMSO.

Day, K. (2001) 'Peer Acceptance and Face Processing Skills.' Unpublished dissertation. University of Stirling.

De Casper, A.J. and Spence, M.J. (1986) 'Prenatal Maternal Speech Influences Newborns' Perception of Speech Sounds.' *Infant Behaviour and Development 9*, 133–150.

Del Prete, T. (1998) 'Getting Back in Touch with Students: Should We Risk It?' *Professional School Counselling 1*, 62–65.

Dermer, M. and Thiel, D.L. (1975) 'When Beauty May Fail.' *Journal of Personality and Social Psychology 31*, 168–176.

De Roiste, A. and Bushnell, I.W.R. (1996) 'Tactile Stimulation: Short and Long Term Benefits for Pre-Term Infants.' *British Journal of Developmental Psychology 14*, 41–53.

De Vries, J.I., Visser, G.H. and Prechtl, H.F.R. (1982) 'The Emergence of Fetal Behaviour: 1. Qualitative Aspects.' *Early Human Development 7*, 301–322.

DeYoung, M. (1988) 'The Good Touch/Bad Touch Dilemma.' *Child Welfare 67*, 60–68.

Diamond, R. and Carey, S. (1977) 'Developmental Changes in the Representation of Faces.' *Journal of Experimental Child Psychology 23*, 1–22.

Dion, K., Berschied, E. and Walster, E. (1972) 'What is Beautiful is Good.' *Journal of Personality and Social Psychology 24*, 285–290.

Dittrichova, J. (1969) 'Development of Sleep in Infancy.' In R.J. Robinson (ed) *Brain and Early Development*. London: Academic Press.

Dodd, B. (1979) 'Lip-Reading in Infants: Attention to Speech Presented in- and out-of-Synchrony.' *Cognitive Psychology 11*, 478–484.

Dodd, B. (1987) 'The Acquisition of Lip-Reading Skills by Normally Hearing Children.' In B. Dodd and R. Campbell (eds) *Hearing by Eye*. London: Lawrence Erlbaum.

Doherty, M.J. and Anderson, J.R. (in press) 'A New Look at Gaze: Preschool Children's Understanding of Eye-Direction.' *Cognitive Development*.

Doherty-Sneddon, G. and Kent, G. (1996) 'Visual Signals in Children's Communication.' *Journal of Child Psychology and Psychiatry 37*, 949–959.

Doherty-Sneddon, G. and McAuley, S. (2000) 'Influence of Video Mediation on Adult–Child Interviews: Implications for the Use of the Live Link with Child Witnesses.' *Applied Cognitive Psychology 14*, 379–392.

Doherty-Sneddon, G., Anderson, A.H., O'Malley, C., Langton, S., Garrod, S. and Bruce, V. (1997) 'Face-to-Face and Video Mediated Communication: A Comparison of Dialogue Structure and Task Performance.' *Journal of Experimental Psychology: Applied 3*, 1-21.

Doherty-Sneddon, G., Bruce, V., Bonner, L., Longbotham, S. and Doyle, C. (2002) 'Development of Gaze Aversion as Disengagement from Visual Information.' *Developmental Psychology 38*, 438–445.

Doherty-Sneddon, G., McAuley, S., Bruce, V., Langton, S., Blokland, A. and Anderson, A.H. (2000) 'Visual Signals and Children's Communication: Negative Effects on Task Outcome.' *British Journal of Developmental Psychology 18*, 595–608.

Dumas, G. (1932) 'La Mimique des Aveugles.' *Bulletin de l'Academie de Medicine 107*, 607–610.

Duncan, S. (1972) 'Some Signals and Rules for Taking Speaking Turns in Conversations.' *Journal of Personality and Social Psychology 23*, 283–292.

Eberts, E.H. and Lepper, M.R. (1975) 'Individual Consistency in the Proxemic Behaviour of Preschool Children.' *Journal of Personality and Social Psychology 32*, 841–849.

Ekman, P. (1972) 'Universals and Cultural Differences in Facial Expressions of Emotions.' In J. Cole (ed) *Nebraska Symposium on Motivation*, Vol. 19. Lincoln: University of Nebraska Press.

Ekman, P. (1979) 'Non-Verbal and Verbal Rituals in Interactions: About Brows: Emotional and Conversational Signals.' In M. Von Cranach (ed) *Human Ethology: Claims and Limits of a New Discipline*. Cambridge: Cambridge University Press.

Ekman, P. (1982) *Emotion in the Human Face*. Cambridge: Cambridge University Press.

Ekman, P. and Friesen, W.V. (1969) 'Nonverbal Leakage and Clues to Deception.' *Psychiatry 32*, 88–105.

Ekman, P. and Friesen, W.V. (1978) *Facial Affect Coding Scheme (FACS): A Technique for the Measurement of Facial Action*. Palo Alto, CA: Psychologists Press.

Ekman, P., Roper, G. and Hager, J.C. (1980) 'Deliberate Facial Movement.' *Child Development 51*, 886–891.

Ellis, H.D., Shepherd, J.W. and Davies, G.M. (1979) 'Identification of Familiar and Unfamiliar Faces from Internal and External Features: Some Implications for Theories of Face Recognition.' *Perception 8*, 431–439.

Field, T. (1981) 'Infant arousal, attention and affect during early interactions.' *Advances in Infancy Research 1*, 57–100.

Field, T.M. (1998) 'Touch Therapy Effects on Development.' *International Journal of Behavioural Development 22*, 779–797.

Field, T.M., Grizzle, N., Scafidi, F., Adrams, S., Richardson, S., Kuhn, C. and Schanberg, S. (1996) 'Massage Therapy for Infants of Depressed Mothers.' *Infant Behaviour and Development 19*, 107–112.

Field, T.M., Kilmer, T., Hernandez, R.M. and Burman, I. (1999) 'Preschool Children's Sleep and Wake Behaviour: Effects of Massage Therapy.' *Early Child Development and Care 120*, 39–44.

Field, T.M., Lasko, D., Mundy, P. and Henteleff, T. (1997) 'Brief Report: Autistic Children's Attentiveness and Responsivity Improve after Touch Therapy.' *Journal of Autism and Developmental Disorders 127*, 333–338.

Field, T., Pickens, J., Fox, N.A., Gonzalez, J. and Nawrocki, T. (1998) 'Facial Expression and EEG Responses to Happy and Sad Faces/Voices by 3-Month-Old Infants of Depressed Mothers.' *British Journal of Developmental Psychology 16*, 485–494.

Fisher, R.P. and Geiselman, R.E. (1992) *Memory Enhancing Techniques for Investigative Interviewing: The Cognitive Interview*. Springfield, IL: C.C. Thomas.

Flavell, J.H., Botkin, P.T., Fry, C.L., Wright, J.C. and Jarvis, P.E. (1968) *The Development of Role-Taking and Communication Skills in Children.* New York: Wiley.

Flin, R.H., Bull, R., Boon, J. and Knox, A. (1990) *Child Witnesses in Scottish Criminal Prosecutions.* Report to the Scottish Home and Health Department. Glasgow: Glasgow College of Technology.

Flin, R.H., Kearney, B. and Murray, K. (1996) 'Children's Evidence: Scottish Research and Law.' *Criminal Justice and Behaviour 23,* 358–376.

Foa, U.G. (1961) 'Convergences in the Structure of Interpersonal Behaviour.' *Psychological Review 68,* 341–353.

Freedman, N. and Hoffman, S.P. (1967) 'Kinetic Behaviour in Altered Clinical States: Approach to Objective Analysis of Motor Behaviour during Interviews.' *Perceptual and Motor Skills 24,* 527–539.

Freud, S. (1915) *The Unconscious.* Standard Edition. Vol. 14. London: Hogarth Press.

Freud, S. (1926) *Inhibitions, Symptoms and Anxiety.* Standard Edition. Vol. 20. London: Hogarth Press.

Fry, A.M. and Willis, F.N. (1971) 'Invasion of Personal Space as a Function of the Age of the Invader.' *Psychological Record 2,* 385–389.

Fry, R. and Smith, G.F. (1975) 'The Effects of Feedback and Eye Contact on Performance of a Digit-Coding Task.' *Journal of Social Psychology 96,* 145–146.

Fullwood, C. and Doherty-Sneddon, G. (in prep.) 'The Effects of Video-Mediated Gazing Behaviour on Recall and Participant Perceptions of a Salesman and Product.' In preparation for *Journal of Experimental Social Psychology.*

Gale, A., Lucas, B., Nissim, R. and Harpham, B. (1972) 'Some EEG Correlates of Face-to-Face Contact.' *British Journal of Social and Clinical Psychology 11,* 326–332.

Gardner, R.A. and Gardner, B.T. (1969) 'Teaching Sign Language to a Chimpanzee.' *Science 165,* 664–672.

Gervais, J., Tremblay, R.E., Desmarias-Gervais, L. and Vitaro, F. (2000) 'Children's Persistent Lying, Gender Differences, and Disruptive Behaviours: A Longitudinal Perspective.' *International Journal of Behavioural Development 24,* 213-221.

Gillberg, C. (1989) 'Early Symptoms in Autism.' In C. Gillberg (ed) *Diagnosis and Treatment of Autism.* New York: Plenum.

Glenberg, A.M., Shroeder, J.L. and Robertson, D.A. (1998) 'Averting the Gaze Disengages the Environment and Facilitates Remembering.' *Memory and Cognition 26,* 651–658.

Goldin-Meadow, S. (1999) 'The Role of Gesture in Communication and Thinking.' *Trends in Cognitive Science 3,* 419–429.

Goldin-Meadow, S. and Butcher, C. (2000) 'Pointing toward Two-Word Speech in Young Children.' In S. Kita (ed) *Pointing: Where Language Culture and Cognition Meet.* Cambridge: Cambridge University Press.

Gomez, J.C. (1991) 'Visual Behaviour as a Window for Reading Minds of Others in Primates.' In A. Whitem (ed) *Natural Theories of Minds: Evolution, Development and Simulation of Everyday Mindreading.* Oxford: Blackwell.

Gooch, D. (1999) 'Distance, Intimacy and Compliance: An Investigation of Compensation Behaviours in Pre-School Children.' Unpublished dissertation. University of Stirling.

Goodman, G.S., Bottoms, B.L., Schwartz, K., Beth, M. and Rudy, L. (1991) 'Children's Testimony about a Stressful Event: Improving Children's Reports.' *Journal of Narrative and Life History 1*, 69–99.

Goodwyn, S.W. and Acredolo, L.P. (1993) 'Symbolic Gesture versus Word: Is There a Modality Advantage for the Onset of Symbol Use?' *Child Development 64*, 688–701.

Goodwyn, S.W., Acredolo, L.P. and Brown, C.A. (2000) 'Impact of Symbolic Gesturing on Early Language Development.' *Journal of Nonverbal Behaviour 24*, 81–103.

Graham, J.A. and Heywood, S. (1976) 'The Effects of Elimination of Hand Gestures and of Verbal Codability on Speech Performance.' *European Journal of Social Psychology 5*, 189–195.

Grandin, T. (1984) 'My Experiences as an Autistic Child and Review of Related Literature.' *Journal of Orthomolecular Psychiatry 13*, 144–174.

Hall, E.T. (1966) *The Hidden Dimension.* New York: Doubleday.

Harlow, H.E. and Harlow, M.K. (1972) *The Young Monkeys.* Albany, NY: Delmar.

Harris, L. (1968) 'Looks by Preschoolers at the Experimenter in a Choice-of-Toy Game: Effects of Experimenter and Age of Child.' *Journal of Experimental Child Psychology 6*, 493–500.

Harris, P.L., Olthof, T. and Terwogt, M.M. (1981) 'Children's Knowledge of Emotion.' *Journal of Child Psychology and Psychiatry 22*, 247–261.

Hatfield, E. and Sprecher, S. (1986) *Mirror, Mirror, on the Wall.* Albany, NY: State University of New York Press.

Hess, E.H. (1965) 'Attitude and Pupil Size.' *Scientific American 212*, 46–54.

Hitch, G.J., Halliday, S., Schaafstal, A.M. and Schraagen, J.M.C. (1988) 'Visual Working Memory in Young Children.' *Memory and Cognition 16*, 120–132.

Home Office with Department of Health (1992) *Memorandum of Good Practice for Video Recorded Interviews with Child Witnesses for Criminal Proceedings.* London: HMSO.

Hood, B.M., Willen, J.D. and Driver, J. (1998) 'An Eye Direction Detector Triggers Shift of Visual Attention in Human Infants.' *Psychological Science 9*, 131–134.

Ikatura, S. and Tanaka, M. (1998) 'Use of Experimenter-Given Cues during Object-Choice Tasks by Chimpanzees (Pan Troglodytes), an Orangutan (Pongo Pygmaeus), and Human Infants (Homo Sapiens).' *Journal of Comparative Psychology 112*, 119–126.

Iverson, J.M. and Goldin-Meadow, S. (1998) 'Why People Gesture as They Speak.' *Nature 396*, 228.

Izard, C.E. (1978) 'On the Development of Emotions and Emotion-Cognition Relationships in Infancy.' In M. Lewis and L.A. Rosenbaum (eds) *The Development of Affect.* New York: Plenum.

Izard, C.E. (unpub.) 'The Biological and Social Functions of Facial Expressions: Darwin's Legacy to the Psychology of Emotions.' Unpublished dissertation. University of Delaware.

Jecker, J.D., Maccoby, N. and Breitrose, H.S. (1965) 'Improving Accuracy in Interpreting Non-Verbal Cues of Comprehension.' *Psychology in the Schools 2*, 239–244.

Johnson, S., Slaughter, V. and Carey, S. (1998) 'Whose Gaze Will Infants Follow? The Elicitation of Gaze-Following in 12-Month-Olds.' *Developmental Science 1*, 233–238.

Jones, S.E. and Yarborough, A.E. (1985) 'A Naturalistic Study of Meanings of Touch.' *Communication Monographs 52*, 19–56.

Jump, V.K. (1999) 'Effects of Infant Massage on Aspects of the Parent–Child Relationship: An Experimental Manipulation.' *Dissertations Abstracts International: Section B: The Sciences and Engineering 60* (4-B), 1886.

Karmiloff-Smith, A. (1992) *Beyond Modularity: A Developmental Perspective on Cognitive Science.* Cambridge, MA: MIT Press.

Keller, H. and Zach, U. (1993) 'Developmental Consequences of Early Eye Contact Behaviour.' *International Journal of Child and Adolescent Psychiatry 56*, 31–36.

Kendon, A. (1967) 'Some Functions of Gaze Direction in Social Interaction.' *Acta Psychologica 26*, 22-63.

Kendon, A. (1970) 'Movement Coordination in Social Interaction: Some Examples Described.' *Acta Psychologica 32*, 101–125.

Kestenbaum, R. and Gelman, S.A. (1995) 'Preschool Children's Identification and Understanding of Mixed Emotions.' *Cognitive Development 10*, 443–458.

Kirkland, J. and Smith, J. (1978) 'Preferences for Infant Pictures with Modified Eye-Pupils.' *Journal of Biological Psychology 20*, 33–34.

Kowtko, J., Isard, S. and Doherty-Sneddon, G. (1991) *Conversational Games in Dialogue.* University of Edinburgh: HCRC Publications.

Kraut, R.E. and Poe, D. (1980) 'Behavioural Roots of Person Perception: The Deceptive Judgements of Customs Inspectors and Laymen.' *Journal of Personality and Social Psychology 39*, 784–798.

La France, M. and Ickes, W. (1981) 'Posture Mirroring and Interactional Involvement: Sex and Sex Typing Effects.' *Journal of Nonverbal Behavior 5*, 139–154.

La Frenier, P. (1999) 'Les modèles évolutionistes peuvent-ils bénéficier des recherches développmentales sur la Théorie de l'Esprit?' *Enfance 51*, 327-335.

Langton, S.R. and Bruce, V. (1999) 'Reflexive Visual Orienting in Response to the Social Attention of Others.' *Visual Cognition 6*, 541–567.

Lawton, M.B. (1998) 'Physical Contact between Teachers and Preschool-Age Children in Early Childhood Programs.' *Dissertation Abstracts International Section A: Humanities and Social Sciences 59*, 0413.

Levine, M.H. and Sutton-Smith, B. (1973) 'Effects of Age, Sex, and Task on Visual Behaviour during Dyadic Interaction.' *Developmental Psychology 9*, 400–405.

Longbotham, S. (2001) Unpublished thesis. University of Stirling.

Lorenz, K. (1942) 'Die angeborenen Formen moglicher Erfahrung Z.' *Tierpsychol 5*, 235-409.

McGrew, W.C. (1972) *An Ethological Study of Children's Behaviour.* New York: Academic Press.

McGurk, H. and MacDonald, J. (1976) 'Hearing Lips and Seeing Voices.' *Nature 264*, 746–748.

McNeill, D. (1985) 'So You Think Gestures are Nonverbal?' *Psychological Review 92*, 350-371.

McNeill, D. (1992) *Hand and Mind.* Chicago: University of Chicago Press.

McNeill, D., Cassell, J. and McCullough, K.E. (1994) 'Communicative Effects of Speech-Mismatched Gestures.' *Research on Language and Social Interaction 27,* 223–237.

Main, M. and Solomon, J. (1990) 'Procedures for Identifying Infants as Disorganised/Disoriented during the Ainsworth Strange Situation.' In M. Greenberg, D. Cicchett and E.M. Cummings (eds) *Attachment During the Preschool Years.* Chicago: University of Chicago Press.

Markman, E.M. (1981) 'Comprehension Monitoring.' In P. Dickson (ed) *Children's Oral Communication Skills.* New York: Academic Press.

Maurer, D. and Salapatek, P. (1976) 'Developmental Changes in the Scanning of Faces by Human Infants.' *Child Development 47,* 523–527.

Mazur, S. and Pekor, C. (1985) 'Can Teachers Touch Children Anymore? Physical Contact and Its Values in Child Development.' *Young Children 40,* 10–12.

Mehrabian, A. (1969) 'The Significance of Posture and Position on the Communication of Attitudes and Status Relationships.' *Psychological Bulletin 71,* 359–372.

Meins, E. (1998) 'The Effects of Security of Attachment and Maternal Attribution of Meaning on Children's Linguistic Acquisitional Style.' *Infant Behaviour and Development 21,* 237–252.

Meltzoff, A.N. and Moore, M.K. (1977) 'Imitation of Facial and Manual Gestures by Human Neonates.' *Developmental Psychology 198,* 75–78.

Merrison, A.J., Anderson, A. and Doherty-Sneddon, G. (1994) *An Investigation into the Communicative Abilities of Aphasic Subjects in Task Oriented Dialogue.* Edinburgh: Human Communication Research Centre (internal publication).

Millot, J.L., Brand, G. and Schmitt, A. (1996) 'Affective Attitudes of Children and Adults in Relation to the Pupil Diameter of a Cat: Preliminary Data.' *Anthrozooes 9,* 85–87.

Moore, C. and Corkum, V. (1998) 'Infant Gaze Following Based on Eye Direction.' *British Journal of Psychology 16,* 495–503.

Morton, J. and Johnston, M.H. (1991) 'Conspec and Conlern: A Two-Process Theory of Infant Face Recognition.' *Psychological Review 98,* 164–181.

Murray, K. (1995) *Live Television Link: An Evaluation of Its Use by Child Witnesses in Scottish Criminal Trials.* Edinburgh: HMSO.

Newton, P., Reddy, V. and Bull, R (2000) 'Children's Everyday Deception and Performance on False-Belief Tasks.' *British Journal of Developmental Psychology 18,* 297–317.

Oakley, A. (1982) 'Obstetric Practice – Cross-Cultural Comparisons.' In P. Stratton (ed) *Psychobiology of the Human Newborn.* Chichester: Wiley.

O'Reilly A.W. (1995) 'Using Representations: Comprehension and Production of Actions with Imagined Objects.' *Child Development 66,* 999–1010.

Otteson, J.P. and Otteson, C.R. (1980) 'Effect of Teacher's Gaze on Children's Story Recall.' *Perceptual and Motor Skills 50,* 35–42.

Pascales, O., de Schonene, S., Morton, J., Deruelle, C. and Fabre-Grenet, M. (1995) 'Mothers' Face Recognition by Neonates – A Replication and Extension.' *Infant Behaviour and Development 18,* 79–85.

Patterson, M.L. (1973) 'Compensation in Nonverbal Intimacy Behaviours: A Review.' *Sociometry 36,* 237–252.

Patterson, M.L. (1976) 'An Arousal Model of Interpersonal Distance.' *Psychological Review* 83, 235–245.

Paulsell, S. and Goldman, M. (1984) 'The Effect of Touching Different Body Areas on Prosocial Behaviour.' *Journal of Social Psychology 122*, 269–273.

Pechman, T. and Deutsch, W. (1982) 'The Development of Verbal and Nonverbal Devices for Reference.' *Journal of Experimental Child Psychology 34*, 330–341.

Peery, J.C. and Crane, P.M. (1980) 'Personal Space Regulation: Approach-Withdrawal-Approach Proxemic Behaviour during Adult–Preschooler Interaction at Close Range.' *Journal of Psychology 106*, 63–75.

Peignot, P. and Anderson, J.R. (1999) 'Use of Experimenter-Given Manual and Facial Cues by Gorillas (Gorilla Gorilla) in an Object-Choice Task.' *Journal of Comparative Psychology 113*, 253–260.

Perrett, D.I., Hietanen, J.K., Oram, M.W. and Benson, P.J. (1992) 'Organization and Functions of Cells Responsive to Faces in the Temporal Cortex.' In V. Bruce and A. Cowey (eds) *Processing the Facial Image*. New York: Clarendon Press.

Peters, J.M. (1996) 'Paired Keyboards as a Tool for Internet Exploration of Third Grade Students.' *Journal of Educational Computing Research 14*, 229–242.

Phillips, W., Baron-Cohen, S. and Rutter, M. (1992) 'The Role of Eye Contact in Goal Detection: Evidence from Normal Infants and Children with Autism or Mental Handicap.' *Development and Psychopathology 4*, 375–383.

Piaget, J. (1951) *Plays, Dreams and Imitation in Childhood*. New York: Norton.

Piaget, J. (1972) *The Child's Conception of the World*. Totowa, NJ: Littlefield, Adams.

Povinelli, D.J. and Eddy, T.J. (1994) 'The Eyes as a Window: What Young Chimpanzees See on the Other Side.' *Current Psychology of Cognition 13*, 695–705.

Premack, D. (1983) 'The Codes of Man and Beasts.' *Behaviour and Brain Sciences 6*, 125–167.

Premack, D. and Woodruff, G. (1978) 'Does the Chimpanzee Have a "Theory of Mind"?' *Behaviour and Brain Sciences 4*, 515–526.

Provine, R.R. (1989) 'Contagious Yawning and Infant Imitation.' *Bulletin of the Psychonomic Society 27*, 125–126.

Rime, B. and Schiaratura, L. (1991) 'Gesture and Speech.' In R. Feldman and B. Rime (eds) *Fundamentals of Nonverbal Behaviour*. New York: Cambridge University Press.

Rubin, Z. (1970) 'Measurement of Romantic Love.' *Journal of Personality and Social Psychology 16*, 265–273.

Saarni, C. (1979) 'Children's Understanding of Display Rules for Expressive Behaviour.' *Developmental Psychology 15*, 424–429.

Sackett, G.P. (1966) 'Monkeys Reared in Isolation with Pictures as Visual Input: Evidence for an Innate Releasing Mechanism.' *Science 154*, 468–473.

Saxe, G.B. and Kaplan, R. (1981) 'Gesture in Early Counting: A Developmental Analysis.' *Perceptual and Motor Skills 53*, 851–854.

Saywitz, K.J. and Nathanson, R. (1993) 'Children's Testimony and Their Perceptions of Stress in and out of the Courtroom.' *Child Abuse and Neglect 17*, 613–622.

Scaife, M. and Bruner, J.S. (1975) 'The Capacity for Joint Visual Attention in the Infant.' *Nature 253*, 265–266.

Schaffer, H.R. (1971) *The Growth of Sociability*. Harmondsworth: Penguin.

Schaffer, H.R. and Emerson, P.E. (1964) 'Patterns of Response to Physical Contact in Early Human Development.' *Journal of Child Psychology and Psychiatry 5*, 1–13.

Scheman, J.D. and Lockard, J.S. (1979) 'Development of Gaze Aversion in Children.' *Child Development 50*, 594–596.

Schlesinger, H.S. and Meadow, K.P (1972) *Sound and Sign: Childhood Deafness and Mental Health.* Berkeley, CA: University of California Press.

Schwartz, G.E., Fair, P.L., Salt, P., Mandel, M.R. and Kleiman, G.L. (1976) 'Facial Expression and Imagery in Depression: An Electromyographic Study.' *Psychosomatic Medicine 38*, 337–347.

Sellen, A.J. (1995) 'Remote Conversations: The Effects of Mediated Talk with Technology.' *Human–Computer Interaction 10*, 401–446.

Skeels, H. (1966) 'Adult Status of Children with Contrasting Early Life Experiences.' *Monograph of the Society for Research in Child Development 31*, 3.

Souza-Poza, J.F. and Rohrberg, R. (1972) 'Body Movement in Relation to the Types of Information (Person- and Non-Person Oriented) and Cognitive Style (Field Dependence).' *Human Communication Research 4*, 19–29.

Spitz, R.A. (1946) 'Hospitalism: A Follow-Up Report on Investigation Described in Volume I, 1945.' *Psychoanalytic-Study-of-the-Child 1946*, 2, 113–117.

Sroufe, L.A. and Warren, S. (1999) 'Infant Attachment and Developmental Psychopathology.' Unpublished data, Institute of Child Development, University of Minnesota, Minneapolis.

Steiner, J.E. (1977) 'Facial Expressions of the Neonate Infant Indicating the Hedonics of Food Related Chemicals Stimuli.' In J.M. Weiffenbach (ed) *Taste and Development: The Genesis of Sweet Preference.* DHEW publication no. NIH77-1068. Washington DC: US Government Printing Office.

Stern, D. (1977) *The First Relationship.* London: Open Books.

Stewart, C.A. and Singh, N.N. (1995) 'Enhancing the Recognition and Production of Facial Expressions of Emotion by Children with Mental Retardation.' *Research in Developmental Disabilities 16*, 365–382.

Straub, R.R. and Roberts, D.M. (1983) 'Effects of Nonverbal Oriented Social Awareness Training Program on Social Interaction Ability of Learning Disabled Children.' *Journal of Nonverbal Behaviour 7*, 195–201.

Sugarman, S. (1983) 'Empirical versus Logical Issues in the Transition from Prelinguistic to Linguistic Communication.' In R.M. Golinkoff (ed) *The Transition from Prelinguistic to Linguistic Communication.* Hillsdale, NJ: Lawrence Erlbaum.

Tarrahian, G.A. and Hicks, R.A. (1979) 'Attribution of Pupil Size as a Function of Facial Valence and Age in American and Persian Children.' *Journal of Cross Cultural Psychology 10*, 243—250.

Thompson, J. (1941) 'Development of Facial Expression in Blind and Seeing Children.' *Archives of Psychology 37*, 1–47.

Trevarthen, C. (1977) 'Descriptive Analyses of Infant Communicative Behaviour.' In H.R. Schaffer (ed) *Studies in Mother–Infant Interaction.* London: Academic Press.

Trower, P. (1980) 'Situational Analysis of the Components and Processes of Socially Skilled and Unskilled Patients.' *Journal of Consulting and Clinical Psychology 48*, 327–339.

Volkmar, F.R. and Mayes, L.C. (1991) 'Gaze Behavior in Autism.' *Development and Psychopathology 2*, 61–69.

Vrij, A. (2002) 'Deception in Children: A Literature Review and Implications for Children's Testimony.' In H.L. Westcott, G.M. Davies and R.H.C. Bull *Children's Testimony*. Chichester: Wiley.

Vygotsky, L. ([1934] 1962) *Thought and Language*. Cambridge, MA: MIT Press.

Walden, T.A. and Field, T.M. (1982) 'Discrimination of Facial Expressions by Preschool Children.' *Child Development 53*, 1312-1319.

Walden, T.A. and Field, T.M. (1990) 'Preschool Children's Social Competence and Production and Discrimination of Facial Expressions.' *British Journal of Developmental Psychology 8*, 65–76.

Waters, E., Wippman, J. and Sroufe, L. (1979) 'Attachment, Positive Affect, and Competence in the Peer Groups: Two Studies in Construct Validation.' *Child Development 50*, 821–829.

Watson, J.S. (1973) 'Smiling, Cooing and "the Game".' *Merrill Palmer Quarterly of Behaviour and Development 18*, 323–339.

Watson, O.M. (1970) *Proxemic Behaviour: A Cross-Cultural Study*. The Hague: Mouton.

Werner, H. and Kaplan, B. (1963) *Symbolic Formation: An Orgasmic-Developmental Approach to Language and the Expression of Thought*. New York: Wiley.

Westcott, H., Davies, G. and Clifford, B. (1991) 'The Credibility of Child Witnesses Seen on Closed-Circuit Television.' *Adoption and Fostering 15*, 14–19.

Whittaker, S.J. and Fisher, J.D. (1979) 'Multidimensional Reaction to Therapeutic Touch in a Hospital Setting.' *Journal of Personality and Social Psychology 37*, 87–96.

Willis, D.M. (1979) 'Early Speech Development in Blind Children.' *Psychoanalytic Development of the Child 34*, 85–117.

Willis, F.N. and Hamm, H.K. (1980) 'The Use of Interpersonal Touch in Securing Compliance.' *Journal of Non-Verbal Behaviour 5*, 49–55.

Willis, F.N. and Hoffman, G.E. (1975) 'Development of Tactile Patterns in Relations to Age, Sex, and Race.' *Developmental Psychology 11*, 866.

Wood, D., Bruner, J. and Ross, G. (1976) 'The Role of Tutoring in Problem Solving.' *Journal of Child Psychology and Psychiatry 17*, 89–100.

Woolfe, T., Want, S.C. and Siegal, M. (2002) 'Signposts to Development: Theory of Mind Development in Deaf Children.' *Child Development 73*, 768–778.

Yamada, F. (1998) 'Frontal Midline Theta Rhythm and Eyeblinking Activity during a VDT Task and a Video Game: Useful Tools for Psychophysiology in Ergonomics.' *Ergonomics 41*, 678–688.

Yarbus, A.L. (1967) *Eye Movement and Vision*. Trans. Basil Haigh. New York: Plenum Press.

Yarrow, L.J. (1961) 'Maternal Deprivation: Toward an Empirical and Conceptual Re-Evaluation.' *Psychological-Bulletin 58*, 459–490.

Zuckerman, M. and Driver, R.E. (1985) 'Telling Lies: Verbal and Nonverbal Correlates of Deception.' In A.W. Seigman and S. Fledstein (eds) *Multichannel Integrations of Nonverbal Behaviour*. Hillsdale, NJ: Lawrence Erlbaum.

Subject Index

Author Index